Anticipations of Freedom

Anticipations of Freedom

Engaging Stanley Cavell

RICHARD ELDRIDGE

OXFORD
UNIVERSITY PRESS

OXFORD
UNIVERSITY PRESS

Oxford University Press is a department of the University of Oxford.
It furthers the University's objective of excellence in research, scholarship,
and education by publishing worldwide. Oxford is a registered trade mark of
Oxford University Press in the UK and in certain other countries.

Published in the United States of America by Oxford University Press
198 Madison Avenue, New York, NY 10016, United States of America.

CIP data is on file at the Library of Congress

ISBN 9780197841754 (pbk.)
ISBN 9780197841747 (hbk.)

DOI: 10.1093/9780197841785.001.0001

Paperback printed by Integrated Books International, United States of America
Hardback printed by Lightning Source, Inc., United States of America

The manufacturer's authorized representative in the EU for product safety is
Oxford University Press España S.A. of Parque Empresarial San Fernando de Henares,
Avenida de Castilla, 2 – 28830 Madrid (www.oup.es/en or product.safety@oup.com).
OUP España S.A. also acts as importer into Spain of products made by the manufacturer.

To Hannah, Sarah, and Jonathan

Contents

Acknowledgments   xi
List of Abbreviations of Books by Cavell   xv

Introduction: Anticipations of Freedom   1

SELFHOOD AND METHOD

1. Between Acknowledgment and Avoidance   21

2. Cavell and the Achievement of Selfhood   32

3. Conceptual Analysis, Practical Commitment, and
   Ordinary Language   42

AMERICA: HISTORY AND FUTURITY

4. Cavell on American Philosophy and the Idea of America   63

5. Cavell and the American Jeremiad   79

SITES OF ARREST AND RECOVERY:
LITERATURE, MUSIC, AND FILM

6. Cavell and Hölderlin on Human Immigrancy   99

7. Criticism and the Risk of the Self: Stanley Cavell's
   Modernism and Elizabeth Bishop's   114

8. "This Most Human Predicament": Cavell on Language,
   Intention, and Desire in Shakespeare   131

9. How Movies Think: Cavell on Film as a Medium of Art   140

10. Imagining Life Together: Psychosexual Intimacy, Social
    Roles, and Contemporary Comedies of Remarriage   156

11. Modernity, Skepticism, and Meaning in *The World Viewed*   166

12. Cavell as Halted Traveler: The Experience of Music   179

13. Cavell and Day for Night   188

Epilogue: Paradoxes and Possibilities of Freedom,
Social and Individual   204

Notes   221
Index   245

... —and, by words
Which speak of nothing more than what we are,
Would I arouse the sensual from their sleep
Of Death, and win the vacant and the vain
To noble raptures ...

—William Wordsworth, "Prospectus to The Recluse"

Acknowledgments

I have been reading Cavell and thinking and writing about his work since 1974. "Aesthetic Problems of Modern Philosophy," "Knowing and Acknowledging," and *The World Viewed* opened up for me the kind of work in philosophy that it was, I thought, both worth doing and mine to do. My oldest and among my deepest debts and gratitudes are to my undergraduate teachers, Stanley Bates and Timothy Gould, who introduced me to those pieces. In graduate school, my dissertation advisors Ted Cohen, Alan Donagan, and Manley Thompson supported me in the work of reading Cavell and reading major figures in the history of philosophy along Cavellian lines. They helped patiently and with encouragement to give that reading shape and to keep it in engagement with clearly defined problems and professional norms. Françoise Meltzer opened up connections to Romanticism, psychoanalysis, and literary theory. Paul Gudel, Stephen Melville, and Jeffrey Wieand were important fellow travelers and interlocutors in coming to terms with and for Cavell's writing.

My colleagues at Swarthmore College, Hugh Lacey, Richard Schuldenfrei, and Hans Oberdiek formed a rich culture of daily philosophical conversation within which I was fortunate to be initiated and to be able to test and develop my ideas, including marking out Cavell's affinities and disaffinities with Hegel and Marx, as well as with Taylor, MacIntyre, Rorty, and Williams, among others. Tamsin Lorraine shared and encouraged my understandings of the historicity of human being and of the importance of aesthetic experience for orientation amidst the currents and eddies of life. For the past two and half decades or so, I increasingly taught Cavell's work, especially *Cities of Words* and essays from *Pursuits of Happiness*, to Swarthmore students. Their responses confirmed my sense of the significance of that work and heartened me in writing about it. There are too many of them to list or even to remember, but I am happy to mention Maisie Wiltshire-Gordon, Chase Fuller, Zachary Weinstein, and Lee Cohen, in the hope that some others may recognize themselves as having been their companions.

Since 2020 the philosophy department at the University of Tennessee, Knoxville has provided a welcoming and supportive new set of colleagues and interlocutors, along with students who responded to the teaching on Cavell on film and literature that I undertook there. Together they provided an ideal environment for completing and revising these chapters.

The American Society for Aesthetics has welcomed my work, including some work on Cavell, for the past forty-four years. Regular encounters and conversations there with Ted Cohen, Stanley Bates, Timothy Gould, Stephen Melville, Jay Miller, Michael Fischer, Nick Pappas, Casey Haskins, Garry Hagberg, Lydia Goehr, Tzachi Zamir, and Gregg Horowitz, among many others, were important sources of insight and energy for going on. More occasional encounters at one or another professional meeting with Charles Altieri, Anthony J. Cascardi, Georg Bertram, and Joshua Wilner were similarly important. J. M. Bernstein shared and gave further shape to common interests in Cavell, Hegel, Kant, and modernism as a semester-long colleague during my visit to Essex and afterward. Andrew Norris was in Philadelphia for a number of years, and both there and thereafter I have regularly learned from his work not only on Cavell and the political, but also on Cavell in relation to Hegel, German thought more broadly, and epistemology. Stanley Cavell was present more irregularly at various conferences, but his astonishing ability to hear and productively to recast my, or anyone's, direction of thought and interest was a singular resource.

The Philadelphia Area Aesthetics Reading Group has been meeting in person or via Zoom for over thirty years now. It is impossible to overstate the importance to my work of the friendships and the relentless, cheerful, deep enthusiasm in thinking philosophically about the arts that its members provided: my thanks to Susan Feagin, Noël Carroll, Espen Hammer, Paul Guyer, Robert Clewis, John Carvalho, Mary Goldstein, Brad Winegar, Kristin Boyce, and John Gibson, along with occasional visitors. Noël (especially in relation to movies), Paul (especially in relation to Kant), and Espen (on nearly everything) shared particular interests in Cavell.

Adam Haslett has modeled for me commitment to the labor and seriousness of art while retaining interest in Cavell and in my own lines of thinking about literature, character, and modernity. More recently, Rafael Azize and I have shared too many conversations to count about Cavell, aesthetic experience, subjectivity, literature, and film. He generously invited me to teach and lecture on Cavell, philosophy and film, and philosophy of literature at the Universidade Federal da Bahia, Salvador, Brazil, where I found uncountable apt responses from Rafael and from his students, friends, and colleagues.

At Oxford University Press, Lucy Randall supported this manuscript and guided it through significant revisions with deft, substantive, and insightful advice that went well beyond what anyone could expect. I am grateful to the press readers for reports that lead to major additions, excisions, and changes. Eight of these chapters have been previously published elsewhere, and two more are forthcoming elsewhere, nearly all of them in unusual and out of the way places. Each has been rewritten slightly to remove some informalities, for cogency of argument and clarity of formulation, and for consecutive reading as chapters of a book. The details of these earlier or forthcoming publications are: "Between Acknowledgment and Avoidance," in *Stanley Cavell*, ed. Richard Eldridge (Cambridge: Cambridge University Press, 2003), pp. 1–14; "Cavell and the Achievement of Selfhood," *Conversations: The Journal of Cavell Studies* 9 (2021), pp. 4–14; "Conceptual Analysis, Practical Commitment, and Ordinary Language," *The Graduate Faculty Philosophy Journal* 39, 2 (2018), pp. 1–23; "Cavell on American Philosophy and the Idea of America," in *Stanley Cavell*, ed. Richard Eldridge (Cambridge: Cambridge University Press, 2003), pp. 172–89; "Cavell and the American Jeremiad," *Journal of Philosophical Research* 39 (2014), pp. 377–91; "Cavell and Hölderlin on Human Immigrancy," in *Ordinary Language Criticism: Literary Thinking After Cavell After Wittgenstein*, ed. Kenneth Dauber and Walter Jost (Evanston: Northwestern University Press, 2003), pp. 299–314; "Criticism and the Risk of the Self: Stanley Cavell's Modernism and Elizabeth Bishop's," in *Stanley Cavell: Philosophy, Literature and Criticism*, ed. James Loxley and Andrew Taylor (Manchester: Manchester University Press, 2011), pp. 92–105; "'This Most Human Predicament': Cavell on Language, Intention, and Desire in Shakespeare," *Conversations: The Journal of Cavell Studies* 5 (2017), pp. 118–28; "How Movies Think: Cavell on Film as a Medium of Art," *Estetika: The Central European Journal of Aesthetics* 51, 1 (2014), pp. 3–20; "Imagining Life Together: Psychosexual Intimacy, Social Roles, and Contemporary Comedies of Remarriage," in *Happiness and Tears, After Cavell*, ed. Paul Deb (Albany: SUNY Press, forthcoming); "Cavell as Halted Traveler: The Experience of Music," in *Music with Stanley Cavell in Mind*, ed. David LaRocca (New York: Bloomsbury, 2024), pp. 131–41; "Cavell and *Day for Night*," in *Cavell and World Cinemas: Beyond Hollywood*, ed. Paul Deb (Edinburgh: Edinburgh University Press, forthcoming). I am grateful to each of the editors and readers for these journals and collections, as well as to an especially insightful anonymous reader of "Modernity, Skepticism, and Meaning in *The World Viewed*," for their comments and suggestions. Thanks to the participants in the Rio Grande do Sul conference on Cavell, Skepticism, and the Ordinary (especially to Eric Ritter for his written comments) and to the participants in the Ottawa conference on Inheriting Cavell for their useful and generous responses to earlier versions of "Cavell and the Achievement of Selfhood." I am grateful to the philosophy department of Middle Tennessee State University, the philosophy department of Seton Hall University, and the Southern Aesthetics Workshop for opportunities to present earlier versions of "Imagining Life Together" to each of them and for productive discussions. Thanks in particular to Kelly Jolley and Eliza Little, my sharp and insightful commentators in the Workshop.

My children Hannah, Sarah, and Jonathan are nearly as old as my first published work on Cavell. How they became interested in things and found directions in life, as well as whether anything I might produce in philosophy (especially on Cavell) might engage with their doings, were much on my mind throughout my writing, not without anxiety. It is, therefore, a special pleasure to report that they each have sensibilities and interests as grownups that resonate to this material in their distinctly individual ways. This is a piece of astonishing good fortune that gives me hope for propitious futurities. Skepticism about how, if at all, philosophy might matter to intelligent, widely read grownups who are not otherwise much engaged with academic philosophy, combined nonetheless with willingness to listen, on the parts of Suzanna Sherry and Paul Edelman also figured productively in my imagination as I read and wrote.

Joan Vandegrift has read (often many times) and believed in almost every word that appears on these pages; her acute eyes and ears improved countless sentences. This is an extraordinary labor of love, faith, and skill without which this book would not exist.

Abbreviations of Books by Cavell

CHU   *Conditions Handsome and Unhandsome: The Constitution of Emersonian Perfectionism.* Chicago: University of Chicago Press, 1990.

CR   *The Claim of Reason: Wittgenstein, Skepticism, Morality, and Tragedy.* New York: Oxford University Press, 1979.

CT   *Contesting Tears: The Hollywood Melodrama of the Unknown Woman.* Chicago: University of Chicago Press, 1996.

CW   *Cities of Words: Pedagogical Letters on a Register of the Moral Life.* Cambridge, MA: Harvard University Press, 2005.

DK   *Disowning Knowledge.* Cambridge: Cambridge University Press, 1987.

HT   *Here and There: Sites of Philosophy*, ed. Nancy Bauer, Alice Crary, and Sandra Laugier. Cambridge: Harvard University Press, 2022.

IQO   *In Quest of the Ordinary: Lines of Skepticism and Romanticism.* Chicago: University of Chicago Press, 1988.

LDIK   *Little Did I Know: Excerpts from Memory.* Stanford: Stanford University Press, 2010.

MWM   *Must We Mean What We Say?* New York: Charles Scribner's Sons, 1969.

PDAT   *Philosophy the Day After Tomorrow.* Cambridge, MA: Harvard University Press, 2006.

PH   *Pursuits of Happiness: The Hollywood Comedy of Remarriage.* Cambridge, MA: Harvard University Press, 1981.

PP   *A Pitch of Philosophy: Autobiographical Exercises.* Cambridge, MA: Harvard University Press, 1994.

SW   *The Senses of Walden.* New York: Viking, 1972.

TNYUA   *This New Yet Unapproachable America: Lectures After Emerson After Wittgenstein.* Albuquerque, NM: Living Batch Press, 1989.

TS   *Themes Out of School: Effects and Causes.* San Francisco: North Point Press, 1984.

WV   *The World Viewed.* Cambridge, MA: Harvard University Press, 1979. First edition 1971.

Introduction

Anticipations of Freedom

In being capable of forming and participating in culture, human beings are interesting animals. Satisfactions, enjoyments, dissatisfactions, and despairs that reach well beyond the sensory are open to them as incipiently self-conscious, social, and creative beings. As John Stuart Mill famously puts it in the second chapter of *Utilitarianism*, "Human beings have faculties more elevated than the animal appetites, and when once made conscious of them, do not regard anything as happiness which does not include their gratification."[1]

It by no means follows, however, that these faculties are successfully gratified and that distinctively human happiness is achieved. Neither the normal diurnal course of nature nor culture unfreighted with conflicts makes us a present of this. Active inheritance and the productive reformation of practices and commitments are required. As Hegel puts it,

> what we *are* we are at the same time in history. . . . The possession of self-conscious rationality . . . has not been gained suddenly nor has it grown merely out of the soil of the present. On the contrary, it is essentially an inheritance and, more precisely, the result of labour, the labour of all the preceding generations of the human race. The arts of the externals of our life, the mass of means and skills, the arrangements and customs of social and political associations, all these are the result of the reflection, invention, needs, misery, and misfortune, the will and achievement of the history which has preceded our life of today.[2]

No one actualizes rational faculties and achieves self-conscious satisfactions in activity independently of cultural formation and historical embeddedness.

Nor, in fact, do we fully and coherently possess and exercise self-conscious rationality in our contemporary courses of practical life. As Hegel elsewhere trenchantly notes, "The life of Spirit"—a shared, self-conscious life of satisfying, reason-responsive commitment and activity—"is not a life that shies

Anticipations of Freedom. Richard Eldridge, Oxford University Press. © Richard Eldridge 2026.
DOI: 10.1093/9780197841785.003.0001

from death and preserves itself from devastation, but rather one that bears death and sustains itself in it."[3] Contra Hegel's optimism about the resolution of fundamental, social-institutional conflicts, however, it is also by no means clear that "the present has cast off its barbarism and unjust arbitrariness, and truth has cast off its otherworldliness and contingent force, so that true reconciliation . . . has become objective . . . in the *state*, in *nature*, and in the *ideal world*."[4] Reconciled life is clearly not at hand. Polarization, massive economic inequality, mutual suspicion, and mistrust of the presumptively liberal institutions that would house and ameliorate these conditions are pervasive. Possibilities of meaningful work are undermined by the deskilling of labor in necessary service industries (nursing home care; big box retail; fast food; lawn service; home and office cleaning; low-level clerical work). Enjoyments are sought in hedonic consumption and the pleasures of ownership rather than in significant activity. As Elizabeth Anderson describes the internationally dominant neoliberalism of market solutions, with politics reduced to little but a play of contending self-interested factions, "the ethos of society is driven by competitive acquisition—a toxic, zero-sum form of esteem competition."[5] The institutions of the formation of culture and practical commitment that might enable more fully reconciled life are foundering. Yet insofar as we continue to possess the faculties of forming and participating in culture anew, we cannot but continue to hope for life otherwise, effectively realized in humanly satisfying activities and relationships, or what Hegel understands as freedom in being *bei sich selbst in einem anderen*, at home in one's activities, roles, and relationships.[6]

All this is what Stanley Cavell is intimating in writing, in the opening sentences of his early essay "Aesthetic Problems of Modern Philosophy," that

> The Spirit of the Age is not easy to place, ontologically or empirically; and it is idle to suggest that creative effort must express its age, either because that cannot fail to happen, or because a new effort can create a new age. Still, one knows what it means when an art historian says, thinking of the succession of plastic styles, "not everything is possible in every period."[7]

The Spirit of the Age—a tangled ensemble of routes of cultural practice as they stand and as they are open to active inheritance and modification—is not easy to place because it is not a kind of thing that is simply there physically to be measured or discerned in the sortal perception of overt qualities and measurable quantities. It is, rather, expressed in what people do with at least implicit potential awareness, as a rising of an arm must be grasped as an intentional raising that is a warning or a blessing or a dismissal as may be. Intentional, meaningful doings can be misunderstood or contested and repudiated, and it is not obvious that newly initiated doings, issuing from a contested practical background, will coalesce into shared repertoires and mutual understandings. And yet one must, will, do something—undertake to make new sense with others so far as possible, from within where one is.

Hegel undertook, implausibly, to trace and to ground without drawing on prior presuppositions a superintending logic of cultural development that would yield satisfying forms of active life in which all might participate and whose worth might be recognized and accepted. Absent this possibility, however, there remain a number of alternative, less than happy ways of responding to contested practical-cultural inheritances.[8] Reactive fundamentalism in the face of what is perceived as chaos is always a possibility, but its primary resources for the resolution of cultural contestations are violence, shunning, and radical religious conversion. Or one might attempt to stand on pure rationality, in a position free of all cultural entanglements and putatively able to judge their worth—a stance that implausibly rests on a spatial conceit of detachment that denies temporality, embodiment, and historicity and that risks smugness and irrelevance: there is no cosmic exile. Or one might revert to liberalism: let a hundred flowers bloom; let a hundred schools of thought contend, and hope for the best. Put thus baldly, however, there will be no institutions of fair cooperation and competition, leaving only proliferations of contending rights claims (property as earned entitlement vs. property as socially distributed, equal possibility of livelihood; abortion as murder vs. pregnancy-termination as a self-standing decision to be honored; absolute freedom of expression vs. a right to be recognized and emotionally unscarred) and the sways of power.[9] In the absence of some significant, lived procedures of mutual, affirmative appreciation that at least mediate disagreements, arguments in favor of objective values that might be used to adjudicate contending rights claims are likely to be bootless, or, worse yet, taken to be little more than further weapons for partisans.[10] As Plato saw and as recent political history shows, just life requires not only written institutional designs but also suitable characters on the parts of citizens and authorities. Meanwhile all three of these stances will be surrounded by an awareness of significant diversity that is undeniable: a lived sense of absence of productive orientation to and by common ends and practices, or an experience of what Georg Lukács called transcendental homelessness, a sense of powers of meaning-making divided and blocked, that will frequently enough issue in both despair and renewed, antagonistic self-seeking.

Existentialism, structuralism, and post-structuralism each register the fact of continuing structural social conflict but also fail to offer plausible avenues of address to it. Existentialist insistence on authentic, individual will in the manner of the early Sartre results in a contentless decisionism that, if anything, exacerbates opposition. "Hell is other people,"[11] Sartre famously wrote, insofar as their efforts to objectify their wills are inevitably set against one's own. Heideggerian talk of hearkening to the call of Being is all but contentless, and his suggestion that one might immerse oneself resolutely in "the nation . . . returning to itself for the fulfillment of its vocation"[12] is at best dangerous and at worse genocidal. Lévi-Straussian structuralism maintains an air of scientific detachment in gazing on oppositions that it sees as everywhere proliferating themselves in different shapes, while itself eschewing normative commitment. Foucault proposes that one might simply awaken to the fact that one occupies a position in relation to "the specificity of the politics of truth in our societies"[13] and then act—a suggestion that leaves everything to contending plays of power.

More recently, that distinctively human being is actualized in a historical world of living practice that is marked by contestation has been accepted by a number of important figures who undertake to overcome the limitations of fundamentalism, detached rationalism, and abstract liberalism as well as existentialism, structuralism, and post-structuralism. In a series of important books, Robert B. Pippin has located the human subject as living essentially in what he describes as "the fractured cultural world of post-Hegelian Western and now World Spirit."[14] One actualizes one's distinctively human powers of reflection, choice, and meaning-making by forming what Pippin calls a practical identity, understood as an ensemble of commitments that are coherently expressed and endorsed by oneself and others over time. Only in this way is it possible for an "action to count as mine" by "fit[ting] intelligibly within a whole complex of practices and institutions within which *doing this now* could have a coherent meaning."[15] As a result, however, of the fractures and structural oppositions present in modern life, no one wholly succeeds in forming and sustaining a practical identity. "The form of modern bourgeois life in general might impose psychological demands on individuals that produce internal, unreconcilable 'collisions'" that "everyone faces, between who one takes oneself to be and who one might discover one is."[16] In the tragic perspective on modern life that Pippin endorses, "there is no unity [either personal or social] intimated or pointed to that could give us some hope for resolution."[17] The best that can be done is not to resolve internal and external conflict, but instead to understand its depth and pervasiveness. This is the task and achievement, according to Pippin, of modernist art and its forms of "aesthetic intelligibility" that are marked by "unintelligibility, untruth, absurdity, and self-negation"[18] in telling the truth about how things are. Ambitious art can "help us understand something better, like the distinct forms of suffering inflicting on people in late capitalism,"[19] while leaving us in practice frozen within insuperable oppositions.

Here Pippin's insights into the aesthetic registering of suffering and failure in the modern and modernist arts are real and important. But one may also wonder whether Pippin underrates both the satisfactions experienced by artists (painters, poets, filmmakers, composers, performers, and all the rest) in the generation of artistic forms that embody attentiveness to practical life, the abilities of audiences to share in these satisfactions imaginatively, and the at least sometimes available forms of satisfaction within practical life that are *en mésure* achievable (and experienced by artists and audiences, among others). Bereft of final answers and caught within insuperable oppositions we may be, yet some good enough accommodations may sometimes be available, at least for some and for a time. (Are there no such things as happy marriages or honorable careers at all?)

Like Pippin, Lydia Goehr is struck by the pervasiveness of structural opposition in modern social life, or by what she calls "the terrible history of prejudice and persecution that has worked its way through lives lived for the sake of art, truth, reason, and divinity"[20] as people have attempted to organize social life authoritatively. (Plato is an arch-enemy here.) Rather than undertaking to resolve structural oppositions—an effort whose wages are tyranny—we should avoid "the path toward a complete explanation" and instead practice "a wit of incongruity ambiguity, and inversion" that undoes all settlements in favor of continuing improvisations.[21] Let a hundred flowers bloom; let a hundred schools of thought contend—not for the sake of arriving at doctrinal truth, but rather taking the form of an accumulation of "*a micrology of telling details*" that focuses on "all the finger- and footprints [of repression and violence] in images and texts."[22]

This view, too, has its insights and charms. The persistent phenomena of social oppression that Goehr focuses on are real, and diagnostic insight and reactive improvisation are important-enough forms of response to them. Yet her stance, put into generalized practice, also threatens to take the form of an aesthetic-cultural-political libertarianism that leaves individuals doing their critical and reactive bests but nonetheless caught in an economic free-for-all of all against all, with little trust or mutual respect across opposed routes of witty improvisation. Against this, it seems both possible and reasonable to hope and work for qualified, reasonable-enough general settlements and, again, to pursue honorable if not final satisfactions.

With substantially more optimism than is present in either Pippin or Goehr, Charles Taylor proposes that we can learn from major modern lyric poetry how to face up to and overcome structural oppositions, so as to find at-homeness in the world in the form of "contact with a continuing cosmic order" that includes an awareness of nature and other human beings that is "shot through with joy, significance, inspiration."[23] Taylor concedes that there is an "essential fragility" to "the epiphanies which works of art bring about."[24] The work done by poetry is "epistemically limited, since it [can] not aspire to the clarity and finality of philosophy."[25] Frequently a cosmic connection is "powerfully evoked as failed, even unattainable," as in Hölderlin and Mallarmé in particular.[26] Yet he finds nonetheless that "what is being delivered and sought here [in the poems he considers] is our proper relation to the spatiotemporal world."[27] "Art reveals . . . some metabiological flows," where "metabiological reality is about what really constitutes human flourishing."[28] Rilke, for example, shows us how to "perceive the glory of the *erlebbare* [livable] world, the world in its human meaning, which our praising brings to completion."[29] Baudelaire's poems "offer a connection to a larger pattern in time which can inspire, even exalt us, and put an end to spleen."[30]

One should not scant the importance of the resonances that powerful lyric poems can sometimes evoke in their readers, and visionary address to our conflictual situations is surely needed. Yet different readers resonate with different poems, including some paratactically organized poems of itinerancy, alienation, and lack of closure (except in power of attention to the chaos). And meanwhile reading poetry is itself an activity that is surrounded by all the continuing stuffs of prosaic, productive, and conflicted social life. In all its oppositions, the world, it seems, is too much with us, and, whatever occasional senses of felt belonging are sometimes available, in getting and spending agonistically we continue to lay waste our powers. And yet, as Pippin, Goehr, and Taylor all see in different ways, we continue to be at least sometimes reflectively aware of our situation and to bear a sense of possibilities of address to it, even if not of final resolution.

That we face and can address the problem of 'knowing how to go on,' with one another and with ourselves, within an omnipresent condition of continuing cultural contestation and difference, with available powers of attention and commitment neither fully actualized nor externally grounded, is the guiding, dominant theme of Stanley Cavell's long career. To the extent that he thematizes and enacts a distinctive mode of address to this situation in a way that avoids the limitations, perils, and pitfalls of fundamentalism, detached rationalism, abstract liberalism, existentialism, structuralism, and post-structuralism, his work has a unique and uniquely powerful claim on us. He offers achievements and models of heightened attention, mostly to works of art and philosophy, but through them to life, coupled with intensities and satisfactions that are beyond the natural-sensual while also remaining tethered to it, and without escapism from conflict into abstraction and emptiness. Philosophy manifests itself in his writing as an *activity* of attentiveness and articulation, not a doctrine.[31] It faces conflict, sometimes resolving it, sometimes articulating persisting differences in a way that makes mutual respect possible, and sometimes falling short and leaving things to other modes of interaction.

> Morality . . . provides *one* possibility of settling conflict, a way of encompassing conflict which allows the continuance of personal relationships against the hard and apparently inevitable fact of misunderstanding, mutually incompatible wishes, commitments, loyalties, interests and needs, a way of mending relationships and maintaining the self in opposition to itself or others. Other ways of settling or encompassing conflict are provided by politics, religion, love and forgiveness, rebellion, and withdrawal. (CR, 269)

It is not everything, but it is not nothing, either. Philosophy or morality *as* critical, moral conversation that explores perceptions, affections, and aversions,[32] *not* standing on definitions and undivided authority, is a central way, though not the only way, of going on with life as a modern subject and of finding one's selfhood more fully actualized, with others, within a course of activity.[33]

Cavell's sense of being always already thrown (*geworfen*) and caught within unmasterable but addressable difference, opposition, and temporality is shaped by both his early family life and his specific cultural and political circumstances. As a child, he was caught between the frequently harsh authority of the father and the sharing of musical transports with the mother—a fact reflected in his subsequent massive involvement with Freud. Growing up in Atlanta and Sacramento, he was confronted with racial differences and the legacy of slavery on a daily basis. As a Jew, he, like his father, felt a specific sense of immigrancy in the United States in contrast with the Anglo-Saxon descendants of the Puritans. His sense of possibilities of address to these divisions that are nonetheless available is shaped by his early experience of playing jazz in mixed race-combos, by the sheer experience of music as sensuously embodied, temporally unfolding meaningfulness, by identifications with figures in movies "working for the world's good" (WV, 62), and more broadly by a sense of America as a place of open possibilities, with chances for anyone to strike out for the frontier and get on with life anew.

These early personal inheritances lie behind and are then further articulated in Cavell's receptions of ordinary language philosophy, first from Austin, his teacher at Harvard, and then from Wittgenstein. What initially knocked Cavell off his horse in Austin's work was the combination of heightened attentiveness to language and life, resulting in a felt conviction in what it made sense to say when, coupled with the democratic availability of this attentiveness and sense of conviction to anyone. Against the conceits of traditional philosophy, putatively grounded in acquaintance with some form of undeniable realities, itself vouchsafed by a distinctly philosophical method, Austin offered nothing more and nothing less than an ear for common language in use, which, when activated in oneself and others, might issue in a sense of orientation within the sways of common life. Or it might not: there are, for Austin, no methodological or metaphysical guarantees that what any particular person reports about what *we* say when will be either shared or found to resolve philosophical perplexities. Difference is accepted as at least a standing possibility, and the appeal to what we say when remains always invitational, not coercive. Austin's parables of dying donkeys, artfully snatched bombes, and treadings on snails and babies offer the chance of agreement in language and practice, achieved by way of shared imaginative investment, but never the certainty of it. In this they offer, as Cavell saw, in analogizing the claims of the ordinary language philosopher with the claims of both the perceptualist critic of the arts and the modernist artist in "Aesthetic Problems," the possibility, but not the guarantee, of sharing a stance on life via imaginative participation that is also afforded by literature, especially lyric. In Wordsworthian terms, the work of the poet-critic-ordinary language philosopher might "make ... incidents and situations from common life ... interesting, [with] the understanding of the Reader ... enlightened and his affections strengthened and purified," thus working through confusion and alienation to achieve onwardness within ordinary life, democratically and without coercion.[34]

As Timothy Gould aptly notes, there is a shift in emphasis in Cavell's work after *The Claim of Reason* from Austinian elaborative-invitational appeals to what we say when in more or less ordinary situations to the reading of major visionary texts that seem to read us, their audiences, by giving surprising voice to what we might then find ourselves newly wishing to say, thus motivating new, perfectionist routes for the expression of our powers, now against the grain of the ordinary.[35] In the course of reading, Cavell finds himself stopped by and resonating with the words of the text that absorbs him. "Cavell now finds the writer coming *before* the reader [including Cavell himself] with the words that the reader will find himself in need of."[36] By articulating his animated responsiveness to the texts he reads, Cavell enacts an "aspiration to representativeness" in opening to *his* readers the possibility of sharing in his responses and animations.[37] Cavell's own "authorial voice," Gould adds, "is suited to activate and revise Austin's appeals to ordinary language,"[38] precisely by being formed in responsiveness to words formed by agents seeking routes out of inattentiveness, dullness, and lack of animation in life, rather than being grounded in anything exterior to words and their uses. For Austin, responsiveness to fully meaningful words meant a return to ordinary life as a sphere of intelligible activity, in contrast with the false blandishments formed under what he called "the *ivresse des grands profondeurs*."[39] For Cavell, this responsiveness increasingly means resistance to and departure from a desiccated ordinary. "Our only chance to avoid becoming the ghostly counterpart of our ghostly voices is to become the auditor of a still less audible voice."[40]

In contrast, hence, with the relative optimisms of Hegel, Austin (who continued to hope for a systematic philosophical science and settled agreements), and Wordsworth ("what we have loved, /Others will love, and we will teach them how"[41]), Cavell retains a sharper, more modernist sense of the persistence of difference. To be in quest of the ordinary, as a place from which one necessarily departs and to which one hopes to return, as to a home, once it is refigured, is to be always never quite fully at home in it. Or as Cavell memorably puts it in *In Quest of the Ordinary*:

It is [my] history of devotion to the discovery of false necessity that brought me to the ambiguity of the title I give to these lectures, *In Quest of the Ordinary*; to the sense that the ordinary is subject at once to autopsy and to augury, facing at once its end and its anticipation. The everyday is ordinary because, after all, it is our habit, or habitat; but since that very inhabitation is from time to time perceptible to us—we who have constructed it—as extraordinary, we conceive that some place elsewhere, or this place otherwise constructed, must be what is ordinary to us, must be what romantics—of course including both E. T. and Nicholas Nickelby's alter ego Smike—call "home." . . . Romantics are brave in noting the possibility of life-in-death and of what you might call death-in-life. My favorite Romantics are the ones (I think the bravest ones) who do not attempt to escape these conditions by taking revenge on existence. But this means willing to continue to be born, to be natal, hence mortal. (IQO, 9, 143)

Within this situation of natality not yet achieved, enhanced energies of onwardness will continue to flow only from a sense of individual, blended perception, affect, and interest, made palpable in words, that will not be everywhere shared and that may at times leave one isolated in one's tastes and commitments, compelled to strike out on one's own. As Espen Hammer puts it,

Cavell is . . . interested in . . . the radically new way of conceiving of philosophical activity that existentialism proposes. Adding to the interesting complexities . . . is the fact that while Kierkegaard figures as Cavell's main spokesman for existentialism, he also instances Wittgenstein—and by implication himself insofar as his work from this period onwards becomes increasingly defined in terms of his ongoing engagement with the *Philosophical Investigations*—as a thinker with a decisive existentialist bent.[42]

Or, in Espen Dahl's formulation, "as Cavell sees it, [the] situation [in the modernist arts] is mirrored in philosophy: after Kierkegaard, Nietzsche, and Wittgenstein, there is no simple answer as to how one should establish and continue to write philosophy; its past conveys no reliable answer for how to proceed, its future relevance cannot be known, and its attraction of an audience has become a goal rather than a given."[43]

Cavell's modernist-existentialist sense of himself, and of each of us one by one, as being thrown into the world without any guiding certainties, with both the individual responsibility for what we make of ourselves in taking on our ungrounded inheritances and the anxieties that come with that responsibility, marks the sentences that constitute what is likely the most cited passage in all of Cavell's writing.

> We learn and teach words in certain contexts, and then we are expected, and expect others, to be able to project them into further contexts. Nothing insures that this projection will take place (in particular, not the grasping of universals nor the grasping of books of rules), just as nothing insures that we will make, and understand, the same projections. That on the whole we do is a matter of our sharing routes of interest and feeling, senses of humour and of significance and of fulfillment, of what is outrageous, of what is similar to what else, what a rebuke, what forgiveness, of when an utterance is an assertion, when an appeal, when an explanation—all the whirl of organism Wittgenstein calls "forms of life." Human speech and activity, sanity and community, rest upon nothing more, but nothing less, than this. It is a vision as simple as it is difficult, and as difficult as it is (and because it is) terrifying. (MWM, 52)

The terror—a terror that much academic philosophy simply denies or represses, thus denying, too, temporality, natality, and life—is that of lacking fixed foundations for commitment while nonetheless remaining called to distinctly human satisfactions.

And yet, too, beyond existentialism and its sharp perceptions of ungrounded self-responsibility, there is also for Cavell the partly, but only partly, self-restorative activity of taking one's perceptions and affections seriously, testing them by bringing them to formulation and interrogating their alignments and misalignments with the perceptions and affections of others. (In an encomium written upon the occasion of the awarding of an honorary degree to him by the University of Chicago, Ted Cohen once described Cavell as having had "the courage of his affections.") Subjectivity—understood as a measure of embodied, individual difference in perception, affection, and commitment—is unavoidable; that is the truth of skepticism. But one can work with and through that subjectivity, and in doing so achieve measures of distinctly human satisfactions and good enough cathexes of one's energies to meaningful activity that might be shared by some.

> To speak of our subjectivity as the route back to our conviction in reality is to speak of romanticism. Perhaps romanticism can be understood as the

natural struggle between the representation and the acknowledgment of our subjectivity (between the acting out and the facing off of ourselves, as psychoanalysts would more or less say).... Hence Wordsworth competing with the history of poetry by writing out himself, writing himself back into the world. (WV, 22)

As in Wordsworth, working through one's subjectivity begins from an initial sense of being halted or arrested—perhaps by something oddly entrancing, perhaps by something horrific—and so pulled out of routine. In Plato's *Symposium*, Aristophanes observes that "When a person meets the half that is his very own, whatever his orientation, whether it's to young men or not, something wonderful happens: the two are struck from their senses by love, by a sense of belonging to one another, and by desire, and they don't want to be separated from one another, not even for a moment."[44] Echoing and building on this, Alexander Nehamas describes a moment of arrest in the midst of otherwise ordinary life.

Imagine yourself, then, on a street, in a restaurant or a gallery, at a party, during a lecture, a concert, or a game. You cast your eyes around, recognizing perhaps some people you know, stopping for a moment to glance at an outfit or two, lingering when you notice people talking to one another, distinguishing, so to speak, foreground from background, those you are explicitly aware of from others who mean nothing to you. And then, all of a sudden, everything becomes background—everything but a pair of eyes, a face, a body, pushing the rest out of your field of vision and giving you a moment of awe and a shock of delight, perhaps even passionate longing. For a moment, at least, you are looking at beauty.[45]

One is called by this moment of arrest to do something: to engage with its object further, to attempt to understand it and to make sense of this experience, testing it for whether its power will last and, if it does, for what that might mean for one's future life. As Nehamas argues, it is like this, too, with the experience of works of art: arrest by the work precedes and motivates interpretation. Andrew Bowie describes a moment of arrest by the saxophone-playing of Johnny Hodges in similar terms,[46] arguing, like Nehamas, that one is moved by this arrest to come to terms with something: to test it, study it, and learn from it. Such experiences are among the stuffs of anyone's life. To ignore or repress them is to live according to routines and formulas, without enchantments.

For Cavell, it is like this, too, with the texts he reads, and his articulation and enactment of his own responses—his manifestation of a responsive persona—models the formation of fuller investments in life, avoiding both the hubris of claiming finality and the reduction of articulable and potentially life-sustaining enchantments to passing moments of merely sensual reaction. Following Cavell in this hence makes possible the building of a fuller life. By articulating one's perceptions, affections, aversions, and evaluations, thence testing these articulations for their authenticity, stability, and breadth of imaginative endorsement by others, one might accomplish an adult form of *paideia* or a formation of character and of direction of interest without fundamentalism and the denial of difference. One might find oneself bound to oneself and to at least some others in courses of activity and attention motivated by these perceptions, affections, aversions, and evaluations, and one might at least appreciate the presence of this process of binding via articulations and their testing in the lives of others, even where there are standing disagreements. In doing so, one might achieve with at least some others and within a democratic society of difference some measure of expressive freedom: not simple liberty or absence of coercion, not mere volition, not only Kantian autonomy self-legislated under abstract principle, and not Hegelian freedom as fully reconciled life, but a blend of self-assertion and continuing, qualified mutual endorsement within meaningful, satisfying activity.

The available contents and directions of perceptions, affections, aversions, and evaluations will inevitably in part be made available and inflected by the articulations of others. No one learns even to recognize a wombat or a wallaby under concepts, let alone a third strike or a tort or an atonement, via untutored sense-perception alone, without training. No one is without parents or other caregivers whose expectations and demands both model and inhibit courses of activity and interest. Conflict between more or less impersonal imperatives for social order and unruly libidinal energies is not to be overleaped in the formation of the ego as a locus of conflict and choice. Inevitably, any human subject with multiple interests and directions of desire—formed via articulation, resolved into activity via choice, and integrable up to a point in an ongoing course of significant life—will participate in a logic of succession, requiring actively taking up and refiguring multiple, contested inheritances.[47]

When, then, things go well enough with the inheritance, the articulation, and the resulting expression of perceptions, affections, aversions, and evaluations in activity, as they sometimes can, then a we of some circumference might achieve the distinctly human satisfactions of "consent[ing] to our present state as something we desire, or anyway desire more than we desire change" (CR, 465), and others differently minded might at least appreciate and value the process of achieving that materially specific and temporalized consent. Without active, concrete engagement with this possibility, meaningful democracy, expressive freedom, and distinctly human satisfactions will all be lost. Cavell's writings enact and model a way forward.

The chapters that compose this volume concentrate on Cavell's philosophical anthropology—his accounts of human being in the world and of the expression and stultification of human powers in sociohistorical, cultural life. Within these accounts, the problem of following a rule is a continuing figure for the problem of expressive freedom, of knowing how to go on in the direction of enhanced self-unity and reconciled life under more coherent commitments; the truth of skepticism is a continuing figure for persisting incompleteness and difference.

In concentrating on this philosophical anthropology, this volume differs from other important book-length engagements with Cavell's work.[48] It takes in view work that Cavell produced relatively late in his career: *Cities of Words: Pedagogical Letters on a Register of the Moral Life* (2004), *Little Did I Know: Excerpts from Memory* (2010), and the posthumous collection *Here and There: Sites of Philosophy* (2022), and it situates this work in relation to Cavell's earlier and better-known writings. While there is a fair amount of Cavell explication, these chapters also extend Cavell's philosophical anthropology, putting it to work in coming to terms with lyric poems, films, and historical phenomena with which Cavell did not directly engage, thus arguing for why that philosophical anthropology matters via the illuminations of these phenomena that it makes available.

The chapters are organized under the broad headings of "Selfhood and Method," where Cavell's distinctive way of pursuing fuller selfhood is considered, "America: History and Futurity," where the general cultural and historical contexts of his work are brought into view, and "Sites of Arrest and Recovery," where either particular moments of arrest and responsive recovery in Cavell are considered, or the Cavellian-Wordsworthian trope of arrest and recovery is enacted in criticism. (Crucially the form of recovery is cadential rather than doctrinal, a matter of settling in and with one's

experience, knowing that things will change, rather than denying temporality by claiming finality.) Recurring themes bind these chapters to one another in multiple ways: immanent criticism as the scrutiny of dialectically
related individual and social commitments; the standing ontological fact of
human immigrancy in being cast into language and possibilities of reflection; skepticism as a continuing apt register of alienation and nonfinality;
Cavell's Freudian sense of the human entry into language; the specific plights
and possibilities of modernity; America and Americanness as figures for
the possibility of onwardness; literature and film as vehicles of response to
human immigrancy and for the achievement of expressive freedom. This
volume's subtitle, *Engaging Stanley Cavell*, is meant to suggest all of (i) Cavell
as an object of study; (ii) Cavell's work as a lens through which to view topics
in philosophy; (iii) Cavell's work put in juxtaposition with some major figures in literature, film, and philosophy: Rorty, Kripke, Hölderlin, Kant,
Schiller, Marx, Truffaut, Collingwood, Freud, the canonical figures of analytic philosophy, and, especially, Wordsworth and Hegel; (iv) Cavell treated
in relation to major currents in American religious, political, cultural, and
literary history, and (v) Cavell's persona as enacted in his writing, as he
works through his attractions and aversions, as itself an object of interest
and identification.[49] Its main title, "Anticipations of Freedom," casts Cavell's
approaches to the problem of fuller selfhood and his substantive readings as
materials to which his readers and the readers of these chapters might resonate in their pursuits of more fully human satisfactions and involvements
in life. Reading the genitive construction "Anticipations of Freedom" objectively, these chapters track thoughts and responses that take freedom as their
not yet (fully) actualized object; reading the genitive construction subjectively, they track the freedom that is to be found within fuller thoughtfulness
and anticipatory responsiveness to life.

In holding together these five ways of engaging with Cavell, these chapters
thus articulate a polyphony of interrelated Cavellian themes. (1) For
reflective-discursive beings such as we are, there is (often) a felt experience of anxiety and alienation that is bound up with the inheritance of language and the formation of the ego. (Some readers find Cavell to monger
alienation excessively. Surely not every life is everywhere either marked by
crises or sunk in boredom. I have felt the force of this worry [see especially
Chapter 4]. But any life will have its sometime crises and losses, and Cavell
identifies available pursuits of happiness, involving shared onwardnesses
achieved [see Chapters 4, 10, 12, 13].) (2) As a result, there is in human life a

standing fact of immigrancy or unnaturalness—especially felt individually in adolescence and historically in modernity, with its radical division of labor and consequent mutual opacities, though possible for anyone at moments of crisis—that is poised against possibilities of fluency, grace, and mutual improvisation. (3) These latter possibilities—productive responses to the truth of skepticism—are significantly and exemplarily enacted in the arts and in mutual improvisations, which then stand as provocations to and possibilities for their receivers. (4) Consequently philosophy's best modes of response to alienation, immigrancy, and skepticism are best inflected and informed by works of art (and criticism) and vice versa. Philosophy thematizes modes of artistic engagement with particulars, art concretizes thematic engagements, and each occasions, overlaps with, and interacts with the other. Philosophy— or one kind of (Socratic) philosophy: the pursuit and achievement so far as possible of fluency, stability, satisfaction, and mutual recognition in the exercise of distinctively human powers—is not properly a body of theory modeled on the sciences. Self-understanding is not a species of knowledge of objects, and philosophical self-understanding aims at the awakening and the animation of interest in practices and relationships, posed against despair or death-in-life under routines that are not one's own. In weaving together these themes over the full range of Cavell's work, early and late, major and less well-known, these chapters offer an extended account and analysis of what might be called Cavell's lived sense of human being in the world and its tragedies and triumphs.

Together, these four thematic ideas and the five modes of engaging Cavell through which they emerge present a systematic picture of Cavell's work that embodies a distinctive account of its continuing interest. Like many of the modernist philosophers and writers whom he admires and considers, Cavell is concerned to resist modern drift, alienation, despair, and lack of wholeheartedness in life, and he is concerned to further this resistance always by beginning *in medias res*, himself initially caught up in drift and alienation, and without appeal to any external super-realities of the kind that were once thought to afford meaningful orientation (the Good, the motions of divine Nôus, the will of God). The shape of contemporary culture and the alienations and despairs it engenders, especially among the young, combined with continuing, widespread suspicion of dogmatic assurances, explains much of the appeal and importance of Cavell's democratic perfectionist pursuits of meaningful onwardness.

In his early essay "The Availability of Wittgenstein's Later Philosophy," Cavell writes that

Our problem is not that we lack adequate methods for acquiring knowledge of nature but that we are unable to prevent our best ideas—including our best ideas about our knowledge of nature—from becoming ideologized. Our incapacity here results not from the supposed fact that ordinary language is vague; to say so is an excuse for not recognizing that (and when) we speak vaguely, imprecisely, thoughtlessly, unjustly, in the absence of feeling, and so forth. (MWM, 68–69)

One should note here the echo of "A Plea for Excuses" by J. L. Austin—Cavell's teacher—in the string of adverbs that Cavell offers to characterize our incapacities as well as the fact that the failures these adverbs describe are failures of life and action, not only of speech. Soon after this passage, Cavell adds that

the breaking of . . . control . . . . [stemming from] subjection to modes of thought and sensibility whose origins are unseen or unremembered . . . is a constant purpose of the writing of the later Wittgenstein. . . . Like Freud's therapy, it wishes to prevent understanding which is unaccompanied by inner change. (MWM, 72)

In a culture in which, more than ever, friendship and intimacy threaten to be reduced to transactionality, practical reason to instrumental consideration of means to ego-centered and uncriticized ends, and enjoyment of life, activity, and relationship to the accumulation of punctual satisfactions of preferences, we stand more in need of this kind of therapy—this kind of philosophy and criticism and art that break control as subjection and forge control as self-assuredness in attention and activity—than ever before. The wager of these chapters is that they might help more of us to see how engaging with Cavell's writing might contribute to it.

SELFHOOD AND METHOD

1

Between Acknowledgment and Avoidance

In an early essay, Stanley Cavell writes that the problem of the ordinary language philosopher—a problem from which he himself takes his bearings—is "to discover the specific plight of mind and circumstance within which a human being gives voice to his condition" (MWM, 240). What can this mean? What is a *plight of mind and circumstance*? How does *giving voice* constitute a response and address to a general human condition that is instanced in a specific way?

Since it is a plight *of mind* that is in question, it is already evident that Cavell must be concerned with something more than simply a physical or biological state of being a human being, even if the mind is itself inextricably lodged in both bodily and cultural circumstances. Nor is the problem of giving voice simply that of unburdening oneself of an idiosyncratic emotion: *giving voice* implies not brute discharge alone, but further a making intelligible of how the human condition is present in one who has been moved to speak. Nor will just any speech do; *giving voice* implies an achievement of expressiveness that is beyond the communication of bits of information about the material world.

Instead, to be moved to give voice to a plight of mind and circumstance—to manage that achievement—is to express a specific sense of just how, here and now, one's human capacities for free and fluent voicing and action are somehow both enabled and inhibited by one's culture and one's life with others as they stand. One seeks, as Cavell elsewhere puts it, "freedom of consciousness, the beginning of freedom, . . . freedom of language, having the run of it, as if successfully claimed from it, as of a birthright" (TNYUA, 55). One seeks to have one's performances—one's uses of concepts in thought, in utterance, and in action, which are all internally related—be both one's *own* as expressions of one's independent personality and desire, against the sways of the common, and reasonably *endorsable*, by both others and oneself, as valuable expressions of common possibilities and necessities.

Anticipations of Freedom. Richard Eldridge, Oxford University Press. © Richard Eldridge 2026.
DOI: 10.1093/9780197841785.003.0003

This is no small task, and Cavell emphasizes the persistence of the effort to achieve such expressiveness, as against both simpler, dogmatic recipes for its achievement and naturalist-quietist scantings of the adventure of the human. Rather than sketching and defending any definite account of human flourishing, Cavell notes that there are certain "arguments that must not be won" and that philosophy might be conceived of as "the achievement of the unpolemical, of the refusal to take sides in metaphysical positions" (PP, 22).

This is not a refusal to take sides or to enact commitments as such, but rather "a refusal of, say, disobedient to, (a false) ascent; or transcendence" (TNYUA, 45) as a ground of commitment. Against false ascent, Cavell poses *philosophy as descent*, the necessary faithfulness of philosophy to the common and the ordinary, as the only available loci of repertoires of language, thought, conceptual life, and human action. But it is also true that "the (actual) everyday [is—or can be experienced as, for Cavell, following Wittgenstein—] . . . a scene of illusion and trance and artificiality (of need)" (TNYUA, 46). *Philosophy as ascent* is also called for. Hence what is pursued, in and through the pursuit of fully expressive action, aiming at exemplariness of voicing, is an eventual or transfigured ordinary, a fit common habitation for the human.

Since, however, one takes one's bearings and possibilities of thought, action, and expression from within the ordinary as it stands, as a scene of both possibilities and (false) necessities, of both affordances and inhibitions, it follows that philosophizing, the effort to enact more humanly expressive possibilities, will be "a spiritual struggle, specifically a struggle with the contrary depths of oneself" (TNYUA, 37). One will find oneself, at times, pursuing a thought, vision, or course of action that is not generally shared, hence seeking abandonment of or departure from the common. But then one will also find oneself, at times, recoiling from the solipsistic madness of apocalyptic vision and returning to the common, accepting it as cure.[1] Neither movement, in Cavell's perception, can be complete or final. What is left, to adapt Dieter Henrich's useful characterization of Friedrich Hölderlin's stance, is the thought "that conscious life is at once shaped and unbalanced by the basic *conflicting* tendencies orienting it. And the formative process of life aims at finding a balance and a harmony amidst this strife, in which no one tendency is entirely suppressed or denied in its own right."[2] For Cavell, as for Hölderlin, these conflicting basic tendencies include at least the pursuit of independent selfhood and the pursuit of communion, community, love, and the common. Seeking both, one is left between *avoidance* (of others, of the common, of what is common with others in oneself, as decayed, vulgarized, inhibiting, and empty) and *acknowledgment* (of others, of the common, of what is common with others in oneself, as what alone enables thought, recovery, conversation, and restoration).

To find oneself in such a plight is, in Cavell's reading, central to what it is to be "a creature complicated or burdened enough to possess language at all" (CR, 140). Not everyone will feel or accept this, will feel or accept the burden or complication of seeking expressive freedom and the run of language, thought, and action. The demands of daily life or of sheer survival are too pressing for some to notice this plight; others are reasonably distracted by scientific, political, artistic, intellectual, and other problems that are genuinely absorbing. But then it is also true that these problems themselves may include problems of human aspiration that touch on this plight of mind, that those who are pressed or absorbed in daily life may suffer from quiet desperation, silent melancholy, or distractedness, all covertly legible in their pursuits and entertainments, and that in certain nights of the soul a sense of this plight may come to consciousness, even if it is then often reasonably suppressed in the name of decency, work, or common life.

We come to language as something that is already there before us in the practices of our elders. The criteria for calling something what it is are there in practice before we are, and we cannot come to thought and linguistic practice without them. This fact has both positive and negative sides. "I have to accept [criteria], use them," if I am to enter into linguistic and conceptual practice at all, but "this itself makes my use of them seem arbitrary, or private—as though they were never shared, or as if our sharing of them is either a fantastic accident or a kind of mass folly" (CR, 83). Their presence and availability in practice are not grounded for me in any kind of unmediated knowledge of ultimate realities and of the relation of words to them. If words and the criteria for their use then seem ungrounded or arbitrary, I can feel my dawning powers in their exercise to be uncertain. My exercise of these powers may seem liable to drift away from others' and then to repudiation, and I can wish to do better. I can indulge in a fantasy of absolute power in my uses of (to me) primitive words, fully grounded in necessarily private acts of inner "recognition." Or I can indulge in a fantasy of powerlessness or "necessary inexpressiveness" (CR, 351), in which my uses of words occur "according to laws of nature" in and through me, without implicating me in responsibility for their finding or missing understanding in any audience.

Yet these fantasies of cognitive omnipotence and of necessary inexpressiveness come to nothing, can't be worked out. "We cannot really imagine ..., or rather ... there is nothing of the sort to imagine, or rather ... when we as it were try to imagine this we are imagining something other than we think" (CR, 344). The discovery of either private, perfect, absolute "inner recognitions" or fully law-governed natural processes in me cannot be stated within ordinary language without returning us to the very scene of risks and responsibilities we had sought to escape. Ordinary criteria "*are* the terms in which *I relate what's happening*" (CR, 93), and I must draw on them if I am to think and speak at all. This is not to deny that there can be innovations in language in the form of new technical terms or new turns of metaphor. It *is* to deny that language as such could have such bases in individual acts or events apart from the common. Public words and the criteria for their use *are* there before us, and they *are* the only things we have to go on. In Stephen Mulhall's useful summary, Cavell's thought is that

> if the ground of the inheritability of language, the basis of the continued existence of the speech community and its members, is the capacity of human beings to see and hear themselves in the words and deeds of other human beings, then the continuance of that community cannot be guaranteed either by nature or by grammar; it rests solely upon our capacity to take and maintain an interest in one another and in ourselves.[3]

Though we can succeed in taking and maintaining such an interest, we can also fail, and we can feel the responsibility for success or failure to be an undue burden. Hence we live, in Cavell's perception, in simultaneous satisfaction with and disappointment in criteria and the ordinary (see CHU, 83, 92), engaged in "a continuous effort at balance" (CR, 44) between escape into independence and personal assertion, on the one hand, and return to accommodation, habit, and domestication on the other. The reason for this joint disappointment and satisfaction is that there is within us "the human drive to transcend itself, make itself inhuman" (TNYUA, 57). "Nothing could be more human" than "the power of the motive to reject the human" (CR, 207), than to seek somehow—whether in perfect individual cognitive omnipotence (even if within a narrow domain) or in perfect submission to the ordinary and natural—to perfect one's satisfactions and overcome one's disappointments. "The threat, or the truth, of skepticism [is] that it names our wish (and the possibility of our wishing) to strip ourselves of the responsibility we have in meaning (or in failing to mean) one thing, or one way, rather than another" (IQO, 135). There is inherent in the human and "inherent in philosophy a certain drive to the inhuman . . . [that is] somehow itself the most inescapably human of motivations."[4]

For beings who are freighted with such wishes and responsibilities, arising in and through engagement with the ordinary, the ordinary itself is, in a phrasing Cavell adapts from Heidegger, "at bottom . . . not ordinary; *it* is extra-ordinary, uncanny."[5] For Cavell, "the uncanniness of the ordinary is epitomized by . . . the capacity, even the desire, of ordinary language [that is, of we who use it] to repudiate itself" (IQO, 154). Nothing within ordinary thinking or linguistic practice *guarantees* its continuation; how it goes on is up to us, we who are initiated into it and go on within and from it, and this can seem terrifying. Yet ordinary thinking and linguistic practice are necessary media for the presence of things to discursively thinking, judgmental subjects, and we do not have the power to alter prior patterns of language and thought *tout court*. These patterns have a certain sway over us, and this too can seem terrifying. Both "the repudiation of the world" as a scene of perhaps false necessities, and of perennial risks, and "its revelation of the world" are "internal to" ordinary language (TS, 34). As discursive, acting, judging subjects, we wish for more—more mastery, more grounding, more surety—from the ordinary. Yet the ordinary (together with its possible successors) remains the only scene for our lives as such subjects. We are hence in relation to the ordinary both at home and not at home; it is uncanny. "The human necessity of the quest for home and the human fact of immigrancy are seen together as aspects of the human as such" (PP, 47).

Inhabiting our relation to the ordinary, therefore, are opposed drives toward both its acceptance and its overcoming. The ordinary and our relation to it in turn enable—and may even present themselves as requiring—the working out of both drives. It is possible, and sometimes necessary if solipsistic madness is to be foregone and thought and reasonable action are to be continued at all, to consent "to become intelligible" (IQO, 114). Acknowledgment of the common—both the current common and the perfected common that can arise out of it alone—is possible. To refuse that acknowledgment altogether and instead to insist on pure independence of thought is to fall into skepticism not as insinuating possibility, but as mad discovery, or to fall even further into the all-too-human avoidances and rages of Othello and Lear. In Wittgenstein's phrasing, "Knowledge is in the end based on acknowledgment"[6] of the common, of what is among us.

Acknowledgment is available, and there is no thought or reasonable action without it. Even genius, whatever departures from the common it enacts in an exemplary way, must be "the name of the promise that the private and the social will be achieved together" (IQO, 114), that a perfected ordinary will be the site of return and redemption. The remarrying pairs canvassed in *Pursuits of Happiness* arrive at such an achievement, and it is—sometimes—a genuine possibility of significance for us.

But then, too, a certain avoidance—what Cavell, following Emerson, calls "aversiveness" or "daring to say" (see IQO, 112)—is also possible and sometimes necessary. "Emerson calls the mode of uncreated life," in which we are dominated by a fallen social world and seem to ourselves not to be authors of our lives, "'conformity.' . . . Each of the modem prophets [—Cavell lists Mill, Nietzsche, Marx, and Freud as well as Emerson—] seems to have been driven to find some way of characterizing the threat to individual existence, to individuation, posed by the life to which their society is bringing itself" (IQO, 11). In the face of such threats, there are times to be "the one who goes first" (IQO, 119), to refigure what the ordinary might better be. In either case, in moments of either acknowledgment or avoidance on the path of thinking,

> [w]hat I require is a convening of my culture's criteria, in order to confront them with my words and life as I pursue them and as I may imagine them; and at the same time to confront my words and life as I pursue them with the life my culture's words may imagine for me: to confront the culture with itself, along the lines in which it meets in me.
>
> This seems to me a task that warrants the name of philosophy. (CR, 125)

To undertake the task of philosophy is then to attempt to speak, in a phrase of Kant's that Cavell adapts to describe the efforts of both the critic of the arts and the ordinary language philosopher, "with a universal voice."[7] Centrally, this attempt will take the form of making what Cavell calls *a claim of reason*, a claim about what *our criteria are*. One will find oneself saying *what we would say when*: "this is what we call an accident as opposed to a mistake, or this is what we call justice, or love, or knowledge." Such claims of reason are lodged as reminders and vehicles of reorientation—to and on behalf of both others and oneself—when the applications of the concepts expressed by these words are somehow both dimly available and yet attenuated or disputed. As Wittgenstein puts it, "When I think away the normal language-game with the expression . . ., then I need a criterion of identity for it."[8] Such utterances are *claims* all at once to selfknowledge (of what one would say when), to community (to what *we* would say when), and to reason (to what it makes sense to say when).[9] "The philosophical appeal to what we say, and the search for our criteria on the basis of which we say what we say, are claims to community. And the claim to community is always a search for the basis upon which it can [be] or has been established. The wish and search for community are the wish and search for reason" (CR, 20).

Such claims to reason that embody efforts at reorientation of both self and community are distinctive of philosophy and philosophical criticism: the heirs, one might say, of necessary truths as constituting what is distinctive about philosophy. Unlike, however, necessary truths as traditionally conceived—that is, as objects of a fixed intellectual discovery that is always ratifiable by anyone—these claims, for Cavell, can fail in their inherent aim of refiguring rational community. "It may prove to be the case that I am wrong [in making such a claim], that my conviction isolates me from all others, from myself" (CR, 20). This is a standing risk for the modernist philosopher—affiliated with the modernist artist's risk of fraudulence in seeking new routes of artistic work[10]—as one who lives in a modem community "in which history and its conventions can no longer be taken for granted" (MWM, xxii), if they ever quite wholly could.

But such claims can also succeed, as Austin's treatments of accidents versus mistakes and losing control of oneself versus succumbing to temptation perhaps above all demonstrate. We can then find ourselves, with ourselves and one another, possessing our criteria and knowing what we would say when. The magic of philosophy (and of art) lies in the achievement of this reorientation in practice, where and when it can be achieved, and in acceptance of the thought that here or there it will, always, have to be re-achieved again. Without their relation to subjectivity, its standing possibilities of disorientation and inexpressiveness, its standing risks of fraudulence and trust,

> art and the criticism of art [—and, given the analogies, philosophy and the criticism of philosophy—] would not have their special importance nor elicit their own forms of distrust and gratitude. The problem of the critic, as of the artist [—and the philosopher (of a certain kind)—], is not to discount his subjectivity [—and need for new routes of expressiveness and perception—] but to include it; not to overcome it in agreement, but to master it

in exemplary ways. Then his work outlasts the fashions and arguments of a particular age. That is the beauty of it. (MWM, 94)

In a justly famous, perhaps even notorious, passage at the end of the opening section of chapter 4, "Self-Consciousness," of *The Phenomenology of Spirit*, Hegel writes that we have reached a great "turning point." Our thinking about who and what we are at this point "leaves behind it the colourful show of the sensuous here-and-now and the nightlike void of the supersensible beyond, and steps out into the spiritual daylight of the present."[11] What this turning point turns out to involve, very roughly, is the absorption of essentially epistemological questions by essentially political, historical, artistic, and religious questions. Allowing for the foreignness of the idiom, in chapters 1, 2, and 3 of the *Phenomenology* the topics are all ones that would be familiar to contemporary analytic epistemologists and philosophers of mind. How do we apprehend particulars? What is the experience of qualia? In what ways might our consciousness of objects be law-governed? Beginning with chapter 4, however, things are very different. The topics now center around forms of worldly practice in pursuit of the public satisfaction of desire. What is it to live freely? How might agents achieve recognition? What political institutions, forms of art, and religious conceptions that have been developed historically will help us to live freely and to achieve recognition?

Hegel's argument in moving from chapter 3 to chapter 4 is that answering the latter set of questions will settle all the epistemological problems that were raised in the first three chapters and that nothing else will. But *that* stretch of argument—the treatment of "Force and the Understanding" and then of "life"—is as notoriously obscure and difficult as anything Hegel ever wrote.

So is the absorption of the epistemological by the practical a good idea? Ignoring Hegel's argument, there are considerations that point both ways, and it is at least possible to understand contemporary analytic philosophy and contemporary Continental philosophy as taking one of these sets of considerations to have decisive force against the other.

In favor of the practical turn, it might be said that our knowing and our epistemological inquiries into the nature of our knowing arise only when we have already managed some cognitive successes and then begun to reflect on the differences between cognitive success and failure. That reflection must involve historical awareness of alternatives, and it must itself be supported by a certain amount of leisure for reflection, over and above a continuous struggle for bare subsistence. Hence knowing and reflection on knowing seem to take place within historical and practical contexts in which people—embodied human agents, with social relations and social interests—are already trying to do something. Much of Continental philosophy since Hegel has been centrally interested in the histories of human cognitive and social practices, taking it for granted that these practices are deeply interrelated. Satisfaction of our aims—including our cognitive aims—if it is to be achieved must be at least in part also a social and practical achievement.

Against the practical turn, it might be said that language, culture, and sociopolitical life—at least in the richly articulated forms which we humans have them—are all species-specific. Other animals just don't do what we do, linguistically, cognitively, or sociopolitically. If we are the linguistic, cultural, and political animals that we are, this must somehow be because we are the mind/brain-endowed animals we are. Surely, further, we have succeeded in knowing some things about our environment by taking in objects in the right way and doing so independently of and often in the face of any political developments. Mathematics and modern scientific knowledge may be evolving and contested, but they are at least more independent of political considerations than are other regions of cultural life. The science and mathematics of China and the United States look a lot more alike than do their paintings or politics or religious rituals. Surely it is reasonable to try to give some culture-independent account of at least our most basic cognitive achievements. Perhaps it is best to leave political philosophy on its own as a set of problems of social organization, without tendentious, quasi-religious essentialisms: political, not metaphysical. Much of contemporary analytic epistemology and philosophy of mind and language has been centrally interested in explaining the roots of culture in given human endowments and in characterizing our cognitive successes by reference to our species-specific powers.

Rough and tendentious though these sketches of argument are, and granting that there are numbers of interesting and important philosophers who are working somehow between them, these two paradigms do map two large and largely divergent routes of current philosophical imagination. For Cavell, by contrast, the argument between these two paradigms is centrally one of those that cannot and must not be won. Our practical and cognitive lives *are* intertwined—it is no accident that one of Cavell's central terms, *acknowledgment*, is a transcription of Hegel's *Anerkennung*—but neither full satisfaction in shared social practices nor full and self-standing absolute knowing of 'the' way things are, free of practical commitment and risk, is possible. In both social and cognitive practice, there are always resistances and remainders, both socially and within oneself. These resistances and remainders will call for and enable departures from what is already done, either cognitively or socially. New regions of interest and ways of pursuing them will emerge out of them, and these will have to be and can (sometimes) be articulated on behalf of a more perfect ordinary. Investigation into how individuals, by drawing on the capacities of the species, manage this feat will always be invited. Yet these regions of interest and ways of pursuing them can establish their sense—for oneself as well as for others—only insofar as they are acknowledged: taken up and lived out, yet also setting up their own resistances and remainders. We live between acknowledgment and avoidance.

To come to discursive consciousness of self in relation to a set of existent and evolving practices, together with their distinctive resistances and remainders, is to participate, in Cavell's formulation, in "a self's judgmental forming of itself, as something to be further possessed *or* to be overcome" (PP, 150; emphasis added).[12] One seeks unity with oneself and in relation to others in secure mastery of fully reasonable practice—sometimes through acknowledgment by accepting the ordinary and one's legibility within it; sometimes through departure, daring to say, and gesturing toward an eventual, more perfect ordinary. Yet there is no escape from this seeking into either absolute knowing or absolute freedom.

Hence, in living within this condition—timidly or boldly; gracefully or assertively; cleverly, decently, or badly—"each life is exemplary of all, a parable of each; that is humanity's commonness, which is internal to its endless denials of commonness" (PP, 11). To think philosophically about this condition, refusing either its abandonment or its absolute cure, in any region of practice, will be also to participate in it, in one way or another. It will involve aligning one's life and pursuits both with and against other lives and pursuits, as one moves oneself between acknowledgment and avoidance. Central to such alignments will be philosophizing as the work of reading:[13] hence Cavell's endless finding of aspects of himself, and of oppositions to himself, in Plato, Descartes, Emerson, Nietzsche, Luther, Rousseau, Wittgenstein, Poe, Shakespeare, Verdi, Hawks, and Capra. In these thinkers and in their works (and in others, without end), Cavell finds exemplary ways of responding to our "continuing task" (IQO, 111) of finding and enacting our freedom, of "guiding the soul, or self, [together with its practices] from selfimprisonment toward the light or the instinct of freedom" (PP, 4). Such findings and enactments, or such routes of self-creation, imply that in taking them up we both could and "would have to accept responsibility for ourselves, in particular have to consent to our present state as something we desire, or anyway desire more than we desire change" (CR, 465), if we are to find satisfaction within them. This possibility and burden might, Cavell notes, further drive one mad, perhaps into Othello's or Lear's region of avoidance and the refusal of legibility: anything but to have to consent again, and yet again, to the ordinary as *it* stands. Or this possibility and burden might, as in the remarrying of the pairs considered in *Pursuits of Happiness*, enable and motivate acknowledgment and a certain consent to one's state, where these might further sustain their reachievement in a fit enough ordinary, experienced as these paired individuals' daily wit and romance with one another.

When each life is thus seen as a parable of each, whether exemplary or admonitory, there will be no single perfect way of human life, individual or social, even while possibilities of further perfection make themselves available and haunt us. Hence philosophers' 'solutions' to 'problems'—whether of knowing or of social life—will present themselves not so much or so centrally as 'answers' to be accepted or rejected, but as bound up with available styles of response (all of them partial, some of them exemplary or admonitory) to the condition of the human, styles themselves legible as involving both acknowledgment and avoidance. What would it be to deny that human life and mindedness should be so seen? Is such a denial quite coherently possible? Cavell's articulation of the human would *imply* that it is not. Through the work of reading, carried out in relation to life, this articulation can sustain itself as encompassing, generous, perceptive, nuanced, and deep, as fitly so as any it is possible to imagine. In this it offers a style of philosophical thinking—the reading of each life as a parable of each—that may well stand comparison with the visions of the human of the analytic and Continental traditions, or of any of the other visionaries upon whom Cavell has touched. One will have to read to see.

2

Cavell and the Achievement of Selfhood

Here is a passage from the discussion of rhythm in music in Hegel's *Aesthetics* that will, I suggest, help us to make sense of some important ideas in Cavell about the achievement of selfhood.[1] This runs some risk of explicating the obscure, Cavell, by reference to the unintelligible, Hegel, but Hegel also helps us here specifically to focus on the ontology and ontogeny of selfhood.

> The I is not indeterminate persistence and uninterrupted duration, but rather only becomes a self as collection and return into itself [als Sammlung und Rückkehr in sich].[2] It transforms this sublation of itself, through which it becomes an object to itself, into being-for-itself and is now through this relation to itself for the first time self-feeling and self-consciousness, and so forth. This collection essentially involves an *interruption* of merely undetermined change—which is what we had had before us—in that the arising and passing away, the disappearance and renewal of points of time was, prior to this collection, nothing but a merely formal passing over from each now to another similar one and thus nothing but an uninterrupted further movement. In contrast with this empty moving *forward*, the self is that which exists *with itself*, and its collection into itself interrupts the indeterminate succession of points of time, makes cuts in their abstract continuity, and frees the I, which remembers itself in these now discrete moments of its experience and retrieves itself in them, from mere self-externalization and change.[3]

Here neither the I nor the self is a fixed, given, persistent thing, if it is even correct to think of it as a thing at all. Rather, there is a living, embodied human being who first develops an I or sense of self as a locus of agency through collecting its sensations, that is, holding them together as sensations that pertain to a *this* in the world.[4] We might think here of an infant developing not yet conceptually articulated proprioceptive awareness of the position of its hand and of its effects as agent on both the hand's motion and the sensations that accompany it. In a second step, this initial sublation of

Anticipations of Freedom. Richard Eldridge, Oxford University Press. © Richard Eldridge 2026.
DOI: 10.1093/9780197841785.003.0004

itself through which it has become initially but inarticulately aware of it-self as a thing in interaction with things in the world is then extended by memory and the focusing of attention on the object interacted with as dis-tinct from other objects. The object—a hand, a rattle, a plush toy—is held in mind as a recognizable thing under a protoconcept, so that the infant becomes a conscious classifier or proto-claim-maker: a being for itself who *takes* itself, as an object of which it is now aware, to be interacting with rec-ognizable things. All this counts as the interruption, through the emergence of an embodied subject who thinks and does things, of what would other-wise be a mere succession of law-governed events in nature. Instead of an indeterminate succession of mere events, there is now a subject attending to objects recognitively and holding them before itself. Through this interrup-tion or cut in experience, the thus emergent subject is "freed from mere self-externalization and change," freed *to* begin to exercise agency consciously. Interestingly, the reason that this passage occurs in Hegel's discussion of rhythm in music is that the experience of rhythm can feed what the cognitive archaeologist Lambros Malafourdis, echoing Antonio Damasio, calls a "com-plex associative enchainment between the 'internal' and 'external' elements of remembering."[5] The experience of rhythm helps our sensations, sense of agency, and registerings of objects as objects to sync up, thus bringing the world into view for an emergent subject.

That the I or the subject emerges, or that selfhood is achieved, in having a sense of agency in exercise and a somewhat stabilized point of view on things, is, of course, also and even more familiar to us from Freud.[6] Freud adds or makes explicit the further thought that this emergence and achieve-ment are never complete, as the ego remains caught between troubling li-bidinal fantasies and superego commands that are internalizations of the authority of others. Given, further, the varieties of others with whom we must engage and who frequently have conflicting habits of judgment and ex-pectations for us, *how* to exercise agency and stabilize selfhood satisfacto-rily remains a fraught issue for us. The continuing, conflicting pressures on the subject in development are the stuffs of dreams, parapraxes, jokes, and neuroses. Hegel similarly notes the standing possibility of a "rupture . . . be-tween my psychical [or primary process-sensual] and my waking [or ego-centered] being, between my spontaneous natural feeling and my mediated, intellectual consciousness, a rupture which, since everyone embraces these two sides in himself is of course a *possibility* in even the healthiest individual, but does not actually *exist* in everyone."[7]

Cavell's own experience of Freud is as formative for him as the experience of any other writer save perhaps Wittgenstein, and the encounter with Wittgenstein was already prepared and shaped by his prior encounter with Freud. During his brief time at Juilliard in 1947–8, Cavell reports, he found his "ambition to compose music ... replaced as it were by reading Freud ten to twelve hours a day, successively contracting the symptoms of hysteria and of obsession depicted in the *Introductory Lectures*" (LDIK, 185; compare LDIK, 234 and CW, 282). In addition, Cavell himself twice entered psychoanalytic treatment, once in the late 1950s under the pressure of a foundering first marriage and as he was having difficulty completing his doctoral dissertation, once again in the late 1970s as he was encountering the demands of fatherhood for a second time and having trouble transforming the dissertation into what would become *The Claim of Reason* (LDIK, 108–9).

Two thoughts that derive from his encounters with Freud are especially important for Cavell. First, thinking about a succession of minor childhood accidents, Cavell finds himself, he reports,

> responding to a recurrent surmise of mine that whatever happens—whatever is eventful enough for speech—is from the beginning accidental, as if a human life is inherently interrupted, things chronically occurring at unripe times, in the wrong tempo, comically or poignantly. This is not incompatible with Freud's view that there are no accidents. What that now means to me is that we chronically interrupt ourselves—say, we fail to give the right quality or quantity or time to our thoughts or deeds. (LDIK, 30)

What this passage says is that in our efforts at achieving stable, fluent subjecthood, in Hegelian terms, freedom, or being with oneself in another, *bei sich selbst in einem anderen*—we always, in circumstances we can't control, find ourselves getting in the way of ourselves: persisting in awkwardness and anxiety and failing to achieve full at homeness in what we do, as new things always happen. In light of this, it is not apt to regard finding and sustaining senses of value and agency in life as an engineering problem, solvable by grasping and applying a formula. Degrees of uncertainty and anxiety about stability and reception attach inevitably to the formation and expression of selfhood. Or as Cavell remarks, "I remain too impressed with Freud's vision of the human animal's compromise with existence—the defense or the deflection of our ego in our knowledge of ourselves from what there is to know about ourselves—to suppose that a human life can get itself without residue into the clear."[8]

Second, out of this experience of immigrancy in the exercise of conceptually structured agency, there then arises a sense of a need for liberation that Cavell also finds articulated in Freud. "The sufferer," Cavell remarks

> has to be, as Freud characteristically puts the matter, awakened . . . [from] feeling himself a prisoner of his circumstances. This sense of imprisonment, of the need for liberation, is critical both for Wittgensteinian philosophizing and for Emersonian perfectionist aspiration. I have sometimes called it the crisis from which the wish for philosophy and for a morally comprehensible life begins. (CW, 284)

In this remarkable passage, Freud is invoked in order to characterize the motivation of the writerly, self-interrogative styles of doing philosophy—those of Wittgenstein and Emerson—that have been most immediately influential for Cavell's own philosophical writing and in furthering his sense of the contours of genuinely available liberation from chaotic succession and into greater practical self-comprehension, into a more morally comprehensible life. It is worth noting the strikingly Freudian sound of some of Cavell's remarks about the practice of philosophy, early and late:

1. That it "is to be achieved through mapping the fields of consciousness lit by the occasions of a word" (MWM, 103).
2. That it is a matter of "proceed[ing] from the fact *that* a thing is said; that it is (or can be) said (in certain circumstances) is as significant as what it says; its being said then and there is as determinative of what it says as the meanings of its individual words are" (MWM, 336).
3. That its progress is "not as from false to true assertions, or from opinions to proven conclusions (say theses) or from doubt to certainty, but rather from the darkness of confusion to enlightened understanding, or say from illusion to clarity, or from being at an intellectual loss to finding my feet with myself, from insistent speech to productive silence" (CW, 328).
4. "That we are the successors of ourselves . . . and not necessarily succeeding in a given order or direction (but capable of choosing upward or downward or neither), is a reasonable figure of the perfectionist life,

seizing crises of revelation, good or bad, clear or confused, as chances of transformation" (CW, 337).

Beyond various remarks about Freud, Cavell's own most extended and powerful pieces of writing on the development of the emergent subject away from anxiety and toward fluency as an unending task are "The Argument of the Ordinary" in *Conditions Handsome and Unhandsome* and the "Excursus on Wittgenstein's Vision of Language" in *The Claim of Reason*. In the later, 1990 text, Cavell characterizes the "portrait of the human self" in *Philosophical Investigations* as one that, "like Plato's and Freud's visions," presents "a self that incorporates selves" (CHU, 83), thus alluding to the introjection of authoritative others into the formation of the superego that is essential to the emergence of selfhood. Kripke's error in reading Wittgenstein, as Cavell sees it, is that he "evades Wittgenstein's preoccupation with philosophy's desire to underestimate or evade the ordinary" (CHU, 68): fails to recognize, that is, anxieties about selfhood in development in relations with others that themselves drive the human subject, as Wittgenstein depicts it in the first voice of the *Investigations*—one of his contending voices and one of ours—ever anew to seek a ground of perfect authority in conceptual performance and thus to overcome the very possibility of shame. In this way, we live our skepticism, first, as a disappointment with the ordinary's inability to provide that perfect authority, as concept applications and resultant routes of practice and interest remain always in part divided and contested, and, second, in a resultant turn toward fantasized perfect authority in an unmediated encounter with something within.[9] The problem that leads to skepticism is not a self-standing intellectual problem to be solved by clever reasoning, but rather the very need to ask the question "Do I know anything with absolute, unimpugnable certainty?"—a need that is always already motivated by the standing immigrancy of the human subject.

The "Excursus on Wittgenstein's Vision on Language" is oriented around the fundamental thought that "'learning' is not as academic a matter as academics are apt to suppose" (CR, 171). Compare Socrates in the *Symposium*: one does *not* acquire wisdom in practice in the way that water "always flows from a full cup into an empty one when we connect them with a piece of yarn."[10] In particular, learning a language is neither a matter only of information intake and processing nor a matter of being told what a name means or learning new words (CR, 173). Instead, it involves coming to recognize and to take an interest in some things in which others also take an interest and manifesting that interest in a bodily, behavioral repertoire that involves emotion, stance, gaze, and awareness of others as well as simply pronouncing some object *a* to be *F*. How much of all this is learned when is never fully settled—even if broad competence in a normal domain can be determined—insofar as what other, different subjects become interested in and how they may display that interest is itself never fully settled. "The learning is," as Cavell puts it, "never over, and we keep finding new potencies in words and new ways in which objects are disclosed" (CR, 180). Projections of words onto things are both stable enough to admit of being shared enough *and* tolerant of new usages. (Wittgenstein: "the use of [a] word ... is not everywhere bounded by rules."[11]) It is always possible to find oneself with another in certain straits of circumstance where it is unclear whether going on together is possible. Driven by existential anxiety about the authoritativeness of one's claim-making as a subject, skeptics remove themselves from the communicative testing of mutual intelligibility, hoping instead to find absolute assurance within. "Nothing is more human than the wish to deny one's humanity, or to assert it at the expense of others" (CR, 109), precisely by withdrawing from engagement with them. Exactly this unappeasable yet natural wish, together with the situation of the subject that supports it, is what is registered in *Philosophical Investigations* as Cavell reads it.

> Philosophical Investigations is in effect a portrait of the unsatisfiability of the human species with its solutions, a portrait-hardly the first—detailing human life as one of restlessness, exposure, insecurity; and more specifically, of ... its articulation of the modern subject, namely its expected reader, as someone characterized by, among other traits, perversity, sickness, selfdestructiveness, suffocation, lostness, strangeness, etc.[12]

The fact that for Cavell it is within the communicative testing of mutual intelligibility and only within that testing—within the argument of the ordinary—that selfhood as at least partial at-homeness in conceptual and practical agency can be achieved explains Cavell's sense that in philosophy there are certain "arguments that must not be won" (PP, 22). To absent oneself from communicative interaction in a putative reversion to absolute conceptual authority is to abandon all possibilities of reassurance and recognition, even if nothing is more human than to do this. As early as "Aesthetic Problems of Modern Philosophy," Cavell urged that introducing supposedly authoritative formulae in the form of necessarily true statements of necessary and sufficient conditions is often, even typically, a way of stunting one's responsiveness both to difficult phenomena that require patient, ambivalent attention and to others who might respond differently and in doing so help one to notice things one might oneself have missed. In contrast with strict definition mongering, the definitional claims of philosophy ought rather to be modeled on the procedures of the ordinary language philosopher, who issues claims about what we say not in order to foreclose conversation but instead to test the possibility and shape of shared response. "Philosophy's first virtue, as it matters most to me, is," as Cavell puts it, "responsiveness," not doctrinal knowledge (CW, 324). We live and achieve selfhood, to the extent that we can, as assurance in exercises of conceptual and practical agency, always already within a largely shared but never fully fixed and bounded field of concepts and possibilities of interest, always already within a partially open form of life, with possibilities of expressive, vertical development. Cavell specifically warns "against supposing that the ordinary in human life is a given, as it were a place. I would say rather that it is a task, as the self is."[13] Within the field of the ordinary, with both its possibilities of meaning and its tensions, "the human necessity of the quest for home and the human fact of immigrancy are together seen as aspects of the human as such" (PP, 47).

We are now in a position to make fuller sense of a crucial early passage on the achievement of selfhood from *The World Viewed.*

> At some point the unhinging of our consciousness from the world interposed our subjectivity between us and our presentness to the world. Then our subjectivity became what is present to us, individuality became isolation.... Apart from the wish for selfhood (hence the always simultaneous granting of otherness as well), I do not understand the value of art. Apart from this wish and its achievement, art is exhibition. (WV, 22)

Initially, this passage bears some comparison with Pierre Hadot's work on ancient philosophy as a set of spiritual exercises or practices for the cultivation of the self within the various ancient schools rather than a body of systematic theory. Like Cavell, Hadot holds that, especially in its origins, "the philosophical act is not situated merely on the cognitive level"[14] but is rather initiated by "an unhappy disquiet before conversion."[15] Similarly, for Cavell, "the thinkers and artists" whose work he is most concerned to take up in *Cities of Words* each develop and enact "a perspective of judgment upon the world as it is, measured against the world as it may be, [that] tends to express disappointment with the world as it is, as the scene of human activities and prospects, and perhaps to lodge the demand or desire for a reform or trans-figuration of the world" (CW, 1, 2). For both Hadot and Cavell, philosophy begins in unrest, discontentment, disquietude, and belatedness, from within our immigrancy as emergent subjects and from a felt need for orientation to which *theoria* cannot ultimately answer.

According to Hadot, the displacement of spiritual exercises by *theoria* occurred first during the late medieval period with the systematization of theology as a master body of knowledge within the university, and it was then sealed in the early modern period in the work of Descartes.[16] Cavell similarly notes, just a page earlier than the key passage about the achievement of self-hood, that there has been a "human wish, intensifying since the Reformation, to escape subjectivity and metaphysical isolation—a wish for the power to reach this world, having for so long tried, at last hopelessly, to manifest fi-delity to another" (WV, 21). (The allusion here is presumably to the kingdom of God or church triumphant as the object to which we once sought to be faithful.)

But where according to Hadot, this displacement might and should simply be reversed by taking up some elements of Epicurean and Stoic prac-tice, as perhaps Nietzsche also urged,[17] matters are less clear with Cavell. The wish for selfhood—for heightened assurance in exercises of conceptual and practical agency—has intensified since the Reformation rather than being displaced. It is, if anything, more sharply present, intensified, albeit in an ineffective way, in Cartesian and post-Cartesian skepticism and realism—two sides of the same coin for Cavell; two responses to the same initiating unhinging of subjectivity from the world—than in earlier practices of philosophy. There is, one might say, a certain fervor to modern and mod-ernist pursuits of selfhood, as a sense of available grounds for achieving and expressing selfhood within coherent, meaningful, shared practice becomes increasingly attenuated.[18] And, unlike Hadot, there is for Cavell no obvious way out of the bearing of the wish for selfhood unsatisfied, at least in some measure. Nor was there any time in a recognizably human form of life in which that wish was not somehow born by some as freighted with existen-tial anxiety. Achilles and Oedipus, for example, were trying to figure out who they could most coherently, intelligibly, and recognizably be in prac-tice, albeit more under the sways of nature and luck than we are and under more fully shared, thick social scripts than we inhabit. We live among and with others who are different from us in various dimensions of interest and

activity, where these differences, ramifying in modernity with technological development and broad and deep divisions of labor, are sharp enough
to block standing general assurance and to leave its achievement always in
question.

But while there is no obvious place to go either to satisfy or to be free
of the wish for selfhood, there are also possibilities of responsive address
to it that are manifest in the work of major artists and those among the
philosophers who rank with them. Such figures—from Plato to Wittgenstein,
from Shakespeare to Ibsen, from Thoreau to Emerson, from Frank Capra to
Leo McCarey—sometimes find themselves in their work achieving a kind of
fullness of attention to life and its difficult phenomena to which audiences
of considerable circumference can and have resonated, where the object of
resonance is less a formulable solution to the problem of the achievement
of selfhood than a dramatized itinerary of either approach to it or evasion
of it. When one finds oneself as a receptive subject in the grip of such resonance with an artistic work's achievement of apt attentiveness and point
of view, then one has been summoned by the work to a like achievement
and enactment of selfhood (with like and unlike objects of attention). One's
life of habit and routine has been interrupted productively by an encounter
with a fuller, more sublime mode of attention. Making art as a mode of address to the further formation of selfhood mobilizes and exercises powers
of statement, memory, thematization, association, judgment, and craft,
among others, in complex interaction with each other. In doing so, at least
when things go well, it achieves attention to phenomena of shared life, and
it invites and sustains imaginative participation in its modes of attention. It
enacts the achievement of exemplary selfhood.

Toward the end of the Preface to the *Phenomenology of Spirit*, Hegel
wrote: "For it is in the nature of humanity to press onward to agreement
with others; human nature only really exists in an achieved community of
minds."[19] Taken as a biological claim, this remark is outrageously false. The
existence of human nature biologically requires nothing more than being
a living being with forty-six chromosomes. But this obvious falsity is here
a mark of the metaphorical. The next sentence reads: "the anti-human, the
merely animal consists in staying within the sphere of feeling, and being able
to communicate only at that level."[20] This makes it clear that Hegel's thought
must be, first, that we fail to exist as distinctly human *subjects* insofar as we
fail to achieve and maintain selfhood through exercises of conceptual and
practical agency that win sufficient assurance and recognition, and, second,

that we can do better. That it remains our task to do this ever anew and ever incompletely—the fate of reason, or of our being self-conscious, reflective beings—is a thought that has nowhere been kept more alive and movingly pertinent to us than in the work of Stanley Cavell, a post-Hegelian, post-Freudian thinker of the emergence of selfhood, always incompletely, in the inheritance of culture and in selfhood's finding of good enough modes of satisfaction in exemplary artistic responsiveness to its situations.

3

Conceptual Analysis, Practical Commitment, and Ordinary Language

It is widely and correctly accepted that the analytic philosophy of the past 120 or so years began with the reaction of Moore and Russell against the British absolute idealism of J. M. E. McTaggart, F. H. Bradley, George Stout, and James Ward. To cite just one of many well-known passages from later in his career in which Russell comments on that reaction:

> [Moore] took the lead in rebellion, and I followed, with a sense of eman-
> cipation. . . . With a sense of escaping from prison we allowed ourselves to
> think that grass is green, [and] that the sun and stars would exist if no one
> was aware of them. . . . The world, which had been thin and logical, sud-
> denly became rich and varied.[1]

Second, it is also widely and correctly accepted that this reaction took two more or less distinct forms. Moore, followed later by Austin and Ryle, among others, defended the claims of common sense and ordinary experience, frequently expressing puzzlement at the incomprehensible nonsense that he found in the works of various epistemologists and metaphysicians prone to outrageous generalization. In contrast, Russell, followed later by Carnap and Quine, among others, sought to produce an ideal, regimented notation system that could be used to establish the epistemic well-foundedness of the exact natural sciences.

What is less widely accepted—in fact, generally not noted at all—is that there is a sense in which the stances of Moore and Russell, along with the styles of analysis they favored, count as versions of idealism. This becomes clear, however, if one approaches their work through the lens of a vocabulary for describing fundamental styles in philosophy that Norman Kemp Smith puts forward in his lecture "The Present Situation in Philosophy," given in 1919 upon his assuming the Professorship of Logic and Metaphysics at Edinburgh University.[2] In this lecture, Kemp Smith lists skepticism,

Anticipations of Freedom. Richard Eldridge, Oxford University Press. © Richard Eldridge 2026.
DOI: 10.1093/9780197841785.003.0005

naturalism, and idealism as fundamentally distinct ways of doing philosophy, albeit noting that they interact with each other and appear in various
grades of stringency. Skepticism, Kemp Smith argues, "is the enemy of fa-
naticism and of false sentiment in every form" (PSP, 6), and hence is vitally
useful. It is, however, also parasitic, spectatorial, and destructive rather than
constructive: "When the community's stock of error gives out, [the skeptic]
is faced by the specter of unemployment, condemned to idleness until a new
crop has been grown" (PSP, 6). Skepticism is unable to answer to a genuine
and addressable human interest in the construction of a more reasonable
and meaningful life. Naturalism, in contrast, is constructive in endorsing the
modern scientific picture of nature and undertaking to understand human
beings in the terms afforded by successful natural science (PSP, 5). But its
accounts of what it is worthwhile to do tend both to be limited in scope and
to collapse into accounts of what human beings mostly in fact do in certain
circumstances. When naturalism "finds in matter . . . the groundwork of reality" (PSP, 18), then it is unable to provide any constructive explanation of
"the fact that science exists at all" as an achievement alongside "the other
achievements of the human spirit, in the arts, [and] in the moral, social, and
religious life" (PSP, 16) that ought to be continued. Instead, it is limited to
observing that what has happened has happened, perhaps supplemented by
the thought that things are generally better if the priests get out of the way
and let human beings do more or less whatever they naturally tend to do.

In contrast, idealism, in the sense in which Kemp Smith understands
and favors it, does take human scientific, moral, political, and artistic
achievements seriously as achievements, and it undertakes to articulate
the ideals and to describe and further the strategies under which these
achievements have taken place (PSP, 15–16). Unlike Berkeleyan subjective idealism, however, this form of idealism includes no commitment to
any thesis of the mind-dependence of existing objects (PSP, 14). Grass and
trees, and suns and stars, are taken to continue to exist on their own, without
requiring the attention of any human or divine being. Human beings, however, are those beings who, set in a natural and material situation, are distinctively capable of scientific, moral, political, and artistic achievements
through the development and refinement of strategies for accomplishing
more fully meaningful and reasonable human lives, and these strategies express commitments to ideals (PSP, 23).

In precisely this sense, both Moore and Russell, along with those whom
they inspired, *are* idealists. This is clear if one again attends closely to the

language Russell uses in describing the anti-Bradleyan turn: "with a sense of emancipation . . . we allowed ourselves to think that grass is green, [and] that the sun and stars would exist if no one was aware of them." The picture is one of self-consciously taking up a commitment in judging and then expressing that commitment in life conduct that is now found to be more reasonable and meaningful than it had been. This kind of language is echoed with variations throughout the works of Moore, Russell, and their successors, as they urge and practice the taking up of judgmental commitments in the service of a more reasonable and meaningful life.

In fact, idealism of this kind must be accepted as soon as we speak at all of concepts. It is built into the idea of full-blooded concept-possession as a matter of having (a sufficiently large and structured set of) normative commitments. For beings who have such normative commitments, exercised in judging and in judgmentally structured action (as opposed to mere conditioned response), the issue of whether life is going well—whether our practices make sense, whether they are reasonable and support and sustain meaningful life—can always arise. Hence we should not be too quick to suppose that there are fixed and absolute oppositions between idealism, skepticism, and naturalism. In Kemp Smith's sense, we are all, at bottom, idealists in advancing and urging some concepts (and practices) over others (PSP, 3). (There are, of course, also substantive issues about modesty versus ambition with respect to sense-making, of various kinds and pointing in various directions, that genuinely divide explicit idealists from skeptics and naturalists.)

Austin explicitly warns against what he calls "the nonsense [of treating a concept] as an *article of property*, a pretty straightforward piece of goods, which comes into my 'possession,' if at all, in some definite enough manner and at some definite enough moment, [as if it were a piece of] the 'furniture' of my mind,"[3] as a kind of classificatory cookie-cutter within. The reason why any such view of concepts as entities—internal or external—of which I might come into definite possession at a single decisive moment is nonsense is that in principle, according to Austin, the only way we have of establishing anyone's 'possession' of a concept is by establishing possession of some degree of mastery of a concept-word, and establishing that is a rough, context-specific, partly holistic, normative, and ill-bounded affair.[4] For the concept *red*, one might, as Austin notes, establish that someone possesses it by noting a person's apt uses of the word "red" in application to red objects, but then again, the apt use of the word "rouge" might also do, and so might mastery of non-object-sorting general sentences such as "red is darker than pink," and so might misdescribing white objects as red when they are, unbeknownst to the subject, presented in red light.[5] In general, however, what will not do is simply noting the presence of some directly causally effective psychological or material state in the subject. Any cookie-cutter-like state, psychological or material, must be applied in accordance with a technique (which may itself vary with circumstances) in the use of which one has been trained.[6] Correct applications of words are norm-governed, bound by relations of material implication (hence holistically interanimated to some degree), and products of suitable, context-specific attention. They are not mere happenstances of the course of nature, such as distilled water freezing at thirty-two degrees Fahrenheit at sea level or the casting of a shadow by the sun, which take place without the active participation of subjects. Even if the possession of concepts requires some material vehicle in the subject (as surely it does), that possession is emergent, partially holistically structured, sensitive to considerations of correctness, and manifested in multiple active and attentive doings. And even if some concepts—to the extent that we have concepts at all—force themselves on us in virtue of our natural situations and biological endowments ("edge," "object," "motion," "cause," etc.), being in a natural situation and having a biological endowment, together with whatever internal states those facts entail, does not amount to possession of a concept. A naturally given, merely differential responsiveness or Quinean innate quality space[7] is not sufficient for full-blooded concept-possession—partially holistically structured and norm-governed as it is—though it may be a causally necessary pre-condition for it, and we may even wish to speak of possession of proto-concepts in the cases of sentient, differentially responsive non-linguistic animals.[8] Possession of a concept is something that can come in degrees and varieties (does a five-year-old possess the concepts "mammal," "satellite," or "marriage"?), and it inherently involves good enough participation in a shared, reasonable enough, indefinitely bounded practice of using language. To undertake analysis of concepts is to address and hope to clear up incoherencies in that practice and in joint social-conceptual life.

But now, given this picture of conceptual analysis, together with the thought that conceptual analysis so understood is what both Moore and Russell were doing (even if they did not always themselves understand it this way), it may look as if all differences have been erased and as if conceptual analysis were nothing more than a kind of ad hoc social criticism. In order to dispel such impressions, it is important, therefore, to turn to the specific practices of conceptual-practical analysis that appear in the traditions that Moore and Russell inaugurated, and in particular to the conceptions and standards of properly intelligible talk and thought and of a more reasonable and meaningful life that they invoked. Moore is surprisingly explicit that definitions—the products of conceptual analysis—terminate in objects or qualities of common experience. In *Principia Ethica*, in the course of explaining his procedure in undertaking to define "good," he tells us:

> My business is solely with that object or idea, which I hold, rightly or wrongly, that the word ["good"] is generally used to stand for. What I want to discover is the nature of that object or idea, and about this I am extremely anxious to arrive at an agreement.... My point is that "good" is a simple notion, just as "yellow" is a simple notion; that, just as you cannot, by any manner of means, explain to any one who does not already know it, what yellow is, so you cannot explain what good is. Definitions of the kind that I was asking for, definitions which describe the real nature of the object or notion denoted by a word, and which do not merely tell us what the word is used to mean, are only possible when the object or notion in question is something complex. You can give a definition of a horse, because a horse has many different properties and qualities, all of which you can enumerate. But when you have enumerated them all, when you have reduced a horse to his simplest terms, then you no longer define those terms. They are simply something which you think of or perceive, and to any one who cannot think of or perceive them, you can never, by any definition, make their nature known.[9]

Here the picture is that there *are* objects of common experience, whatever these may turn out to be. The activity of analyzing concepts as sortal registers of objects of common experience is driven by a sense, even an anxiety, that many people are not attending to those objects, but are instead distracted by stale and empty dogmas (especially those of Victorian and Edwardian Christianity), and it is intended, further, to guide their attentions and life conduct otherwise.[10] Conceptual analysis is here bound up with an image of liberation from incoherent submission to baseless authority and into passionate engagement with objects and individuals as they really are. Moore flirts with the idea of a systematic metaphysical theory of the ultimate objects of common experience, regarding them somewhat incoherently as physically located, mind-independent, but also essentially anthropocentric qualities (e.g., "patch of a whitish color"),[11] but he never successfully carries out an analysis of statements about common material objects into statements about sense-data, and the appeal of Moorean conceptual analysis to the Bloomsbury circle and other members of the London avant-garde[12] has more to do with its underlying resistance to stultifying and empty authoritarianism than with any definite results achieved. If, for example, "the Good" were (as Moore held it to be[13]) an object of simple intuition of a variably present but unanalyzable property of many different sorts of objects, then anything that intuition might more or less plausibly take to be good without argument will in fact be good, and arguments to the contrary put forward by authorities will fall to the ground in the face of the supposedly available facts.

A similar suspicion of cultural authority gone stale appears in the work of both Austin and Ryle, now directed more at the baseless pretensions of systematic, revisionary epistemology and metaphysics than at religion. Austin seeks to undermine the putatively revolutionary discoveries of skeptics and sense-datum theorists by reminding us of the ordinary uses of the words "know," "seems," "appears," "evidence," and so on.[14] For example, in contrast to fresh pig tracks in a muddy field that do constitute evidence of a nearby pig, we would not ordinarily say and should not say—would not really know what we would mean in saying, at least in normal circumstances—that a pig standing directly before us provides (mere) visual evidence of its presence. In this case, we see the pig itself, and not *via* an inference from sense-data.[15] Hence we do not have to worry in general about whether members of the class of ordinary, "moderate-sized specimens of dry goods" are in fact real, and we confuse ourselves and tie ourselves in knots practically whenever we do so worry.[16] We can get on with our epistemic business in such serious contexts as laboratories and law courts, leaving general skepticism to one side. Ryle's account of the "logical geography" of "mental-conduct concepts" is similarly shaped by the guiding aim of remaining faithful to "the verbs, nouns and adjectives, with which in ordinary life we describe the wits, characters, and higher-grade performances of the people with whom we have to do."[17] These verbs, nouns, and adjectives are, Ryle claims, "regularly and effectively used" within ordinary life, and we can and should prefer those usages, however intricate and delicate a business it may be to map them properly, to the misbegotten regimentations of systematic, revisionary, more or less Cartesian philosophers.[18]

While this general turn toward the ordinary and away from traditional religion and philosophy that is played out in various ways in Moore, Austin, and Ryle has had and continues to have significant cultural appeal, it also suffers from a number of considerable problems as a general method for analyzing concepts and doing philosophy. In the first place, correct uses of ordinary language are frequently enough contested and unclear. There are family resemblances, analogical predications (e.g., the head of a wildebeest versus the head of a corporation), unlike determinates of determinables (e.g., pleasure in playing chess versus pleasure in eating ice cream), quality/object ambiguities (e.g., a youth as an identifiable individual versus youth as a time of life), and core and causally extended usages (e.g., a healthy person versus a healthy complexion versus a healthy diet),[19] metaphorical innovations, and the sheer fact of diachronic change in concept-words, concepts, and regions of practice.

Second, varieties of usages and of the concepts they express cannot take place *via* massive and unmotivated leaps, and they may very well be bounded in some ways by our situation in nature. (Could we do without the concepts "edible," "edge," and "motion," to the extent that we have concepts at all?) But then it is natural enough as a result to seek to determine what fixes the boundaries of concept development, so that an impulse to very general, systematic theorizing about the nature and objects of our experience is natural enough to our lives with words. Where does faithfulness to ordinary usage break off and a fall into misbegotten general theorizing begin? This question itself has no fixed, general answer, and an impulse to perfected, absolute control of one's usages of concept-words may be a part of ego-formation as such under conditions of social scrutiny and correction.

Third, in enough cases, though never in all or even in the majority, tangled and contested ordinary language usages of concept words are bound up with tangled and contested matters of on-the-ground practice. Consider debates about race and gender, where pernicious social histories of treatment mark out identifiable class memberships that are indefensible in strictly biological terms. Where and when should we trust the social facts, for which purposes, and where and when should we trust the biology? More prosaically, what is a catch in American football? (What is the NFL catch rule at present? And what should it be?) Less prosaically, what is a democracy? Are fair enough one-person, one-vote elections necessary or sufficient for genuine popular sovereignty in lawmaking? What about the effects of radically unequal economic holdings or gerrymandering on electoral procedures and outcomes? And what, after all, is a "cause"? Is it what is specified in the antecedent of an exceptionless law-formulation? Or, more broadly, what is provided by any satisfactory answer to a why question? Or what are "fairness," "health," or "sanity"? Do we generally have clear paradigm cases from which we can go on confidently and unhesitatingly to stake ourselves to further uses that others will generally accept as reasonable? Do counterfactuals—a form of expression we use often enough—have genuine truth-values? And if so, how? Should we or should we not use them in serious explanatory discourse? None of these problems are likely to be solved by sheer appeal to ordinary uses of ordinary words in central cases, for what is ordinary and central is itself a matter of some contestation. As Donald Davidson once mordantly remarked, "the only concept Plato succeeded in defining was mud [dirt and water]"[20]—an uncontested and clear enough concept, but thus quite unlike the concepts and usages of concept-words that naturally provoke philosophical investigation and debate.

Like Moore, Russell holds that an analysis of propositions must terminate in objects of immediate experience. "Every proposition which we can understand must be composed wholly of constituents with which we are acquainted,"[21] where, according to Russell, the objects of acquaintance are either sense-data or eternally knowable logical forms. Further, like Moore, Russell is concerned both to uphold the claims of ordinary perception and to establish the importance of personal relations that may form without or against the dictates of religious morality.[22] But in contrast with Moore, for Russell, the vindication of the cognitive successes of the modern natural sciences and the consequent rejection of traditional metaphysical philosophy is much more in the foreground. Logical analysis is to exhibit the justificatory basis of the modern natural sciences in claims about sense-data that are known by immediate acquaintance.[23] What Russell calls general truths—a wide class of claims that includes such specimens as "all men are mortal" and Faraday's law of electromagnetic induction[24]—are known on the basis of direct experience plus inductive inference (a species of logical inference, according to Russell at this stage of his career):

General truths cannot be inferred from particular truths alone, but must, if they are to be known, be either self-evident, or inferred from premises of which at least one is a general truth. But all *empirical* evidence is of particular truths. Hence if there is any knowledge of general truths at all, there must be *some* knowledge of general truths which is independent of empirical evidence, i.e., does not depend upon the data of sense.[25]

As with Moore, however, the project of actually exhibiting analyses of general truths into their evidential bases in knowledge of atomic sense-datum facts plus knowledge of logical laws foundered on incoherencies in the conception of sense-data and, in Russell's case, on emerging doubts about the status and reliability of inductive inference.[26] But his early defenses of realism about material entities ("the existing world consists of many things with many qualities and relations"[27]) and of the cognitive achievements of the natural sciences contrasted with the bankruptcy of metaphysical philosophy remained powerfully attractive. "Most philosophers," Russell holds—naming Plato, Spinoza, and Hegel as examples—have been "incapable of giving any account of the world of science and daily life"; they have been "inspired by a certain [malicious] hatred of the daily world" and a wish

> to convict it of unreality in the interests of a super-sensible "real" world. Belief in the unreality of the world of sense arises with irresistible force in certain moods—moods which, I imagine, have some simple physiological basis but are none the less powerfully persuasive. The conviction born of these moods is the source of most mysticism and of most metaphysics.[28]

Rather than indulge in such moods, we can and should, Russell holds, refuse mysticism and metaphysics in the names of the real world and sober science. Whatever the failures of his project of analytically exhibiting the justificatory basis of modern physical science in claims about sense-data, Russell's general conception of analysis both articulated and furthered practical commitments to doing experimental science rather than metaphysics, which found widespread resonances in the practices of others.

Rudolf Carnap continued Russell's effort to vindicate modern science by exhibiting its justificatory bases. In his 1928 *The Logical Structure of the World*, Carnap undertook to produce "a genealogy of concepts ... in which each one has its definite place."[29] "All objects of the constructional system [material things, for example, as well as the concepts that aptly class them] are indirectly constructed from objects of the first level. These *basic* objects form the *basis* of the system."[30] As his career developed, Carnap entertained various candidates for the class of basic objects, moving from phenomenal "elementary experiences"[31] to material objects to (in his 1950 "Empiricism, Semantics, and Ontology") the thought that the question about what is ultimately real might best be regarded as "a practical question, a matter of practical decision concerning the structure of our language."[32]

W. V. O. Quine continued Carnap's pragmatic turn but argued against any permanently fixed class of basic observation statements. As physical theory and laboratory technique develop, what we are able to observe, how we parse these observations, and what we take there to *be* can all change. While there is no sharp distinction between natural science and philosophy, the philosopher who practices "semantic ascent" attends more to general ways of talking about things than to the results of particular investigations:

> It is scrutiny of this uncritical acceptance of the realm of physical objects itself, or of classes, etc., that devolves upon ontology. Here is the task of making explicit what had been tacit, and precise what had been vague; of exposing and resolving paradoxes, smoothing kinks, lopping off vestigial growths, clearing ontological slums. The philosopher's task differs from the others', then, in detail; but in no drastic way as those suppose who imagine for the philosopher a vantage point outside the conceptual scheme that he takes in charge. There is no such cosmic exile.[33]

Everywhere, however, the task of theory construction and revision from within remains governed by the aims of predicting and controlling experiences, or as Quine puts it, of "working a manageable structure into the flux of experience."[34] This aim is unavoidable if we are to survive at all, and it is best fulfilled—more or less obviously, Quine takes it—by the modern experimental sciences rather than by either religion or traditional metaphysics.

While the Russell-Carnap-Quine strand of conceptual-practical analysis has had and likewise continues to have significant cultural appeal, particularly in promoting the natural sciences over metaphysics and religion as paradigms of cognitive achievement, it, too, is troubled by a number of considerable problems. Given that there is no fixed vocabulary of ultimate reference into which to analyze the sentences of the sciences in order to exhibit their justificatory base, the direct, Russellian foundational vindication of science fails. Given the failure of analytical reductions into a favored vocabulary, it is not clear in what sense, if any, the remaining Quinean-Carnapian pragmatic version of the program counts as analytical. Second, as is already suggested by the failure of analytical reductions, theory choice within the natural sciences is frequently enough not a function simply of a crucial experiment or a single decisive piece of data (as Quine saw clearly).[35] More importantly, while problems of the prediction and control of material events within our environments clearly are important, and while some forms of experimental science enhance that prediction and control, those are not the only problems that matter. There are problems of political organization, of economic justice, of the understanding of human beings as plan-forming and reason-mongering agents, of musical composition, dramaturgy, choreography, and poetic expression, and of the ascription of responsibility, all of which the experimental sciences are ill-suited to address. Moreover, as Quine saw, the limitations of the sciences in addressing such problems are inherent ones not to be overcome through the advance of science, insofar as (1) the very notion of subjects having a point of view on things is crucial to addressing them, and (2) a point of view is not a measurable something that the properly experimental physical sciences can grasp.[36] For this reason, Quine dismisses these problems as pseudo-problems that we would do well to leave behind us, replacing them at best with paler, more scientifically tractable counterparts.[37] Yet we remain radically unclear about how in practice to do without the concepts of intention, belief, responsibility, choice, regret, desire, hope, fear, and all their cousins;[38] the realities these concepts putatively track seem ineliminably part of our ongoing lives with one another. How we might live in practice without these concepts and without practical normative commitments to their use remains a significantly open problem, so that the aim of conceptual analysis to point us toward more coherent, reasonable, and meaningful life conduct remains unfulfilled.

In reaction to the failure of Russellian foundational analysis, but, *contra* Quine, in commitment to the ineliminability and genuinely reality-tracking character of intentional and moral idioms, P. F. Strawson urges and practices what he calls "connective analysis," understood as constructing a

> model of an elaborate network, a system, of connected items, concepts, such that the function of each item, each concept, could from the philosophical point of view, be properly understood only by grasping its connections with the others, its place in the system—perhaps better still . . . a set of interlocking systems of such a kind.[39]

Here there is no requirement to translate all concept terms reductively into an epistemically privileged vocabulary or to reduce concepts to encounters with items of direct acquaintance. Instead, we might in tracing connections among concepts move "in a wide, revealing, and illuminating circle" (AM, 19–20), and so arrive at a somewhat more reflectively self-conscious grasp of what we are doing when we make use of the concepts that belong to a given family.[40]

Here two questions are immediately pressing: (1) Which, if any, concepts are *basic*, if there is no privileged vocabulary into which to analyze concept-words in general? (2) What are the relations among the distinct networks that compose an interlocking system? In response to the first question, Strawson proposes that a concept is

> basic in the relevant sense if it is one of a set of general, pervasive, and ulti-
> mately irreducible concepts . . . which together form a structure—a struc-
> ture which constitutes the framework of our ordinary thought and talk and
> which is presupposed by the various specialist or advanced disciplines that
> contribute, in their diverse ways, to our total picture of the world. (AM, 24)

He then lists *time, change, truth, identity*, and *knowledge* as examples of basic concepts (AM, 24). Or, even more strongly, there may be some concepts that are not only fundamental in *our* network of concepts but are "essential to any conception (comprehensible to us) of the experience of self-conscious beings" as such, and hence fully necessary for any experience of any self-conscious being at all (AM, 26).[41] We might, then, at least undertake to "arrive at a clear understanding of the most general features of our conceptual structure, as it exists in fact—whether or not it is possible to demonstrate the necessity of those features" (AM, 27), and even the possibility of demonstrating full-blooded necessity for any self-conscious, experiencing being at all should not be ruled out a priori.

Unfortunately, however, Strawson fails to address the second question. Hence, when there are distinct networks—such as the physical description of the world network and the intentionality-responsibility-morality network—in the terms of which competing and incommensurable modes of explanation (e.g., law-governed event causality versus agent causality) are on offer, we then find ourselves in practice no better off than before having begun analysis, with no clear grip on which network of concepts to use when. Strawson addresses the question of how to resolve a clash between the styles of explanation of the physical causality network and the agency-morality network in the final chapter of *Analysis and Metaphysics*, entitled "Freedom and Necessity." He invites us to consider a case in which

> X, let us say, notices that Y's last remark has caused embarrassment to Z
> and, wishing to spare Z's feelings, X himself makes a remark intended to
> change the direction of the conversation. Can we seriously contemplate
> the possibility of being able to give, in terms belonging exclusively to the

exact physical sciences, a complete causal account of the origin of precisely this complex of thought, feeling, and action on X's part? And of every other piece of human behavior of even such modest complexity as this? The idea is absurd . . . because there is no practical possibility of establishing the general principles on which any such calculation would have to be based. (AM, 140)

Here the rhetorical question and the appeal to what we can "seriously contemplate" and to "practical possibility" are whistling in the dark, when the issue is precisely what, if anything, in the way the world ultimately is grounds and justifies the use of a particular explanatory framework in particular circumstances of encounters with particular objects in the world.[42]

In light, then, of the failure on the part of the Moore-Austin-Ryle line to fix our ordinary uses of concept words in the face of contested conceptual and practical commitments, and of the failure on the part of the Russell-Carnap-Quine line either to carry out reduction to a primitive vocabulary or to vindicate the explanatory power of physical science, we might instead try to come to terms with our life in and with ordinary language as a matter of living continuously with contested conceptual and practical commitments, where conflicts are sometimes addressable in particular contexts but rarely, if ever, conclusively resolvable. To become clearer about this, it would help to see how pervasive unclarity about our conceptual and practical commitments is, how early in life it arises, and how deeply connected it is with our developing and shifting relations with other subjects. Arriving at a clearer understanding of this, and so at a kind of philosophical anthropology of human life in and with language, is the task and achievement of Stanley Cavell, in elaborating what he calls "the vision of language underlying ordinary language procedures" (CR, 168), paradigmatically those of Wittgenstein, with his sense of the availability only of contextual, piece-meal elucidation of what we say when, in his "Excursus on Wittgenstein's Vision of Language," chapter 7 of *The Claim of Reason*.[43]

Building on a remark he ascribes to Wittgenstein in *The Blue Book*—"we learn words in *certain* contexts" (CR, 168)[44]—Cavell focuses on scenes of language-learning as they take place between a parent (or other adult) and child. He argues that frequently "we fail to recognize how (what it really means to say that) children learn language *from* us" (CR, 177); we are often "too quick to suppose we know what it is in such situations that makes us say the child is learning something. In particular, too quick to suppose we know what the child is learning" (CR, 171). Our failure to attend to what is really going on in such scenes might take the form of supposing that the child *grasps* a universal, a rule, or a convention—something fixed that makes us call the same things by the same general name. But *grasp* of something, it-self regarded as an internal state (whether neural or tacitly psychological or present to consciousness), is insufficient by itself to yield correct and fluent performance: one must also master a practical technique of application that is suited to the circumstances.[45] Here, mastery of a technique does not itself consist simply in another internal state but in a kind of readiness to adapt to circumstances: to make projective leaps, encouraged by looks and smiles or inhibited by disapproval, which develop within a temporally sustained process of maturation. Cavell offers as examples the temporally developing mastery of the terms "pumpkin," "kitty," "mayor," and "lend" on the part of a child (CR, 169–73). In each case, at certain stages the child may hit the right target, as it were, but do so imitatively and not fully knowing what she is doing or why. When a child calmly strokes a fur piece and says "kitty," is it a mistake or a metaphor? When a child identifies a drawing of a pumpkin in a picture-book, does she know that a pumpkin is a fruit, or even whether it is edible? (What if it is Cinderella's pumpkin-coach?) When a child says "the mayor is making a speech," does she know (necessarily?) what an election is? When a child is told "Let sister use your shovel" and then hands it over (briefly? resentfully?), does she know what borrowing and lending are (CR, 170–2)? Do we know what the child is definitely doing in issuing a linguistic performance in circumstances of developing competence? Is there even a definite answer? Second, especially at early stages of language learning, coming imitatively to use words *more or less* as the grownups do is more like, and is more infused with, imagining, pretending (e.g., pretending to make dinner for one's stuffed animals, or having tea with them),[46] and wishing to please others than we might be tempted to think. "'Learning,'" as Cavell puts it, "is not as academic a matter as academics are apt to suppose" (CR, 171), and we would do well to stop "trying to intellectualize our lives" (CR, 175) and our temporally sustained, open-ended, and imagination-infused developments of practical abilities by positing such things as dispositive inner ("mental state") grasps of universals, rules, or conventions: "what can be said in a language is not everywhere determined by rules, nor is its under-standing anywhere secured through universals" (CR, 180).[47]

If all this—language's temporally extended course of development, its prac-tical flexibility in varying situations, its inflection by emotion, imagination, and pretending under the sways of others—is true of the nature of the language learner's competence, and then, further,

> if there are always new contexts to be met, new needs, new relationships, new objects, new perceptions to be recorded and shared, then perhaps it is as true of a master of a language as of his apprentice that though "in a sense" we learn the meaning of words and what objects, are, the learning is never over, and we keep finding new potencies in words and new ways in which objects are disclosed. (CR, 180)

Are there, then, always new contexts to be met? Is the learning in fact never over? There are at least three reasons to think that the answers are yes. First, there is "the fierce ambiguity of ordinary language" (CR, 180), the fact that all concepts and all concept-words have "an indefinite number of instances and directions of projection" (CR, 185).[48] Cavell memorably illustrates this point in discussing the various—related but different—circumstances of application of the verb "feed," as in "feed the kitty," "feed the swans," "feed the meter," "feed the film into the machine," "feed his pride," and so on (CR, 181–2).[49] Words could not function for us as they do were they not both stably applicable in (a range of) standard cases and tolerant of new projections. A language that consisted *only* of a single name for every particular object, to which object it applied immediately and automatically without imaginative projection, is inconceivable.[50] Of course, in many or most cases in which an elucidation of a specific application condition is called for, we are rightly confident that we are able to say something that will be to the point. For example, "feed one's ego" suggests that with a bit of nurturing, a sense of self-worth and authority can grow naturally, as if beyond one's control; "feed the meter" builds on a similarity between internal mechanical processing, on the one hand, and incorporation and digestion, on the other. Some application conditions may strike us as more prima facie context-independent and closer to a "core" of usage than others, and these can usefully be listed in a dictionary.[51] But always in applying words, projective imagination will be required; the language learner must actively get what is to be done, must see how to go on.

Second, even when in a vast range of circumstances, application conditions for concept-words will be clear enough to a competent speaker, there remain concept-words the application conditions of which *are* contested, at least often enough: for example, "meaning," "language," "belief," "knowledge," "moral judgment," and so on (CR, 175).[52] In each case, there is a temptation to theorize about definite application conditions that might be specified in a formula apt to all circumstances. Giving in to this temptation amounts, according to Cavell, to producing moralistic modes of criticism "that . . . leave the critic imagining himself free of the faults he sees around him" (CR, 175).[53] Instead of moralizing, we would do better to "look and see" (PI, §66), where this will mean patiently attending to details of difficult cases in order to see how the application of a concept-word might be projected, as a matter of reasonably and meaningfully keeping faith with what has been done practically in using words in the past. By the time the details have been rehearsed, the aspects of the case brought into clearer view, and a projection ventured (or withdrawn or made in a qualified way), there will be nothing left for a fixed formula or definition to do.

Third, there is the sheer fact of change in practical life, driven in part by the persisting inventiveness of human beings in coming up with new technological devices for the sake of ease, health, enjoyment, or the control of nature, among other things. As we keep on coming to live in different ways, occasions for new concepts will continue to arise. In 1960 no one yet knew what a meme or a streaming video is. And consider the hyper-fast mutations of slang as markers of distinctive subjectivities.

None of this is to say that something reasonably called conceptual analysis is impossible. But it is important that it is fundamentally an analysis of practical commitment within a context of established but unclear and contested usages, and it is important to think about the form and character of a successful analysis. Given the unavailability of fixed formulae that might control all future usages of concept-words under a kind of necessity apart from practice, what can be achieved is something more like a cadencing of attention and commitment, arising from the rehearsal of details in which an audience shares as it "gets" or "sees" what it is reasonable to do in light of past usages and present circumstances.[54] Developing a view of this kind, Alva Noë has argued that our lives as persons are *organized* in terms of the skills and practical commitments that we inherit in and through our entry into culture. Art, he suggests, seeks "to bring out and exhibit, to disclose and to illuminate, aspects of the way we find ourselves organized"[55] within our inherited and developing skill sets and associated conceptual-practical commitments. It can help us to get clear or clearer about how what we do hangs together or might hang together better. Philosophy, moreover, is akin to art in helping us to see and engage with our practical situations more fully and clearly: "Philosophy is the choreography of ideas and concepts and beliefs. For these too exist only in the organized activity of our thought and talk."[56]

What Cavell calls a "claim of reason"—a claim about what we say when, made from within our ordinary language and in an effort to move from perplexity to clarity—is all at once a claim to reason, to self-knowledge, and to community, as one seeks without any warrant other than the resources of one's ear and practical sense to stage one's putative achievement of clarified attention and commitment as exemplary.[57] (Communion may or may not follow.[58]) Or, as Cavell puts it in *Little Did I Know*, "philosophy, of a certain ambition, tends perpetually to intersect the autobiographical" (LDIK, 2), as one courts exemplarity in what one claims to see more clearly, but can never guarantee in advance of the responses of others that one has done so:

> What I require is a convening of my culture's criteria, in order to confront them with my words and life as I pursue them and as I may imagine them; and at the same time to confront my words and life as I pursue them with the life my culture's words may imagine for me: to confront the culture with itself, along the lines in which it meets in me. (CR, 125)

One lives, as Cavell elsewhere puts it, within "the uncanniness of the ordinary" (see IQO, 153–80), where at any moment (if not at all of them) such convenings may be in order.

This may make it seem as if there are only encounters but no stable results, and as if philosophy is vaporized into a literature of itineraries with temporary starts and stops but no genuine ends. And there is something right about that.[59] One might speak, as Cavell does, "of arguments that must not be won . . . of my conception of philosophy as the achievement of the unpolemical, of the refusal to take sides in metaphysical positions, of my quest to show that those are not useful sides but needless constructions" (PP, 22). Such differences as there are between philosophy and literature as forms of disciplined attention to life have less to do with proof and finality on the part of philosophy and focus on sheer particulars and contingencies on the part of literature than they have to do with philosophy's direct concern with clarifying concepts and practical commitments that are very widely shared but lived out with less than full coherence in various regions of colliding practice. Philosophy focuses on the concepts and practical commitments signaled by the words "justice," "belief," "knowledge," "right," "beautiful," and so on, while literature focuses on specific situations in which those concepts and commitments are lived out, tragically or comically.[60] The miracle is that sometimes exemplary enough cadencing of attention can be achieved as one articulates one's course of working through one's perplexities in living with others amid tangled conceptual-practical commitments.[61] And that may be enough on some occasions to make the game of entering fully textured appeals to what we say worth the candle.[62]

AMERICA

History and Futurity

4

Cavell on American Philosophy and the Idea of America

Here is a common picture of what American philosophy looks like to and within many American philosophy departments.[1] To a considerable degree, it does not exist at all. Most departments do not feel obliged to teach American philosophy as they do modern philosophy (Descartes to Kant) and ancient Greek philosophy. It is normally not part of the requirements for a major. Of course, writings by Americans are mostly what do get taught, but they are taught as just philosophy, not as *American* philosophy. When it is taught, it is taught as a peripheral history course, typically focusing on the major pragmatist thinkers from the late nineteenth to the mid-twentieth century: Peirce, James, and Dewey, with perhaps a turn toward Rorty to round things off. These figures are thought to emphasize the importance of paying attention to what works: to experimental science in the pursuit of knowledge and to liberal reform in politics. The only way to discern what works—in either epistemology or politics—is through trial and error. Epistemology and social theory in any more visionary sense are evaded.[2] Our going practices of experimental science, particularly natural science, have shown themselves to be good enough: neither in need of nor admitting of any further epistemic support from foundationalist theories of justification. In politics, liberal decency, respect for rights, and reliance on markets are about the best we can do. Larger visions of social justice are by and large fantastic and potentially tyrannical, compared to a clear-eyed understanding of how decent people mostly can and do get on socially in order to satisfy their preferences. To the extent that the pragmatist commitment to getting on with what works is taken seriously, it is not so much understood as itself a visionary discovery of the natures of knowledge and justice as it is just taken for granted. Strong voluntarist pictures of human responsibility as including the possibility of getting right what we really ought to do in either the pursuit of knowledge or the arrangement of social life are simply dropped.[3] The naturalist stances of Quine, Rorty, and Dennett, according to which there's little point in making

Anticipations of Freedom. Richard Eldridge, Oxford University Press. © Richard Eldridge 2026.
DOI: 10.1093/9780197841785.003.0007

much of a fuss about free will (in anything other than the Humean sense of political liberty or hypothetical freedom) come to the fore. The key notion is *coping*, and emphatically not *achieving our human destiny*.

This picture of American philosophy in turn both rests on and further articulates larger images of America and of philosophy. America is understood as the place in which freedom is construed as a matter centrally, perhaps exclusively, of individual liberty (as opposed to the actualization of the power to do or be something in particular—for example, to be more fully human or more properly faithful). Most Americans exercise their liberty by pursuing happiness and satisfaction in the private spheres of family life, consumption, and enjoyment. Larger workplace and public identities are taken to be instrumental to satisfactions in these more private spheres, unless, of course, some people just happen to enjoy political work or quasi-familial workplace friendships or workplace activities. The business of politics in America is the fair reconciliation of competitive individual and factional interests. There are not enough goods to go around to enable everyone to satisfy every preference. Government hence properly sets up rules of fair competition, including centrally the laws of property and person and the laws of contract, fair trade, workplace safety, and nonexploitativeness.

Philosophy is understood in relation to this picture of America as committed to the overcoming of *merely personal* interest. People *do* have idiosyncratic interests. Some people devote themselves to fly-fishing; others to cello playing; others to cooking; still others to building bridges. Some people are Methodists; others are Catholics, Jews, Episcopalians, and nonbelievers. But no set of commitments, practical or religious, works for everyone. Older, premodern philosophies were quasi-theologies that attempted to install a favored set of practical or religious commitments as mandatory. They were failed efforts to make a particular form of devotion rationally obligatory. Happily, we are, in philosophy, beyond that project and its potential and actual tyrannies. Whether as the analysis of concepts, as a defense of the achievements of science (in yielding understandings that anyone might make use of or not, as anyone wishes), or as an outline of fair terms of justice and the rule of law that favors no one set of personal interests, philosophy is, above all, *neutral*.[4]

There is a great deal of both truth and value in these pictures of America and of philosophy. It is, nonetheless, Stanley Cavell's perception that to the extent that these pictures are true, they are *made* true by Americans and philosophers adopting them out of conformism, acquiescence, desperation, and complicity in failures to achieve our best possibilities—as philosophers, as Americans, and as human persons. All too often, Cavell proposes (following Emerson), we fail to dare to exist,[5] fail both personally and socially to live in pursuit and achievement of genuine care and commitment.

According to Cavell, philosophy and politics and America all promise more than this. To the pursuit of happiness as the satisfaction of individual preferences, Cavell—following Emerson and Thoreau, in company with Wittgenstein, Heidegger, Plato, and Rousseau—poses a counterimage of happiness as conversion to and achievement of *freedom*, understood not as liberty, but rather as something more like full mastery in what one does and says.[6] What is needed, then, in this view is a kind of *rebirth*: away from instrumentalism and into accession to transfigured commitment and expressive power. It is naturally difficult to describe the kind of transformation that is in question. It is something like the discovery on the part of the modernist artist in the course of her work that her natural talent and instincts can be originally enacted in an intelligible way: to make new sense,[7] against the grain of the old. The thought is that as it stands "we are not free, not whole, and not new, and we know this and are on a downward path of despair because of it; and that . . . for a grownup to grow he requires strangeness and transformation, i.e., birth" (SW, 60). The hope is that "we might despair of despair itself, rather than of life, and cast *that* off, and begin, and so reverse our direction" (SW, 71).

The idea, by contrast, that philosophy should be neutral and should focus on what works—more or less well and from our present vantage point—is then a betrayal of what philosophy has centrally been and still centrally can be. "Philosophy begins with, say, in the Socratic ambition, and may at any time encounter, an aspiration toward the therapeutic, a sense of itself as guiding the soul, or self, from self-imprisonment toward the light or the instinct of freedom" (PP, 4).

The catch, however, is that there are no standing terms available for specifying fully the condition at which transformation or conversion or rebirth aims. A sense of this catch is especially prominent in America, with its founding resistance to any single national religion. This sense also figures in the resistance of certain philosophers, typically the ones Cavell cites as heroes and forebears—Emerson, Thoreau, Rousseau, Plato, and Wittgenstein, most prominently—to academicism and to conclusive formulations of stance, that is, in the drift of these writers toward a certain literariness or poetry. For them the process of discovery of the self to itself takes place in and through an ongoing course of writing. As part of the founding myth of perfection*ism*, as it is exemplified in Plato's *Republic* and then further inhabited by Emerson, Thoreau, and Wittgenstein, Cavell lists the sense that "the self finds that it can turn (convert, revolutionize itself)... [in order to achieve] a further state of that self, where the higher is determined not by natural talent [that is, not by birth] but by *seeking* to know what you are made of and cultivating the thing you are meant to do" (CHU, 6–7; emphasis and interjection added). As it engages in this seeking, the self finds itself caught up in the movement or work of thought and of writing, resistant to what Cavell stigmatizes as "moralism" and dogma and the academic. As vehicle of this seeking, "philosophical *writing* ... enters into competition with the field of poetry, ... not to banish all poetry from the just city but to claim for itself the privilege of the work poetry does in making things happen to the soul, so far as that work has its rights" (CHU, 78). This kind of philosophical writing—both modeled on and in competition with poetry, rather than the treatise or scientific report—expresses both an ambition for conversion in and through process and a distinctly American sense of striking out for the new, of being on the way. Philosophy, from Plato through Emerson through Wittgenstein, then *is* about happiness, but where "the achievement of happiness requires not the perennial and fuller satisfaction of our needs as they stand but the examination and transformation of those needs" (PH, 405). What is sought, through transformation, is not the achievement of a final *state*, but rather "a sort of continuous reaffirmation" (PH, 1432) of self in activity and in relationship. To seek such a continuous reaffirmation, and to see philosophy as seeking it, out of what is perceived as a present state of acquiescence, conformity, complicity, and lack of interest is not neutrally to endorse moderately successful strategies of coping that are already in place. One might say that the perfectionist strain in the thought of Emerson and Thoreau points us toward the possibility and value of falling in love and living in love with what we do, against our present half-heartedness.

Politics, too, then is different, for political thinking and political activity are open to being informed by perfectionist aspirations. "The transformation of the self... finds expression in the imagination of a transformation of society..., where what is best for society is modeled on what is best for the individual soul" (CHU, 7). At the beginning of an important essay relatively early in his turn toward Emerson, Cavell cites "the following pair of sentences, attributed... to William James" that are set in brass in the lobby of William James Hall at Harvard.

THE COMMUNITY STAGNATES WITHOUT THE IMPULSE
OF THE INDIVIDUAL
THE IMPULSE DIES AWAY WITHOUT THE SYMPATHY
OF THE COMMUNITY. (IQO, 105)

This message, which, Cavell remarks, "maybe taken [among other ways] as claiming a transcendental relation among the concepts of community and individual as they have so far shown themselves" (IQO, 105), is what politics as the usual business of factional negotiation tends to forget or repress.

An image and practice of politics that embraces this message incorporates, as politics as usual does not, a role for what Cavell, following Kant, calls *reflective judgment*: "the expression of a conviction whose grounding remains subjective—say myself—but which expects or claims justification from the (universal) concurrence of other subjectivities, on reflection" (CHU, xxvi). It is this kind of reflective judgment that might best record a perception of our present liabilities and call us to something better—for example, away from present practices of "intolerable inequality or discrimination" (CHU, xxvi). The making of reflective judgments and the practice of reflection on them by others point toward politics not as negotiation, but as conversation, a joint exploration of joint possibilities.

The aim of such political conversation is not the satisfaction of individual interests or preferences as they stand, but rather the joining together of the private-erotic with the public-political. This is a tall order; the private and the political do not readily come together. But "while it is the nature of the erotic to form a stumbling block to a reasonable, civilized existence, call it the political, human happiness nevertheless goes on demanding satisfaction in both realms" (PH, 64–5). What we find ourselves engaged in, with one another politically and not just one by one, alone, is "a struggle for mutual freedom" (PH, 17–18).

One immediate consequence of this aim and of our standing failure quite wholly to achieve it is that our sense of being members of our society and culture is likely to take the form of a sense of compromise by and complicity with society as it stands. The social contract as Rousseau and Kant imagine it, as theorists of autonomy (not of preference satisfaction), and as it is lived in America is a matter of *consent*, where "my consent is not . . . modifiable or proportionable (psychological exile is not exile): I cannot keep consent focused on the successes or graces of society; it reaches into every corner of society's failure or ugliness. A compromised state of society, since it is mine, compromises me" (CHU, 107, 28). This experience of compromise and complicity in American society and culture is all too familiar to Americans—aware of the depth both of their Americanness and of the failures of their society and culture to achieve their promises.

Rightly developed—as Rousseau and Kant (rather than Hobbes, say) develop it—social contract theory focuses on this sense of joint membership and complicity. To consent to the social contract is then not to take up an instrument for the pursuit of personal advantage; it is to accept one's responsibility for society and its promise of freedom. Consent implies

> that I recognize the society and its government, so constituted, as *mine*; which means that I am answerable not merely to it, but for it. So far, then, as I recognize myself to be exercising my responsibility for it, my obedience to it is obedience to my own laws; citizenship in that case is the same as my autonomy; the polis is the field within which I work out my personal identity and it is the creation of (political) *freedom*. (CR, 23)

As Stephen Mulhall usefully puts it, Cavell's thought is that the story of a social contract makes explicit the idea that "citizenship is [and is to be] not a constraint on my autonomy but an aspect of it."[8] Society is, in the Rousseauian-Kantian form of social contract theory, "an artifact" to which I am "deeply . . . joined" (CR, 25), both bound up in its promises and complicit in its failures.

> The essential message of the idea of a social contract is that political institutions require justification, that they are absolutely without sanctity, that power over us is held on trust from us, that institutions have no authority other than the authority we lend them, that we are their architects, that they are therefore artifacts, that there are laws or ends, of nature or justice, in terms of which they are to be tested. They are experiments. (SW, 82)

The image of America that Cavell forwards is then that it is a place of these experiments, perhaps the central place. "It had a mythical beginning, still visible, if ambiguous, to itself, and to its audience" (MWM, 344). Out of this beginning there arose "a society whose idea of itself requires that it repudiate the hierarchies and enforcements of the European past and make a new beginning" (PH, 156). Unlike the countries of Europe, America has been from the beginning and remains the nation of no settled tribe or *Stamm*, of no national religion, not even of any national language. It is a place of immigrancy, a place to come to, in order then to strike off in one's own direction.

No doubt this *is* a kind of myth. The settlement and cultivation of America are in historical fact shot through with violence. There were Native Americans here before there were Europeans, and the Europeans introduced the overwhelming disfiguration of slavery. As Cavell himself remarks,

> It is simply crazy that there should ever have come into being a world with such a sin in it, in which a man is set apart because of his color—*the* superficial fact about a human being. Who could *want* such a world? For an American, fighting for his love of country, that the last hope of earth should from its beginning have swallowed slavery, is an irony so withering, a justice so intimate in its rebuke of pride, as to measure only with God. (MWM, 141)

Yet despite this withering irony, in the very face of it, this founding mythology—this mythology of a founding, a new beginning—is nonetheless lived imaginatively in America, when Americans dare to dream. It is a central part of "the inner agenda of [our] culture" that America *is* the place where freedom is to be achieved (PH, 17).

Everywhere intertwined with and enacted in these counterimages of philosophy (as transformative thinking, talking, and writing), of politics (as the conversation and cultivation of freedom), and of America (as the new place for the achievement of freedom—its birthplace) is an image of the human person, fit to live in these practices and in this place. The self is not a thing that is simply given, but a power of becoming responsible for and fully invested in what one does, which power is emergent, paradoxically, through its own activity.

> The fate of having a self—of being human—is one in which the self is always to be found; fated to be sought, or not; recognized, or not. My self is something, apparently, toward which I can stand in various relations, ones in which I can stand to other selves, named by the same terms, e.g., love, hate, disgust, acceptance, knowledge, ignorance, faith, pride, shame. (SW, 53)

If we do not achieve full investment or what Emerson calls Power or Self-Reliance, but instead accept complicity, conformity, desperation, and dullness, then we fail to (dare to) exist. We face, or in conformity evade,

> the issue ... of the self as a thing of cares and commitments, one which to exist has to find itself, which underlies the myth of the self as on a journey (a path in Plato's image, a stairway in Emerson's, a ladder in others'), a journey to, let us say, the truth of itself (not exhausted by its goods and its rights). (PP, 142)

The ideas, first, that we exist in and through our cares and commitments and, second, that we are able to be variously ashamed or proud of them, or faithful in them, or disgusted by them are inflections of the Kantian idea that our consciousness is apperceptively structured. "The *I think*," Kant reminds us, "must *be able* to accompany all my representations; for otherwise something would be represented in me that could not be thought at all, which is as much to say that the representation would either be impossible or else at least would be nothing for me."[9] That is, for any judgment that I make, it is possible for me in reflection to become aware that it is I who have thus judged. The capacity to do this is impersonal, not unique to any individual. It is possessed by all beings who are capable of judgment. That our consciousness has this structure further implies, according to Kant, that we are responsible for our judgments and the actions that flow from them. "The human being, who is otherwise acquainted with the whole of nature solely through sense, knows himself also through pure apperception," so that he is aware of himself as possessing "reason, [which] has causality,"[10] that is, which can give birth to actions, for which we are responsible. When we act out of respect for the moral law, then we exercise our practical reason and power of action appropriately, thereby coming into our own as human agents.

Thoreau picks up this Kantian line of thought, according to Cavell, when he writes, in the "Solitude" section of *Walden*:

> With thinking we may be beside ourselves in a sane sense. By a conscious effort of the mind we can stand aloof from actions and their consequences.
> ... We are not wholly involved in Nature. I only know myself as a human entity; the scene, so to speak, of thoughts and affections; and am sensible of a certain doubleness by which I can stand as remote from myself as from another. However intense my experience, I am conscious of the presence

and criticism of a part of me, which, as it were, is not a part of me, but a spectator, sharing no experience, but taking note of it, and that is no more I than it is you.[11]

We have, then, an impersonal capacity for reflecting on our judgments, and hence for evaluating what we do—for being proud or ashamed or embarrassed or (culpably) ignorant or accepting of it. Hence we should (dare to) seek to *be* proud, upright, and fully committed in what we venture (never knowing whether the world will cooperate with us or not), rather than timid, acquiescent, or ashamed. Thoroughgoing commitment in and to what one does lures us, or should lure us, as we seek to wed uncertain venture to reflective endorsement. Or, as Cavell furthers Thoreau's thought,

> Our first resolve should be toward the nextness of the self to the self; it is the capacity not to deny either of its positions or attitudes—that it is the watchman or guardian of itself, and hence demands of itself transparence, settling, clearing, constancy; and that it is the workman, whose eye cannot see to the end of its labors, but whose answerability is endless for the constructions in which it houses itself. The answerability of the self to itself is its possibility of awakening. (SW, 107–8)

Emerson's sense of the human person is similar, as in "Self-Reliance" he develops Descartes' *cogito* into the thought that, as Cavell has it, "if I am to exist I must name my existence, acknowledge it. This imperative entails that I am a thing with two foci, or, in Emerson's image, two magnetic poles—say a positive and a negative, or an active and a passive" (IQO, 106). That the self in its doubleness or nextness has active and passive sides that might be put together, that it might thus answer to itself in and through its courses of action, is our infinite task and possibility.

Thoreau and Emerson are, for Cavell, the American philosophers who (along with Wittgenstein elsewhere) take up the Kantian image of the human person. In doing so in their specific ways, they point us toward the romance of expressive freedom, the romance of the pursuit of full existence, uprightness, pride, self-reliance, and answerability to self. Not that this romance is concluded or even quite concludable: far from it. Thoreau and Emerson are "philosophers of direction, orientation, tirelessly prompting us to be on our way, endlessly asking us where we stand, what it is we face" (SW, 141–2). "Emerson's writing is meant as the provision of experience for these shores, of our trials, perils, essays" (TNYUA, 92), where this experience is not already in place to be smoothly developed into happiness, but instead takes the form of trials, perils, and essays, from and through which conversion of care and commitment are required.

That Thoreau and Emerson seek new direction—a conversion of, and from within, experience as it stands, in which they are themselves all too caught up—lends to their writing (and to Cavell's) qualities of *aversiveness* to the ordinary transmission of a settled message: a certain sense of tentativeness and self-revision, a foregrounding of the writer's starts and turns and halts. Their writing enacts a sense of *seeking* to be on the way out of present straits and toward happiness, freedom, and self-reliance. As things stand, our getting on the way is enabled, but also inhibited, by imperfect present conditions. Hence for these writers it is a matter (as it typically is for modernist artists) of getting started at all, of figuring out how to "take an interest in our lives" (SW, 67) from within present dullness, conformity, and acquiescence (SW, 67),

> Thoreau calls this everyday condition quiet desperation; Emerson says silent melancholy; Coleridge and Wordsworth are apt to say despondency or dejection; Heidegger speaks of it as our bedimmed averageness; Wittgenstein as our bewitchment; Austin both as a drunken profundity (which he knew more about than he cared to let on) and as a lack of seriousness. To *find* what degrees of freedom we have *in this condition*, to show that it is at once needless yet somehow, because of that, all but necessary, inescapable, to subject its presentation of necessity to diagnosis, in order to find truer necessities, is the romantic quest I am happy to join. (IQO, 9)

Getting on our way from where we are requires, in the perception of Emerson, Thoreau, and Cavell, not escape (from the cave) into the abstract, or into scientific procedures, but engagement with the near, the low, the common, the ordinary. Emerson and Thoreau work "out of the problematic of the day, the everyday, the near, the low, the common, in conjunction with what they call speaking of necessaries, and speaking with necessity" (TNYUA, 81). They write out of "devotion to the thing they call the common, the familiar, the near, the low" (IQO, 4). In doing so, the hope—their hope—is that we might hear "how the language we traverse every day can contain undiscovered treasure" (MWM, 43) that we can work into our lives because it is already worked into our lives (albeit in ways we do not hear), unlike the false promises of ascent on offer in more traditional doctrines.

Out of our present condition, Emerson and Thoreau (and Cavell) propose to teach or provoke us by stumbling ahead of us toward the light of freedom. They are not experts, either in the instruments or means for the satisfaction of desires as they stand or in the specifics of the end to be achieved. There is "no expert knowledge" on offer, "nothing closed to the ordinary human being, once, that is to say, that being lets himself or herself be informed by the process and ambition of philosophy" (PH, 9). What we might best do "may not be measurable from outside" (PP, 142), but only from within the ordinary, the cave, America. We are to be, somehow, "guided by our experience but not dictated to by it" (PH, 10), as we seek to put the active (workman) and passive (watchman) sides of the self together and seek to compose selves together into a perfected conversational culture of freedom—all from where we are.

There are, then, no formulae for the achievement of freedom. Advice about means and instruments does not heighten or deepen commitment. Descriptions of ultimate goods to be achieved are tendentious and in-supportable, in coming from 'outside' where we are. Because there are no formulae, there are no experts in freedom. Though freedom remains, in this perception, central to the inner agenda of our selves and culture, Americans are also skeptical about prophets. They value expertise and sound advice about coping and getting on with the business at hand. If Thoreau and Emerson and Cavell do not offer that, but instead themselves only stumble as writers toward freedom, then Americans are all too likely to scorn them or, if touched by them at all, to be unsettled but unconvinced. This is pretty much Cavell's sense of the place of Thoreau and Emerson in American culture. Cavell notes what he calls "the extraordinary fact that those I regard as the founders of American thinking—Ralph Waldo Emerson and Henry David Thoreau—are philosophically repressed in the culture they founded" (IQO, 181). Given the pragmatist strain in American culture, in competition with its inner agendas of freedom and perfection, this fact is perhaps not so extraordinary after all. Americans are generally not terribly attentive to their history, especially to their philosophical history. When they do pay attention to it, they are, as pragmatic individualists, perhaps reasonably inclined to pay attention to Jefferson, Madison (especially *Federalist* No. 10 on faction and the separation of powers), and Lincoln. These thinkers offer political solutions—deep and abstract, but still political—to political problems, not conversion.[12]

Cavell, however, nonetheless argues that Emerson and Thoreau are *specifically* repressed. "I am taking precisely that condition to signify their pertinence to the present: I do not, the culture does not, *repress* the thought of Schopenhauer or Kierkegaard or Spengler; they were simply not part of our formation" (TNYUA, 82–3). Emerson and Thoreau are "threats, or say embarrassments, to what we have learned to call philosophy" (IQO, 14) and to what in our acquiescence we have come to think of as America. This is *because* the inner agenda of freedom that they forward, and as they forward it in their specific ways (out of allegiance to America, to its future, and to philosophy's) is itself in specific competition with America's pragmatist, competitive individualist, "get on with business" strands of life. They offer "a continuous rebuke to the way we live" (IQO, 35) from within the contested insides of the way we live (and of themselves). As specifically repressed, they remain, like repressions in general, present in our lives and exerting pressure on them.

Cavell's talk of rebuke, prophecy, and conversion to freedom is likely, however, to seem itself empty, tendentious, and 'cracker-barrel,' especially to Americans naturally suspicious of settled terms of religious and cultural achievement. Such talk seems to monger shame and to do so without telling us much about what, specifically, to do. Emerson and Thoreau seem to undo our sense of ourselves as innocent, without outlining any particular route of recovery or restoration, hence to cast our lives as tragic. Their writings can feel like jeremiads. No doubt we should regret American slavery, and no doubt we face many problems of persistent unfairness and lack of opportunity that should be addressed through political means. But should we feel shame toward our past and ourselves, and is conversion the most apt response to the problems we face?[13]

In light, therefore, of this worry about emptiness and shame-mongering, it is especially worth noting that in his own faithfulness to the near, the low, and the common Cavell himself traces the achievement of a genuinely honorable American romantic happiness and freedom. In *Pursuits of Happiness*— his happiest book—Cavell follows the careers of the principal pairs in seven American movies made between 1934 and 1949. His thought here is that the principal characters in these movies—Jean (Barbara Stanwyck) and Charles (Henry Fonda), Peter (Clark Gable) and Ellie (Claudette Colbert), David (Cary Grant) and Susan (Katherine Hepburn), and so on—"take the time, and take the pains, to converse intelligently and playfully about themselves and about one another" (PH, 5). Among the questions that they ask themselves and each other—most explicitly in the case of David in *Bringing Up Baby*, but implicitly throughout—is "What am I doing here, that is, how have I got into this relation and why do I stay in it?" (PH, 130). Cavell emphasizes continuously that the asking and answering of this question are figures for consent to the social contract, that the achievement of settlement in the relationship of marriage is a figure for settlement of and with one's country and culture and self (and vice versa). As though, then, to make the rebukes and promises of America's prophets other than empty and tendentious, these pairs *do* achieve a settlement. Among other things, they discover—on their ways with one another and to their continuous surprise (in the sense that what they turn out to want is not what they had thought they wanted)—that "what they do together is less important than the fact that they do whatever it is together" (PH, 113). Above all, they talk and acknowledge and have fun with one another. To be sure, at least one of the pair in each case has money so that these couples are not in the end constrained by the pinch of necessity (though often one of them has been thus constrained). They do not have to get on with business. They have time for conversation and exploration. This can make their careers seem like fairy tales or fantasies for many of us.

But then the question that these movies raise and honorably answer is: What—survival apart—is getting on with business *for*? Most of us, Cavell argues, find their answers to this, their achievement of a kind of ongoing purposiveness (with one another) without settled purpose (no external aim, room left for continuing exploration) to be something worth endorsing. They achieve an "honorable . . . happiness" (PH, 65) in and through their pursuits. "The pair is attractive, their wishes are human, their happiness would make us happy. So it seems a criterion is being proposed for the success or happiness of a society, namely that it is happy to the extent that it provides conditions that permit conversations of this character, or a moral equivalent of them, between its citizens" (PH, 32). Since the criterion of happiness is satisfied by these pairs, and hence proleptically for Americans as a people, the wages of prophecy and conversion need not be only admonishment, rebuke, and shame. Acknowledgment intertwined with fun is possible.

To be sure, even though it anticipates a more general happiness, the happiness achieved by these pairs is achieved pairwise. The stateroom door closes at the end of *The Lady Eve*, leaving Mugsy (and us) outside the happiness of Jean and Charles; at the end of *It Happened One Night*, the camera pulls away from the outside of the cabin as the lights go out and the trumpet sounds, leaving Ellie and Peter inside their happiness, us outside.

Partly, however, this division of the private, erotic happiness and intimacy of these pairs from larger social life is a function of the fact that there is, unlike what Plato imagines the ideal city might accomplish, no one final achievement of happiness and freedom that is possible for us. Each of us must begin from where we are, all at once within our tangled culture, from our individual talents and possibilities, and with certain specific others, in engagement with the near, the low, and the familiar. This is an American pursuit of happiness and freedom, not a Platonist[14] pursuit of a standing good. Both selves and language-culture are, always, on the way, seeking always a further settlement. Improvisation, exploration, and wit are not to be bypassed in this seeking in favor of submission to a final theory. As Stephen Mulhall usefully comments, Emerson and Thoreau (and Cavell) are committed to "writing in a way which acknowledges the relative autonomy of both language and its individual speakers, their simultaneous dependence upon and independence of each other."[15] Between self-speaker and culture-language there will be interaction, always, including possibilities of departure and return.

Writing that acknowledges this condition, as the writing of Emerson and Thoreau does, then "presents itself" not as the statement of a theory but as "the realization of [Friedrich Schlegel's] vision ... of the union of poetry and philosophy" (TNYUA, 21). It will include narratives of departure and return, accounts of rehearsals and efforts, and of partial (or pairwise) successes and failures. The thoughts about our condition and possibilities that occur within such writing will be provisional. They will aim, and will sometimes succeed partly (but only partly), at offering us terms in which to do better from where we are. Cavell captures this point by focusing on Emerson's sentences from "Self-Reliance": "In every work of genius we recognize our own rejected thoughts. They come back to us with a certain alienated majesty." As Cavell goes on to comment, these sentences propose that

> If the thoughts of a text such as Emerson's (say the brief text on rejected thoughts) are yours, then you do not need them. If its thoughts are *not* yours, they will not do you good. The problem [—or possibility?—] is that the text's thoughts are neither exactly mine nor not mine. In their sublimity as my rejected—say repressed—thoughts, they represent my further, next, unattained but attainable self. (CHU, 57)

To commit oneself, as Cavell does, to the cultivation of such repressed thoughts (of America, of the self, and of their possibilities of freedom) is to adopt what Simon Critchley has usefully characterized as a "weak messianism," wherein one engages in " 'a passive practice', that is, a way of inhabiting the actual everyday with one eye on the eventual every day."[16]

Are the thoughts to which Cavell (after Emerson and Thoreau) proposes to return us *our* repressed ones? Is freedom—as acknowledgment, self-reliance, mutuality, and achieved Power, and happiness in all of this—central to the inner agenda of our selves and our American culture? There *are* some reasons to be doubtful about this. Narratives of possible conversion, however weak, do carry with them risks of authoritarianism, hypocrisy, and the illegitimate repression of our natural and naturally divergent wants and desires. There is good reason, in order not to wallow in guilt and shame, to accept ourselves as just wanting what we want and just getting on with the business of life as best we can. If America promises us no more than the chance to do that, as individuals, perhaps it is not so bad: better this weak promise than the tribalisms and authoritarianisms of Europe and its philosophies and religions. Why should I feel embarrassed that I like, say, Robin Williams, and my wife, and my house, and you don't? Perhaps it is important to me, and should be to you, that these likings are *mine*, not, or at least not necessarily, to be shared.[17] Why should we not, as pragmatism seems to suggest, just go absolutely with what *works*, from where we are, without worrying about mysterious conversion to a higher pursuit of freedom and happiness that might anyway make us too much like one another?

But then—just as with Emerson and Thoreau—it is not clear that this kind of worry is not already internal to Cavell's perfectionism and commitment to the pursuit of freedom. Perfectionism, as Cavell pursues it, "does not seek to impose itself by power"; "the project of Emersonian perfectionism demands no privileged share of liberty and of the basic goods" (CHU, xxii), and there are, again, no experts ready to hand with fixed formulas. To say all this is to say that democratic equality and fairness and political liberty matter and, further, that they matter specifically for the sake of the divergences, explorations, and developments of individual interest and ability and commitment that they enable.

Cavell's sense here—a sense shared with Emerson in his own continuing efforts to join in an American conversation of differing voices, without mastering it—is that there are certain "arguments that must not be won" (PP, 22)—among them the argument between the perfectionist, conversion- and freedom-seeking voice in American life and the voice of the tolerant, the divergent, the useful, and the acceptance of ourselves as good enough as we stand. "The conversation over how good [the] justice [of a good-enough democracy] is must take place and must also not have a victor, . . . not because agreement can or should always be reached, but because disagreement, and separateness of position, is to be allowed its satisfactions, reached and expressed in particular ways" (CHU, 24–5).

What we seek, as individual selves, as friends and couples, and as Americans, is "consent to our present state as something we desire, or anyway desire more than we desire change" (CR, 465). Sometimes this will require just acceptance: acceptance of liberal political arrangements, of divergences within them, of the sheer difference of people other than oneself or of difference within oneself. Sometimes it will require conversion in the form of openness to and commitment to a certain route of cultivation and expressiveness—sometimes for oneself, sometimes for several, sometimes for the nation—in order to overcome present dissatisfactions. After all, "you never know. I mean, you never know when someone will learn the posture, as for themselves, that will make sense of a field of movement, it may be writing, or dancing, or passing a ball, or sitting at a keyboard, or free associating" (IQO, 115). Cavell himself expresses some sense of being pulled between his particular Jewishness and his more general Americanness, as they "inflect each other," suggesting that Thoreau and Emerson are of interest to him precisely because they keep open this mutual inflection of particular and national (in him and in the nation) by providing "a philosophy of immigrancy, of the human as stranger" (PP, xv)—seeking settlement, but never quite finally arriving at it.

So you never know. I would not want the American settlement to continue without furthering America's and our sometimes repressed inner agenda of freedom—without continuing America's romance—just as I would not want that inner agenda to be administered in comprehensive (nonliberal) political enforcements that would always betray that very agenda.[18] You never know.

5

Cavell and the American Jeremiad

I

There are a number of reasons to be skeptical about the existence of an American style in philosophy. Stylistic choices in philosophy are not neutral with respect to content, so that it can be difficult to separate questions of style from questions of content; there may well be as many distinctive styles of philosophy written in the United States as there are distinct topics addressed by America philosophical writers, and therefore no such thing as *an* American philosophical style. Second, no more is any analysis of style neutral. In picking out particular complexes of style, content, and approach for attention, one will inevitably be making normative judgments about what counts as significant philosophy, what displays connections between style, content, and method in a perspicuous way, and so forth. Hence the topic of style, and of American style in philosophy in particular, is not a straightforward empirical question to be answered only by taking up substantively neutral data. Third, America is largely a country of immigrants, who have brought with them heterogeneous problems and styles of address, both in philosophy and in life.

Nonetheless, "it should be apparent by now," Richard Poirier claims, "that in presenting their case, the Americans simply sound different. They sound altogether less rhetorically embattled, less culturally ambitious, than do any of [their] European cousins."[1] Supposing one has some sense of this distinctive pragmatic, problem-oriented, modestly argumentative American philosophical sound, the trick then will be to explore it where one finds it present in a marked way—all the while remembering that any such exploration will be itself selective, critical, and normative with regard to issues about philosophy, especially about what counts as serious or important or influential philosophy (these terms do not mean the same thing) and about American life, especially about what counts as serious or important or influential within it.

One common way of characterizing philosophy, both American analytic and otherwise, takes it as an enterprise of conceptual analysis in

Anticipations of Freedom. Richard Eldridge, Oxford University Press. © Richard Eldridge 2026.
DOI: 10.1093/9780197841785.003.0008

relation to initiating perplexities. It is an effort to think and speak or write more clearly in the interest of increased fluency, power, and at-homeness in one's commitments in having certain concepts that guide and inform our practices. Hence it is a matter of seeking increased fluency, power, and at-homeness within cultural life itself. John Dewey provides a useful formulation of this conception of philosophy in remarking that both the mind/body problem and the problem of the nature and value of art are "like the problem of reorganizing our heritage from the past and the insights of our present knowledge into a coherent and integrated imaginative union."[2] One might also think of Brandom's conception of philosophy as the enterprise of "grooming concepts"[3] or of a generally Wittgensteinian practice of conceptual elucidation. In all three of these views—Dewey's, Brandom's, and Wittgenstein's—concepts are seen first as in circulation within cultural and practical life, not fixed in Platonic heaven, and not forced on us by perception of our environment and neural processes alone. They are seen, second, as commitments we have imposed on ourselves, of course also in response to our environments and to wide ranges of practical problems, to classify and engage with certain phenomena in certain ways, to count certain ways of classifying as appropriate. They are seen, third, as complexly entangled with one another, forming a not quite coherent set that it is not easy to survey. (As Dewey remarked, we do not yet fully have a "coherent and integrated imaginative union" of either practices or concepts.[4]) Hence, fourth, there are occasions—circumstances of perplexity—when the criteria for applying a particular concept will be unclear or contested and in need of elucidatory articulation and, perhaps, revision. Happily, such circumstances of perplexity are not the stuff of every moment of everyday life, but then they also occur often enough, and no culture, arguably no imaginable culture, can be fully free of them.

The philosophers who most interest me—the masters, as it were, in the grooming of concepts, conceptual elucidation, and the articulation of a more coherent and integrated imaginative union of concepts and practical commitments—are those who are alert to the primary fractures or circumstances of complexity that trouble our present set of concepts and present practical commitments and who then imagine, or articulate, or draw out a way forward toward increased coherence and fluency in a convincing way.

This is obviously a tendentious claim. "Not every philosopher," as Friedrich Waismann once wrote, "but where is one to get one's bearings if not from the masters?"[5] Tendentious and partisan though it is, this claim also offers some hope of being both capacious enough and yet focused enough to capture in useful ways some of the most important things that are going on in the writings of clearly major philosophers. Think, for example, of Plato's sensing of the collapse of an older aristocratic-warrior ethic under the pressures of increasing cosmopolitanism and commercial life and his introduction of an ethic of reflective self-command. Or think of Descartes's criticisms of teleological explanations of natural phenomena and his account of the accuracy, coherence, and usefulness of the practices of the new experimental-mathematical sciences. Or think of Frege's turn away from the analysis of psychological processes and to the analysis of public systems of notation, perhaps regimented, in order to analyze thought and inference.

Or, to turn to American examples, consider Quine. Quine's main object, early and late, was to urge that there does not exist any metaphysical, epistemological, or semantic knowledge that is independent of the practices of experimental natural science. As he wrote early on in "Two Dogmas of Empiricism," "Meaning is what essence becomes when it is divorced from the object of reference and wedded to the word.[6]" That is, in both cases, those of traditional metaphysics and of the semantics of intension à la Church, one gets nothing of value. Talk of nominal versus real essences when it is divorced from current conceptual and explanatory commitments on the ground is worthless. There is no way prior to, beyond, or from above those commitments to establish by argument or investigation whether man is really a rational animal or a featherless biped, and from within those commitments, the question is already settled in cognitive practice. Perhaps even more clearly, limit theory as developed by Dedekind and Cauchy is a usable notation system and technique, and we need not worry about the metaphysics of infinitesimals, about how there can be or whether there really are distances or times that are less in magnitude than any finite number but also greater than zero. Introducing the notation system of limit theory, we simply get a better grip on what we have already been up to with some degree of success and on what we might best do in order to get on fruitfully from where we are. Likewise, intentional psychology should, from where we are in our explanatory practices, go the way of infinitesimal talk, in favor instead of talk of dispositions and neural processes, according to Quine. Infinitesimals and intentions are alike "*Entia non grata*," things we can do without once we have a clearer notation system that we can put to productive use in experimental and explanatory practice. Philosophy becomes, in this view, "the task," carried out from within ongoing practices, "of making explicit what had been tacit, and precise what had been vague; of exposing and resolving paradoxes, smoothing kinks, lopping off vestigial growths, clearing ontological slums."[7]

Never mind, for the moment, whether Quine is right about intentions. (I think he isn't.) The broader metaphilosophical observations I am making are (1) that Quine's appeal here is to self-recognition on our part of what it makes more sense to say, that is, what conceptual and practical commitments it makes more sense to have than the particular tangle of them we have at this moment of perplexity, (2) this appeal is made in the context of a problem felt to be pressing, and (3) the appeal is essentially imaginative; it is an appeal to imagine a problem situation differently and to find more sense in it thus imagined.

Or consider a second example from a completely different sphere. In a useful paper entitled "The Concept of Literature," published in 1973, Monroe Beardsley undertakes to define the concept of literature. The result at which he arrives is that a text is a work of literature if and only if it either displays a higher than normal ratio of implicit or secondary meaning to explicit or primary meaning *or* consists of imitation illocutionary acts, that is, not actual assertions, questions, arguments, and so forth, but rather ones that imagined or pretended speakers make. What these two disjuncts of the definition have in common is that satisfying either of them "help[s] to make a discourse self-centered and opaque, an object of attention in its own right."[8] The reason, further, why self-centered and opaque discourses matter for us is that "it is among discourses marked off from the ordinary run . . . that aesthetic goodness is most likely to be found."[9] Again, never mind whether this definition is quite right. (I think it isn't.) The point to which I wish to call attention is what Beardsley is doing methodologically. At the very beginning of his article, he notes that "an enterprise of conceptual analysis may be constructive as well as descriptive" and that "the rectification of boundaries and the establishment of clear titles are themselves aesthetic tasks."[10] What this means is that conceptual analysis must be in part descriptive, in taking seriously actual applications of the term "literature" by a wide variety of speakers. No radical revisionism and no narcissistic mania of privileged metaphysical knowledge that departs unrecognizably from ordinary usage will be allowed in doing the work of conceptual analysis. But the analysis will not be merely descriptive and empirical. It will also be constructive, in developing a new vocabulary (e.g., that of imitation illocutionary acts) in formulating the analysans, as clarity is sought in characterizing our bases of concept-word application, and it may also be critical or normative in part, in favoring certain applications by experienced readers and by those who have reflected on the varieties of things they read, say, over those of other speakers of the language. Finally, conceptual analysis is itself an aesthetic task. Its criterion of success includes not only that of elucidating or clarifying the bases of ordinary usage, but also that of doing so with felt rightness, so that a sense of perplexity and of difference among us in how we apply the term "literature" is eased, and we feel ourselves to be more at home in our practices of concept application. One could object against this procedure that it amounts to little more than rationalizing some subjective preferences about what counts as a genuine work. Beardsley—so it might be argued—starts with a set of favored works W_1 to W_n, constructs a generalization to cover these works, and then supposedly proves that a work of literature has certain features, that is, that W_1 to W_n are genuine literary works. That seems to be not much argument. But the reply to this objection is that the work of identifying and generalizing from sample works is all done openly and in public, that it is open to revision, that it uses the least tendentious but still constructive vocabulary possible, and that it stays close to common experience. Where else should we begin, if not on the ground? And how else should we proceed, if not via careful reflection, with judgments open to revision? If our life on the ground in applying the concept of literature is perplexing and contested, we can nonetheless make some start, and we can hope to form a "we" of more assured and fluent concept-word users out of our critical attention to conceptual practice as it stands. Surely some measure of more fully endorsable orientation in practice is available, against the background of our current situation.

In other words, in a quite different domain and using a quite different vocabulary, the broad understanding of the nature of elucidatory conceptual analysis is exactly what it is in Quine. It addresses a situation of perplexity by entering an imaginative appeal to use a new vocabulary that had been more or less latent within the old in order to make sense of what we have mostly been doing inchoately in applying a term and might now do better, with a greater sense of fluency and assurance.

This, then, is the way of doing philosophy as conceptual analysis as descriptive, historically sensitive, but also critical, normative, and aesthetic engagement with conceptual practice. Perhaps we might even count characterization of philosophy as conceptual analysis as itself a piece of conceptual analysis of the concept of *philosophy* itself, even if a somewhat tendentious one.

II

The further questions that I want to raise are: (1) Is there anything particularly American about this conception of philosophy or way of doing philosophy? Or is it just the way in which philosophy is always and everywhere properly done? (2) What are the virtues and vices, and what are the stylistic marks, of becoming increasingly self-conscious about this way of doing philosophy?

The answer to question (1)—to both parts of it—is yes. That is, my view, again without much argument, is that conceptual analysis so construed is both the way in which philosophy is always and everywhere properly done *and* something distinctly American, and distinctly American for interesting historical reasons. This compound answer commits me to thinking of this practice of philosophy in America as representing the coming into mature self-consciousness of what philosophy itself has always already been, when it has been done well. Again, I am well aware that this is itself a tendentious, critical, normative claim about the concept of philosophy and what philosophy is. But that is where I am. Plato, Aristotle, Augustine, Descartes, and so on are engaging in conceptual analysis so conceived when they are doing the work that mattered most for their audiences in situ and that matters most for us, *and* American philosophers, or some American philosophers, among them Dewey, Quine, Beardsley, and Cavell (to whom I will come) are doing this in an especially explicit and self-conscious way. I add that in my pantheon of heroes both Austin and Wittgenstein practice philosophy as conceptual analysis in this highly self-conscious way, so philosophy's coming to this kind of methodological self-consciousness cannot be exclusively an American phenomenon. And yet it does seem to me to have a prominently marked career in America, where its practitioners include not only Dewey, Quine, Beardsley, and Cavell, but also, with variations, Rorty, James, Emerson, and Thoreau. Why might this be so? What about the history of America in particular might motivate the practice of philosophy as conceptual analysis so conceived?

To pursue this historical question, I have found nothing better to which to turn than the wonderful work of Sacvan Bercovitch on the American jeremiad. Bercovitch argues that, for the New England immigrants fleeing religious persecution, "the term American involves a distinctive blend of the visionary, historic, and figurative modes,"[11] and he argues, further, that this blend continues to inform the American literary and political imagination in fundamental ways throughout the eighteenth and nineteenth centuries and up to the present. To say that visionary, historic, and figurative modes are blended is to say that the place America, historically arrived at, is to be a place where a vision of the ideal is to be made actual, and it is to use a particular figurative, rhetorical mode in order to describe both the task and the process of its achievement. John Winthrop in his 1630 sermon on board the ship *Arabella*, bound for the Massachusetts Bay Colony, took as his text Deuteronomy 30:5: "And the LORD thy God will bring thee into the land which thy fathers possessed, and thou shalt possess it; and he will do thee good, and multiply thee above thy fathers."[12] The sermon that takes up this key text and that serves as an archetype for serious critical discourse for the next almost four centuries is then "a state of the covenant address," a "political sermon . . . to revitalize the errand."[13] The older social and political dispensations of Europe are hostile to the Puritans and have been left behind. The task is to live in the wilderness according to the revealed word. In Perry Miller's phrase, the Puritans undertook to fill their venture "with meaning by themselves and out of themselves,"[14] with reference only to the word and the new world, not to the social and political pasts they had left behind. "The settlers . . . took with them when they left [seventeenth-century England] a sacred and a worldly view of their errand, both a conviction that they were elect and an expectation of the great things they were to do on earth."[15]

Carrying this project forward required, however, both specification and continual monitoring of how the work is or isn't going. An issue is continually held in consciousness by sermonizers and kept before the minds of the public: are we or aren't we fulfilling the errand? How can we part progress from backsliding, from within where we now are in the new world? Hence the American jeremiad, modeled on the prophet Jeremiah's lamentations over the conduct of the people of Israel, was, as Bercovitch puts it, "a ritual designed to join social criticism to spiritual renewal, public to private identity."[16] It blends "catalogues of iniquities" with "an unswerving faith in the errand" and "an unshakeable optimism."[17] The sermonizer as contemporary prophet is the one who sees through present modes of sinfulness and who recovers the way on behalf of the people as a whole. "As prophets of probation, [the American sermonizers] could describe themselves as isolated representatives of the people—historian-seers whose representative qualities were enhanced by their hostility toward those they represented. Alienation and engagement: *by their very contradictions these terms were made to correspond.*"[18]

With the settlement of America outside New England, the coming of the American Revolution, and the development of increasing commercial life and trade both before and after the Revolution, the jeremiad rhetoric became wedded to less immediately religious purposes and more to the projects of nation-building and wealth-accumulation, where these latter are, significantly, still described in redemptivist terms. In Bercovitch's summary,

> The concept of American revolution transformed self-reliance into a function not only of the common good but of the redemption of mankind. In virtually every area of life, the jeremiad became the official ritual form of continuing revolution. Mediating between religion and ideology, the jeremiad gave contract the sanctity of covenant, free enterprise the halo of grace, progress the assurance of the chiliad, and nationalism the grandeur of typology. In short, it wed self-interest to social perfection, and conferred on both the unique blessings of American destiny.[19]

The jeremiad rhetoric's sense of humanity's creation or election for a higher errand, its indictment of current modes of life and thought as a fall away from the terms of the covenant, and its call for conversion or re-commitment to better modes of life and thought all fundamentally structure Emerson's writing. Emerson continually calls for the true American Scholar who does not yet exist, for "Man Thinking" who is characterized by "self-trust," while he sees in fact around him only "the bookworm" or, in a Schillerian figure "man metamorphosed into a thing, into many things," man "subdivided and peddled out, . . . spilled into drops" through the social division of labor.[20] The essay "Nature" begins with a charge of belatedness and paleness against the present and with a call to make a new future through the exercise of natural human powers.

> Our nature is retrospective. It builds the sepulchres of the fathers. It writes biographies, histories, and criticism. The foregoing generations beheld God and nature face to face; we, through their eyes. Why should we not also enjoy an original relation to the universe? Why should we not have a poetry and philosophy of insight and not of tradition, and a religion by

revelation to us, and not the history of theirs? Embosomed for a season in nature, whose floods of life stream around and through us, and invite us, by the powers they supply, to action proportioned to nature, why should we grope among the dry bones of the past, or put the living generation into masquerade out of its faded wardrobe. The sun shines today also. There is more wool and flax in the fields. There are new lands, new men, new thoughts. Let us demand our own works and laws and worship.[21]

In his moment of most ecstatic accession to vision and power, Emerson proclaims the power of nature, present around, in, and through him, to move us into godly life.

In the woods, we return to reason and faith. There I feel that nothing can befall me in life,—no disgrace, no calamity (leaving me my eyes), which nature cannot repair. Standing on the bare ground,—my head bathed by the blithe air and uplifted into infinite space,—all mean egotism vanishes. I become a transparent eyeball; I am nothing; I see all; the currents of the Universal Being circulate through me; I am part or parcel of God.[22]

To his credit, Emerson characteristically swerves into doubt and despair within a few lines or paragraphs of his heights of optimism. In "Nature," he goes on to note that "the same scene which yesterday breathed perfume and glittered as for the frolic of the nymphs is overspread with melancholy today."[23] Nature's power to convert us vanishes as our moods alter into melancholy and our way of life lapses into dull routine, and these movements cannot be stopped. In "Experience," in the next sentence after announcing the existence of "the Power which abides in no man and in no woman, but for a moment speaks from this one, and for another moment from that one," Emerson goes on to ask "But what help from these fineries or pedantries? What help from thought? Life is not dialectics.... Culture with us ... ends in headache."[24] Yet despite the standing presence of uncontrollable alterations of mood and relapses into a fallen ordinary, Emerson continues to indict the present and to court redemption. He stands in pursuit of "the unattained but attainable self,"[25] "ready to die out of nature and be born again into this new yet unapproachable America I have found in the West."[26]

Thoreau takes up the jeremiad rhetorical stance from Emerson and the broader New England context, but he modulates into a register of labor and agricultural life. His criticism of the present is directed at thoughtlessness, aimless expenditures of energy, especially in commerce, and distracted fear-fulness. "The mass of men," he writes in *Walden*, "lead lives of quiet desper-ation"[27] "men labor under a mistake . . . as serfs of the soul; . . . by a seeming fate, commonly called necessity, they are employed, as it says in an old book, laying up treasures which moths and rust will corrupt and thieves break through and steal. It is a fool's life."[28] "By closing the eyes and slumbering, and consenting to be deceived by shows, men establish and confirm their daily life of routine and habit everywhere, which is still built on purely illu-sory foundations."[29]

In the face of this fallen present, Thoreau resolves to learn for himself what recovery or conversion, if any, to a more fit way of life might be possible, thus casting himself, in learning on his own against the grain of his culture as it stands, both as a prophet, seer, or visionary, and as one in and through whom change is to happen. "I went to the woods because I wished to live deliber-ately, to front only the essential facts of life, and see if I could not learn what it had to teach, and not, when I came to die, discover that I had not lived."[30] The change that is to happen involves a characteristically Thoreauvian mix-ture of self-reliant handicraft labor with independence and originality of reading, thought, and writing. He praises, "the pantaloons which I now wear [which] were woven in a farmer's family,—thank Heaven there is so much virtue still in man; for I think the fall from the farmer to the operative as great and memorable as that from the man to the farmer,"[31] and he calls for culture instead of or beyond potatoes. "When we want culture more than potatoes, and illumination more than sugar-plums, then the great resources of a world are taxed and drawn out, and the result, or staple production, is, not slaves, nor operatives, but men,—those rare fruits called heroes, saints poets, philosophers, and redeemers."[32] Like Emerson, Thoreau worries about his reception and effect within the culture he is confronting. His flights of confidence remain marked by doubt. "I am obliged to say to you Reader," he writes, "that the seeds which I planted, if indeed they *were* the seeds of those virtues [viz. 'sincerity, truth, simplicity, faith, innocence, and the like'] were wormeaten or had lost their vitality, and so did not come up."[33] Yet, as in Emerson, Thoreau's fundamental commitment to the work of the crit-ical indictment of the habits and thoughts, the practices and concepts, of his present joined to the exemplary envisioning of habits, thoughts, practices, and concepts otherwise, transfigured and redeemed, remains in place.

And it is this jeremiad tradition, modulated into a key of greater so-briety and professionalism and directed to more specific problems, that we find still recognizably present in Dewey, Quine, and Beardsley, among others. A present life of practice and concepts, perplexing in some degree, is to be attended to and engaged with honestly and critically, with the aim of increased coherence and fluency, somehow envisioned from within present perplexities, without reversion to fundamentalisms of intellectual intuition, the will of God, or a dialectical method that departs from the ordinary. Elucidatory conceptual analysis, carried out from within the ordinary, in the hope of reforming it, is, among other things, an inheritor of the American jeremiad rhetorical tradition.

III

The second question I proposed to take up is: What are the virtues and vices, and what are the stylistic marks, of becoming increasingly self-conscious about this way of doing philosophy? Stanley Cavell's writings, early and late, are marked by the development of this increasing self-consciousness of the inheritance of the American jeremiad rhetorical tradition blended with elucidatory conceptual analysis as Cavell took it up from Austin and Wittgenstein. Hence we can trace the virtues and vices and the stylistic marks of this increasing self-consciousness as they develop within his work.

Cavell gets his faithfulness to the ordinary—but to an ordinary clarified and redeemed in and through eliciting what one, or we, really want coherently to say in response to a circumstance of perplexity—initially from Austin. This faithfulness to the actual ordinary and pursuit of a redeemed ordinary has a number of features that distinguish it prominently both from traditional metaphysical-epistemological thought and from pragmatism. Unlike traditional metaphysical thought, it accepts a standing sense of belatedness and complex inheritance in coming to be a subject or ego in and through accession to language. (Cavell's engagement with Freud is also an important source here.) There is no standpoint outside this belatedness and complex inheritance from which subject identity might be maintained in distantiation from the impurities of the ordinary. Hence there is a pronounced suspicion of metaphysical-epistemological thinking that proposes the availability of such a stance, however much it remains human to wish for such a standpoint in the face of present perplexities. Unlike pragmatism, but like traditional Platonic and religious thought, however, there is also a sense that we do not at present know our interests, so that conversion of interest may be required in order to overcome current distress. Getting on with business as usual is not the fixed order of the day. Third, there is the pursuit of exemplarity in the effort to make a movement toward increased clarity and assurance in stance. An individual must say something, must venture a claim about what we say, in the hope that this claim will be taken up by others and that shared felt rightness in usage will have been articulated, even while one knows that such a claim, as an orientation-seeking articulation, is open to challenge and repudiation. The claim to what we say is, as Cavell later puts in *The Claim of Reason*, a claim all at once to reason, self-knowledge, and community. Hence the view is neither communitarian nor purely individualist, but (for want of a better term) perfectionist. The individual undertaking to articulate what we say is undertaking to serve as the exemplary or representative bootstrapping device for hauling both self and community out of their present mutual straits and toward greater clarity and assurance in both concept-applications and action. One seeks, as Cavell later puts it, to guide "the soul, or self, [together with its necessary companions] toward the light or the instinct of freedom" (PP, 4), via a movement into "freedom of consciousness, the beginning of freedom, ... freedom of language, having the run of it, as if successfully claimed from it, as of a birthright" (TNYUA, 55).

These features—a sense of belatedness or complex inheritance in coming to be a subject, suspicion of traditional metaphysical-epistemological thinking that cultivates distantiation from existing practices, plus openness to conversion via the pursuit of exemplary individuality—are prominently on view in Cavell's early essays in *Must We Mean What We Say?* In the title essay, Cavell describes a claim about what we say as a *categorical declarative*, and he notes that the speaker who issues one "is certainly not *instituting* norms, nor is he *ascertaining* norms; but he may be thought of as *confirming* or *proving* the existence of norms when he reports or describes how we (how to) talk" (MWM, 22). Here to resist talk of either instituting norms (constructivism) or ascertaining norms (realism), and to propose instead confirming them is to resist any simple and absolute dichotomy between invention and proposal (instituting), on the one hand, and discovery (ascertaining) on the other. Instead one is, in pursuit of exemplarity, articulating and confirming norms one will stand by, from where one is, in a bootstrapping movement from a moment of perplexity into a moment of greater clarity and satisfaction.

The aesthetic dimensions of this activity are nowhere clearer than they are in "Aesthetic Problems of Modern Philosophy." The title records a controlling ambiguity. The essay takes up two problems about art that arise within modern philosophy: are poems paraphrasable? and is serial music really (hearable as) music? But the argument of the essay goes on to develop the thought that one of the reasons we have difficulty finding satisfactory answers to these questions is that we repress or leave unarticulated the character of our aesthetic experience of difficult poems and pieces of music. That is, modern philosophy falls into perplexities and difficulties because of its repression of—its problems with—the aesthetic. Instead, then, of pursuing distantiated knowledge of concepts (e.g., what a poem or a piece of music really is, absolutely) we should and would do better to refuse formulaic, one-line answers and to describe more carefully the ways in which we are and are not involved with some difficult modern works. That is, instead of saying, for example, either with Cleanth Brooks that a poem is by definition unparaphrasable or with Yvor Winters that a poem, to be a poem, must be paraphrasable, must express a stateable thought, we should rather attend to the aesthetically dense, singular movements of something like thought at the edge of thought that are present in Wallace Stevens's modernist lyrics. By doing so, and only by doing so, we might hope to find increased satisfaction in giving words to our experience of these works, rather than stunning ourselves into dullness with empty formulae.

Surrounding this large argument is a set of Wittgensteinian remarks on the aims of philosophy and on the kinds of satisfactions philosophy may afford. The essay opens with two somewhat cryptic sentences. "The Spirit of the Age is not easy to place, ontologically or empirically; and it is idle to suggest that creative effort must express its age, either because that cannot fail to happen, or because a new effort can create a new age. Still, one knows what it means when an art historian says, thinking of the succession of plastic styles, 'not everything is possible in every period'" (MWM, 73, citing Heinrich Wölfflin). Here Cavell is committed all at once to the existence of something like ages or historically circumscribable regimes of sense-making that lack any fixed logic and are difficult to discern, to the thought that the task of philosophy in or as criticism is that of finding or founding the contours of an age or one's place within it, and to the idea that this is possible, yet may itself require creative effort, not just the recording of data or empirical facts. When one achieves, as an artist, as a critic, or as a philosopher, a breakthrough to sense-making out of an experience of initial perplexity, then what has happened is that the subject, as a self-bootstrapping device, has found a satisfying, exemplary articulation of experience and orientation within it. Or as Cavell puts it, "the problem of the critic, as of the artist, is not to discount his subjectivity, but to include it; not to overcome it in agreement, but to master it in exemplary ways....All the philosopher, this kind of philosopher, can do is to express, as fully as he can, his world, and attract our undivided attention to our own" (MWM, 94, 96). In this activity, it is not Sancho Panza, rooted in a domesticated ordinary and prone to accept authorities of station, but rather "Quixote who is the patron saint of the critic, desperate to preserve the best of his culture against itself, and surviving any failure but that of his honesty and his expression of it" (MWM, 88) and thence going on in this desperation despite the risks of folly.

As Cavell moves in the 1970s through his initial writing on movies and his work on Thoreau into the completion of *The Claim of Reason* in 1979, he increasingly identifies the sense of openness, standing incompletion, and risky improvisation in the self's use of the self to court increased coherence with Wittgenstein rather than with Austin. The distinct writerliness of the text of *Philosophical Investigations* in its play of voices becomes for Cavell an enactment of continuing temptations, wishes, and fantasies, intermingled with moments of articulation of what we say that provide good enough, but never absolute, orientation and release from perplexity. The encounter with *Walden* and then with Emerson begins to make more explicit the jeremiad character of the rhetoric of Cavell's form of conceptual analysis. Two crucial methodological passages from *The Claim of Reason* show this character markedly. The first is from the end of Part III, "Knowledge and the Concept of Morality," the oldest stratum of writing of the text. There Cavell writes about moral argument that "its rationality lies in following the methods which lead to a knowledge of our own position, of where we stand; in short, to a knowledge and definition of ourselves" (CR, 312). This passage makes explicit the connection between conceptual analysis—here the analysis of what makes a reason a moral reason, of what a moral argument *is*—and the pursuit and achievement of self-knowledge, figured as confidence in stance.

The second, longer passage occurs at the very end of Part I, "Wittgenstein and the Concept of Human Knowledge," at the end of chapter 5, "Natural and Conventional." It records a sense of a standing slippage or friction between what is conventional and what is natural, together with a sense of some available possibilities of their fitter alignment, that is, of more natural, fluent, assured life within a framework of convention and culture refigured from within.

The jeremiad rhetorical style is prominent. The occasion for philosophy is upon him, Cavell writes, when

I . . . feel that my foregone conclusions were never conclusions *I* had arrived at, but were merely imbibed by me, merely conventional. I may blunt that realization through hypocrisy or cynicism or bullying. But I may take the occasion to throw myself back upon my culture, and ask why we do what we do, judge as we judge, how we have arrived at these crossroads. What is the natural ground of our conventions, to what are they in service? It is inconvenient to question a convention; that makes it unserviceable, it no longer allows me to proceed as a matter of course; the paths of action, the paths of words, are blocked. In philosophizing, I have to bring my own language and life into imagination. What I require is a convening of my culture's criteria, in order to confront them with my words and life as I pursue them; and at the same time to confront my words and life as I pursue them with the life my culture's words may imagine for me: to confront the culture with itself, along the lines in which it meets in me. . . .

In this light, philosophy becomes the education of grownups. The anxiety in teaching, in serious communication, is that I myself require education. And for grownups this is not natural growth, but *change*. Conversion is a turning of our natural reactions, so it is symbolized as rebirth. (CR, 125)

This passage shows, self-consciously, with the discourse directed by the subject seeking clarity to the subject frozen in false commitments, elucidatory conceptual analysis fused with jeremiad rhetoric. The occasion for betaking oneself to thought is a sense of perplexity, of a blocked path or being brought to a halt, with movement blocked, within the culture within which one finds oneself. The sense of halt stems from a sense that the way things are done in a certain region of culture—a set of constitutive conventions—is stiltedly artificial and inhospitable to the exercise of genuinely human powers, so that the conventions embody something like a breach of covenant. The paths that are sought are simultaneously paths of words and of actions, paths of language and of life. The halt is experienced as occurring at a crossroads— an allusion to Paul on the way to Damascus—where conversion is sought. Accomplishing this conversion will require a feat of imagining, of seeing things otherwise, accomplished originally from within where one has been halted. And the achievement that is sought courts exemplarity—a convening of my culture's criteria, and its consequent redirection, not one's own psychic turning alone—in a bootstrapping hauling of the subject and the culture forward together.

Under the increasing presence of Emerson, this fusing of elucidatory conceptual analysis with jeremiad rhetoric becomes even more marked in subsequent writings. In *In Quest of the Ordinary*, Cavell characterizes the condition that calls for philosophy in a string of complementary terms drawn from Thoreau, Emerson, Coleridge, Wordsworth, Heidegger, Wittgenstein, and Austin.

> Thoreau calls this everyday condition quiet desperation; Emerson says silent melancholy; Coleridge and Wordsworth are apt to say despondency or dejection; Heidegger speaks of it as our bedimmed averageness; Wittgenstein as our bewitchment; Austin both as drunken profundity (which he knew more about than he cared to let on) and as a lack of seriousness. To find what degrees of freedom we have in this condition, to show that it is at once needless yet somehow, because of that, all but necessary, inescapable, is the romantic quest I am happy to join. (IQO, 9)

In *Little Did I Know: Excerpts from Memory* the turn to autobiography—the subject's rehearsals of its plights and possibilities, and of its encounters with them, both remembered and in present reflection—is explicit. The text is broadly organized around the trope of the mother as the figure of trance and expressive fluency, exemplified in her piano-playing, and also of outsiderliness in that very musical trance and in other tendencies to withdrawal, and around the trope of the father as the figure of interruption, rivalry, and so of shocks into ego formation and into the pursuit of substitute sources of the mother's trance and expressiveness. It ends, heartbreakingly, with a paradigm scene of moral conversation, where each party is exploring and commenting on possibilities of stance in present culture, on which possibilities they may or may not agree. The son, Stanley, is talking in the hospital with his roughly eighty-three-year-old father, who has just had a pacemaker implanted and who is disturbed by what he regards as the unsuitable fuss and busyness of it all.

> "They are just doing their job. Placing a pacemaker
>   has become a standard medical procedure."
> "You mean I don't have a choice."
> "I don't know."
> "Tell them to stop."
> "That's not my job."

Wondering whether my father would question the philosopher about what a son's responsibility is, or what a wife's is, or what a doctor's is, I was about to say that I would tell the doctor about our talk, but my father had fallen asleep. His position appeared awkward to me. I walked out to find my mother. (LDIK, 548)

Here a moral conversation has taken place—an exchange of perceptions and accompanying reasons, motivated not by the guarantee of agreement under a method, but by the hope of agreement, and in any case amounting to exploring one another's positions and possible courses of action in relation to current concepts of dignity, medical treatment, responsibility, and care. Acknowledgment of differing positions and responsibilities and of differing conceptions of them is, perhaps, almost achieved, but then broken off by the father's falling asleep. The son then walks out—puts himself into motion, overcoming a halt—in order to seek the figure of trance, fluency, and expressiveness. All this is meant as an exemplary bodying forth to sense, in words, of what it is, now, in America in 1977 (the moment of the hospital change) or 2004 (the moment of writing) or 2009 (the moment of revision), to be a responsive and responsible human subject, brought to a halt and then again able to move in difficult circumstances.

IV

What, then, are the virtues and vices of this form of elucidatory conceptual analysis that has self-consciously taken the figures of the American jeremiad rhetoric on itself and moved, with them, into the register of autobiography? What happens, evidently enough, is the foregrounding of an itinerary of encounters, moods, emotions, and thoughts (which may include passages of argument with oneself or others, where the arguments can be seen to have a more or less deductive structure) over abstracted structures of argument themselves. Just as no culture and set of conventions are final, there are no fixed *arché* from which deductive arguments might proceed and stand on their own, independent of particular investments by particular situated subjects. Hence there is a prominent writerliness to Cavell's prose, philosophical and autobiographical, as he tracks his swerves of encounter, mood, emotion, and thought. While including bits of dialectic with oneself and others, the larger structures of the writing become increasingly narrative, recording readings of other texts, conversations, associations, moments of halt or of movement recovered. Concepts are shown as under pressure in the courses of encounters and other circumstances of perplexity. There is a pronounced drift toward showing and toward antinomianism, and away from the announcement and defense of settled doctrine. Futurity is held continuously in view, as the time for the working out of more fit possibilities of life, individual and communal, where these possibilities are themselves brought into view in and through the envisionings of the exemplary individual. One can, as a philosopher, worry about this. Attention to encounter, mood, and emotion can displace more impersonal movements of thought and argument that remain committed to holding reasons spatially in view, as though they were continuously available to anyone. "Can philosophy become literature and still know itself?" (CR, 142), one might ask, in all sincerity. Perhaps it is all too American, too individualist, too rhetorical, too religious, too literary, and just not philosophical enough, where the philosophical is equated with the neutral and the general.

But then when one is, as a reader, caught up in these antinomian itineraries, the more immediately problem-oriented procedures of elucidatory conceptual analysis that are to be found in Dewey, Quine, or Beardsley may look too regimented, too impersonal, as though problems were being taken up from nowhere, without acknowledgment or awareness of their circumstances of arising in life. Whether one should, as a philosopher, practice elucidatory conceptual analysis more in the style of Quine and Beardsley or more in the style of Cavell and Wittgenstein (as Cavell reads him) is not a question that it is easy to answer. Perhaps both styles—the more neutral and careful version in Quine and Beardsley, and the more passionate, self-consciously critical and jeremiad version in Cavell—are both American enough and worthwhile enough to attract and to hold our interest. I would not want to live without the practical seriousness in focusing on problems, the transparency in laying out considerations, and the argumentative honesty of Quine and Beardsley. But no more would I want to live without the passionate sense of lived problems, the hesitancy about dogmas and rigid formulae, and the open orientation toward futurity of Cavell.

SITES OF ARREST AND RECOVERY

Literature, Music, and Film

6

Cavell and Hölderlin on
Human Immigrancy

Describing the ambition of ordinary language philosophy and taking it as
his own, Stanley Cavell remarks that the ordinary language philosopher's
"problem [in proceeding from what is ordinarily said] is to discover the specific plight of mind and circumstance within which a human being gives
voice to his condition" (MWM, 240). This ambition can be variously pursued
in autobiographical writing, in poetry, and in criticism, as well as in ordinary
language philosophy.

One way to pursue it would be to arrive, or to claim to arrive, at a final
discovery of the human condition: to announce, for example, that we are
immortal souls capable of eternal knowledge, in substantial union with a
mortal, material body; or that we are nothing but congeries of atoms; or that
we are made in the image of a God of justice and love, thence to take one's
bearings from that announcement. This is roughly the way of dogmatic philosophy, in seeking final results—ultimate characterizations of our condition, vouchsafed to us from an encounter with the dictates of reason alone, or
with reality as such, material or divine, as the case may be.

One does not have to be a hyperbolic skeptic to be suspicious of this ambition, articulated and worked out in this way. What are the criteria of an
encounter with reason or reality alone? How might any such announcement,
even to oneself, be trusted? But there is another, more distinctly critical way
to follow this ambition, proceeding, as it were, from within the continual
having of it. This latter way eschews the ultimacy of any discovery of our condition in favor of tracing—and sharing in—swerves between self-composure
and self-abandonment on an eccentric path: as though one found oneself
along with other human beings whose expressions of their plight one might
read as neighbors to one's own, always in medias res between nothingness
and at-homeness with oneself, others, and the world, in living without full
composure according to reason and the nature of things. Here the ambition to discover our condition so as to take one's bearings persists, but this

Anticipations of Freedom. Richard Eldridge, Oxford University Press. © Richard Eldridge 2026.
DOI: 10.1093/9780197841785.003.0010

condition is experienced as a continuing plight within which one comes to voice and judgment, rather than as an object of knowledge that voice and judgment might master.

This latter way of thinking within a continuing ambition of human self-discovery is not easy to articulate. (Any characterization of how one might or must so think itself uneasily verges on dogmatism.) The claim that this way of thinking is appropriate to what we are cannot be justified by any argument that would satisfy anyone committed to standards of demonstrative proof independent of any appeal to a transfiguration of perception. Some might see that this is how things are—that we always live thus in medias res—and some might not. But there can be no demonstrative rational proof of the ultimate correctness of this critical view.

This perception of our condition can, however, be filled in persuasively by elaborating readings of various responses to that condition.[1] Such elaborated readings might invite acknowledgment, even if they are unable to command it, and in doing so might serve to keep open lines of reflection and conversation with others and within oneself, rather than short-circuiting them into avoidance and repression. Or they may not. That there is at least a way of thinking philosophically and poetically and critically, through the elaboration of readings of our condition, aiming at acknowledgment, and that this way of thinking is a distinctive and potentially valuable realization of philosophy and of our condition are things that I will try to suggest by juxtaposing some Wittgensteinian thoughts about the strangeness of language as our almost habitation, Cavell's diagnoses of philosophy's motives, and some pieces of Friedrich Hölderlin's philosophy and poetry. Such a juxtaposition might help fill in a distinctively romantic shape of thinking so conceived, pointing toward romantic articulations—at once philosophical, poetic, and critical—of our condition under which we might acknowledge ourselves to fall and which we might come to see to be in play in literature, in criticism, and in human life.

I

When we are not thinking philosophically, or not otherwise overcome by wonder at the sheer existence of the world before us, we find words to be familiar objects of use. They come to the tongue and hand as thought comes to the mind. But it is also possible, when in the grip of philosophy or wonder, for words to strike us as strange. Wittgenstein notes this experience of the strangeness of words: "Suppose I had agreed on a code with someone, 'tower' means bank. I tell him. 'Now go to the tower'—he understands me and acts accordingly, but he feels the word 'tower' to be strange [*fremdartig*] in this use, it has not yet 'taken on' the meaning." Or the effect of strangeness can be produced by simply repeating a word: you would be missing something "if you did not feel that a word lost its meaning and became a mere sound if it was repeated ten times over."[2] What are the sources and meanings of this joint familiarity and strangeness?

Spoken and written words are there in one's early childhood environment as aural and visual stimuli if not yet as objects of recognition as words, before one comes to master any of them. They circulate among others who are in control of their own bodies and who attend to their own needs. A dim half recognition—not yet voiced and conceptually structured—of one's dependence on these others inhabits this not yet conceptually conscious quasi-experience of one's environment. (Cavell, in describing this condition in which speech and conceptual thought are yet beyond and above us, notes with approval Rousseau's remark that the first encounter in the state of nature with another human being will "produce the name 'giant.'") [PP, 3, citing Rousseau's *Essay on the Origin of Language*].)

Then, after a time, speech and thought come, at first haltingly and in specific domains and then with an astonishing rapidity of fluency and generality. What has happened? One has come to share with others—in part at least, and mysteriously—a world of speech, thought, and recognitive perception. Wonder at the joint familiarity and strangeness of words is bound up with wonder at this accomplishment. How have I, by trafficking in unseen ways, with these sounds and marks—how have I come to do this thing? If I concentrate on these sounds and marks as sounds and marks, then they seem awkward and inert. If I simply use them in accomplished speech and writing and thought, then a grasp of an external basis of their life passes me by, as I am caught within their flow. Just how and how far do I share a world of speech and writing and thought with others? What have I done?

One way to respond to this primitive perplexity—the way of dogmatic philosophy, or of what Cavell calls "skepticism"—is to attempt to settle it intellectually: to articulate and confirm rationally an exact account of the nature and limits of this achievement, so as to still any latent anxieties. (A second way is simply to repress this perplexity. This is not always or even often dishonorable, but it involves giving oneself over wholly to conventions of thought and language. These conventions might prove untrustworthy, or one might feel one's life in subscribing to them not to be the fruit of one's own will.) This intellectual effort has a natural appeal. If we could know how we, and others, have come to language and thought, and we could know how far we share conventions, and how apt those conventions are to the world and to our thinkings, then the risks we run in speaking would be diminished, even settled. Instead of facing moments of repudiation and misunderstanding as we venture forth in words ("That is not it at all, / That is not what I meant, at all"),[3] we might speak and think in full assurance that all is in order in our speech and thought, in their relations with the world and with others. Dogmatic philosophy, or skepticism, by raising questions about how we come or might come (or fail to come) to well-founded thought and language, keeps open the primitive quasi-experience of our accession to language in which, it may well seem, we all share. This accession remains marked by unsureness about its nature and anxiety over its potential repudiability. In Cavell's phrasing, skepticism "names our wish (and the possibility of our wishing) to strip ourselves of the responsibility we have in meaning (or in failing to mean) one thing, or one way, rather than another" (IQO, 135).

To the extents—and how shall these extents be measured? from what position and with what perceptions?—that our perplexities with language and with our thinking are primitive and that skepticism and dogmatic philosophy arise out of them, they are unavoidable unless we repress them. The human experience of coming to language and thought moves us toward querying their bases philosophically in hopes of perfecting away our risks. In Cavell's formulation,

> there is inherent in philosophy a certain drive to the inhuman, to a certain inhuman idea of intellectuality, or of completion, or of the systematic... that exactly because it is a drive to the inhuman, it is somehow itself the most inescapably human of motivations. The quest for the inhuman is an essential part of the motivation to skepticism. And it is a reason why... skepticism is forever an inherent aspiration of the thing we know as human.[4]

The philosophical effort to discover in something given (intellect, or matter, or God) the bases of language and thought emerges here as an all too human "attempt to convert the human condition, the condition of humanity, into an intellectual difficulty, a riddle" (CR, 493), something to be solved and done with. Sometimes this effort will take the form of positing a power of inner recognition, prior to all instructions and stimuli—a fantasy of a private language. "This may be seen as part of philosophy's denial of my powerlessness (over the world, over others, over myself, over language) by demanding that all power seem to originate with me, and in isolation." Or sometimes it will take the form of seeing actions and utterances as nothing but materially caused events, caught up in nature's own meaningless course. "It may be seen as philosophy's denial of my power (such as it may be) by sublimizing the power of the world, or say nature" (PP, 112–13).

Either way, and whether or not the philosophical effort is worked out in any specific, articulate shape, it may well seem that we live caught between fantasies of perfect power in thought, action, and speech, on the one hand, and of freedom from responsibility and escape into powerlessness by way of acceptance of or submission to the world, on the other. If one has this perception of our "betweenness" in exercising our powers in the world—our immigrant not quite at-homeness, not quite homelessness—then it may seem important not to deny this perceived fact of the continuance of fantasies, drives, ambitions, wishes, and frustrations: "I say this struggle with skepticism, with its threat or temptation, is endless: I mean to say that it is human, it is the human drive to transcend itself, make itself inhuman, which should not end until, as in Nietzsche, the human is over" (TNYUA, 57).

It seems impossible to escape the sways of context and the ways of others in having words that are there before one. Without those sways and ways, there are no criteria of recognition, no chances of thought speaking only to itself alone. There is no room to insert thought between the world and these sways and ways. "[I]t *makes no sense* at all to give a general explanation for the generality of language, because it makes no sense at all to suppose words in general might not recur [—in actual usages—], that we might possess a name for a thing (say 'chair' or 'feeding' and yet be willing to call *nothing* (else) 'the same thing'" (CR, 188). This means, among other things, that the risks of misfiring in attempting to extend words to new things as others do are, even if necessarily rarely realized (at least in extreme forms), necessarily also perennial. "[I]f utterances *could* not fail, they would not be the human actions under consideration, indeed not the actions of humans at all" (PP, 85).

Nor, however, are we given over wholly to powerlessness and to unthinking submission to the natural. We bear responsibility, to ourselves and to others, for how we extend our words and how we think and act. There arises for us a question about what we ought to do or desire, or what it is best for us to do or desire, no matter what we in fact do or desire. (Thus Heidegger: "*Dasein* is an entity which does not just occur among other entities. Rather it is ontically distinguished by the fact that, in its very Being, that Being is an *issue* for it.")[5] In this questioning (or its suppression), and in the bearing of responsibility, the self displays itself "as a thing existing in perpetual relation to itself . . . as a thing of cares and commitments, one which to exist has to find itself" (PP, 142). In thinking and speaking, as things that we do and for which we bear responsibility, we find ourselves caught up in the "self's judgmental forming of itself, as something to be further possessed or overcome" (PP, 150). To be so caught up is to be cast always en route toward the perfection of action and responsibility, toward a kind of horizonal, fully expressive action, in which thought and gesture inform one another wholly, in transparency to each other, to oneself, and to others, to be cast on a "journey to freedom" (PP, 143).

Between self-standing, perfect power and abandonment to powerlessness, there is the fact—if it is a fact—of human immigrancy, as we ever seek at-homeness in the world, in our bodies, in our actions, in our thoughts: seek perfect expressiveness. "[T]he human necessity of the quest for home and the human fact of immigrancy are seen together as aspects of the human as such" (*PP*, 47).

II

Within this conception (or perception) of the standing immigrancy of the human, a critical path in reading and thinking will involve trying to find "ways to prevent [the impulse to self-scrutiny] from defeating itself so easily" (*CR*, 176), either in complacent intellectual revelation or in self-dramatizing intellectual skepticism. Instead of arriving at final results that would either cure our immigrancy or absolutize it skeptically so as to kill our ambition to overcome it, thinking must rather come to terms with it, in what Cavell describes as "the achievement of the unpolemical, of the refusal to take sides in metaphysical positions" (PP, 22). Managing this achievement will involve *reading* the texts and lives of others, and one's own texts and life, as expressions of this immigrancy and of the motives with which we inhabit it. In this perception philosophers—and poets, and critics, and people generally—"have left us with a trail of images of themselves preparing for philosophy or recovering from it" (PP, 3). These images can be read in the discernment of the ambitions, wishes, strategies, and frustrations that motivate them.

Reading these images, and doing so in awareness of one's participation in the human motives that animate them, will differ from any interpretive procedure controlled by a definite method that yields predictable results. It will be unlike de Manian deconstruction, which finds always the same aporias and indeterminacies and so theatricalizes our positions as readers and subjects by calling attention to ourselves rather than to the specific play of motives and pursuits in the text and subject under consideration, as the shapes of these motives and pursuits vary historically. "To conclude that such issues are undecidable . . . theatricalizes the threat, or the truth, of skepticism" (IQO, 135). It will be unlike some sorts of New Historicist criticism that reduce texts to reflections of a social life with a logic untainted by subjectivity, involving power dynamics independently laid down and of which the interpreter is master. Instead, both social life and one's own stances in reading will be seen to involve plays of motives and fantasy that are already present, or present under transformations, in the text under study. And it will be unlike formalist New Criticism in connecting the paradoxical self-crossings and self-reference of literary form with historically modulating plays of human motives to pursue freedom and expressiveness rather than taking texts as self-standing objects of purely absorptive-perceptual interest. (Arguably, the best New Criticism is not formalist in this way.) One will see not only the form but the human subject—that is, oneself—in the form and in its expression of one's own motives under variation.

Reading in discernment of the human motives that give birth to philosophy, motives in which one shares, will mean adopting a stance *next* to the text, between sheer submission to it and sheer control over it. It will mean both noting and oneself reenacting the play of energy and limit in the text, thus revealing it as a precursor of one's own response to it. Unlike method-driven criticism, it will involve suspending one's sense of what the answers to philosophical questions must be, keeping open the space of the unpolemical expression of our plight. "[T]he reader would have to ask himself or herself 'Do I know what philosophy can—and cannot—do?'"[6]

Yet criticism or reading here will also be more than a collection of scattered and unrelated aperçus. While the (philosophical) motives to freedom, expressiveness, and the subliming away of responsibility that are under discernment are tangled and self-criticizing, for they involve commitments both to independence and common attachment, and while the fruits that their pursuits may lead to remain unclear, they are nonetheless, in this perception, not accidental. They are essentially connected with our lives as subjects, as creatures who are minded and in possession (we know not how) of language. (It is Wittgenstein's sense of his having a share in these motives that, for Cavell, finally distinguishes his writing from Austin's [see PP, 113]). Hence the thought arises, when, in reading, one shares in these essential motives, "that the human is representative, say, imitative, that each life is exemplary of all, a parable of each" (PP, 11).

What one may variously call motives to philosophy, or to freedom, or to expressiveness, or to intimacy wedded to independence, or to a kingdom of ends, are worked into the very structure of our conceptual consciousness, into our being *able* to reflect on our judgmental activity and to deliberate. These motives have to do with "the formation of moral consciousness as such" (PP, 142), indeed with the formation of judgmental consciousness as such, where judgments are always among our deeds, hence bound up with matters of responsibility and possibilities of reflective assessment.[7] We have the sense of ourselves as both in need of and open to guidance, as we assess or can assess our doings. This is enough for philosophy, as a way of both thinking about and sharing in the terms of these assessments of what we do freely and what dully, or under constraint, or without interest, to get started. "[P]hilosophy begins with . . . and may at any time encounter an aspiration toward . . . a sense of itself as guiding the soul, or self, from self-imprisonment toward the light or instinct of freedom" (PP, 4).[8]

Insofar as we share in these tangled motives to freedom, or to philosophy, there is for us "no assurance of, or only relative finality to, human identity" (PP, 121) as possessors of rational and deliberative capacities and capacities for a free life. We are cast, both with others and with ourselves, between acknowledgment and avoidance, between accepting the common as our home and aversively asserting our own independence. (This is perhaps the place to remark that Cavell almost follows Hegel's great turning point, in which the desire to know is seen as absorbed into a prior desire for a free life with oneself and with others. It is no accident that a central term for human achievement in both Cavell and Hegel, in seeing problems of knowledge as the obverse face of problems of human relations, is "acknowledgment" [*Anerkennung*]. The difference is that, for Cavell, the desire for a free life remains an ideal that is irrepudiable, but less than clearly fully satisfiable, so that the desire for a free life is continually threatened with collapse back into a desire to know how to lead a free life that is not yet present.[9] The threat or truth of skepticism cannot be evaded by a turn to the practical.) Lacking more assurance than this, but not simply despairing of finding any, we will find ourselves asking the questions that Cavell asks and that, within this perception, the most serious writers will be seen to find inevitable as they go about their recountings: Am I known (to myself and to others)? What have I done? How am I now to go on?[10]

III

So much can be gleaned from a Wittgensteinian vision of language and mind in conjunction with a Cavellian reading of it. Is it convincing? There can be, again, no neutral, demonstrative argument in favor of it, independent of the focusing or transfiguring of a perception of our condition. But it may help to elaborate the depth and imaginative appeal of this vision of our immigrant condition to see how much it shares with Hölderlin's philosophical romanticism and its consequences in Hölderlin's poetic practice. The following features are central to both a Cavellian-Wittgensteinian and a Hölderlinian understanding of the immigrancy of human conceptual consciousness.

First, there is a specific inheritance of and responsiveness to Kant's critical turn, in particular to Kant's sense that there are human rational powers whose possession calls us from within our mindedness toward a somehow free and elevated life. The apt exercise of these powers is, however, betrayed by any effort to guide them by reference to some given external reality to be discovered. Instead, the possession of these powers is to make us capable of a certain orientation toward and with one another and the world, from within our having of them. Cavell notes that:

> In Kant's interpretation of a fundamental Platonic picture, the individual self has as it were internalized the sensuous and the super-sensuous worlds—Plato's unreal and real realms. These are now two "standpoints" which it is the condition of being human to be able to adopt in succession, in opposition to each other. . . . In Kant's *Foundations* the turn from one realm to the other takes place in every moral judgment each time you stop to think, to ask yourself your way. . . . [A]fter Kant, the journey to freedom has been cut short—to a half step—you see how to take it, and where it lies, or you do not. (PP, 143)

Similarly, Hölderlin describes in his letters his own sense of the importance of Kant's intimation of possibilities of elevation from within, both for himself and for his culture.

> The new circumstances in which I live are now the best ones imaginable. I have much leisure for my own work, and philosophy is once again my almost exclusive occupation. I have taken Kant and Reinhold and hope to collect my spirit in this element which was dispelled and weakened by fruitless efforts of which you were a witness.... Kant is the Moses of our nation who leads it out of the Egyptian apathy.[11]

Second, there is a sense of mixed fallenness from and elevation out of nature, a sense of an arche-separation from self-enclosed nature in the having of conceptual-judgmental consciousness and deliberative capacities. For Cavell, there is no general explanation—no philosophical explanation over and above the humdrum facts of teaching and training and imitating and, mostly, going on from them—of how we come to possess language and to be distinctively minded in that possession. Once that happens, we are both cursed with partiality, or not quite at-homeness in our mindedness in language and culture, and blessed with possibilities of perfection. For Hölderlin, "*Judgment*. In the highest and strictest sense, is the original separation of object and subject . . . that separation through which alone object and subject become possible, the *arche*-separation."[12] Despite its pains, this arche-separation dimly enables us to do something, to live freely and in celebration of our mindedness in nature, if we can but learn to express aright what is highest, to live religiously, in Hölderlin's poetic sense of the term. "Here there can yet be spoken about the uniting of several religions into one, where each one honors his god and all together honor a communal one in poetic representations, where each one celebrates his higher life and all together celebrate a communal higher life, the celebration of life [as such]."[13]

　Third, in bearing the possibility and problem of a higher, free life, there is a specific sense of wandering. Our reorientation is to arise from the release of our latent capacities and possibilities, but these capacities and possibilities are crossed or tangled, admitting of no ready, univocal expression guided by knowledge of an external object. Cavell holds that "we live lives simultaneously of absolute separateness and endless commonness" (PP, vii). In consequence, attachment or reattachment to the common can come as either a balm for painful isolation or a confinement that compromises independence; assertions of apartness can either mark out a new and vital expressive path or enact a fall into narcissistic emptiness. There is no way to know specifically how to go forward fruitfully—no criterion of a life of freedom that is vouchsafed to us by external objects—independently of trying one's powers in a mixture of engagement with and departure from the common, and then waiting. (The truth of skepticism names our wish to know, and our impossibility of knowing, in advance how to go forward fruitfully, with absolute assurance.)

Hölderlin holds that "the infinite, like the spirit of the states and of the world, cannot be grasped other than from an askew perspective."[14] The infinite, the spirit of the world, cannot be seen straight on so as to yield direct and reliable knowledge of how to enact it. We are cast, always, on "an eccentric path,"[15] in pursuit simultaneously of love and selfhood, community and autonomy. In Dieter Henrich's memorable summary of Hölderlin's sense of human life,

> Conscious life is at once shaped and unbalanced by the basic conflicting tendencies orienting it. And the formative process of life aims at finding a balance and a harmony amid this strife, in which no one tendency is entirely suppressed or denied in its own right. The preface to the fragment of *Hyperion* already identifies the highest and most beautiful state humanly attainable as the ability to withstand what is greatest, and yet to be humbled by what is smallest.... [Man] is bound to a world that, like himself, originates in opposition. For the sake of unity he strives actively beyond each of its boundaries. Yet in it he at once confronts the beautiful—an anticipation of the unity that is lost to him and that he seeks to restore. As he embraces the beautiful, the complete truth, which lies at an infinite distance, is realized for him within limits. He is thus captivated by it, and for good reason. But he must not forget that his active nature is called upon to overcome the finite. In the conflict of love and selfhood he runs his course, either errantly or with self-understanding.[16]

An eccentric path moves jaggedly about a self-divided center—the longed-for unification of love and selfhood; the common and the individual, the passional and the reflective—drawn by it into abrupt movements, as a moth is drawn to a flame, but never mastering or possessing it.

IV

What would it be to move along such an eccentric path, or to run one's course, with *understanding*? There can be no univocal and formulable answer to this question. Any univocal and formulable answer would have to rest on a complete conceptual grasp of the self-divided center that draws yet escapes us. A univocal and formulable answer would put an end to our wandering or immigrancy. In the romantic vision of our condition as always *in medias res*, always on an eccentric path, any claim to have arrived at a final conception of how to live with understanding must appear as a piece of hubristic dogmatism that is belied by the fact of our movement. Instead of answers, there can at best only be enactments, or expressions, or acknowledgments, of our immigrancy and of the possibilities that we bear and that captivate us. At best, these might know themselves, or those who give birth to them might know them to be enactments, expressions, or acknowledgments of a subject's position on a path, rather than items of external knowledge. How might such a piece of self-knowledge show itself?

Here is one short, poetic fragment of Hölderlin's—"The fruits are ripe . . . [*Reif sind* . . .]"—that seems to me to show such self-knowledge. It comes from a collection of fragments reconstructed by D. E. Sattler in editing the Frankfurt edition of Hölderlin's works and given the title *Aprioritat des Individuellen*,[17] as though this collection of fragments addressed the question of what necessities govern any individual human life. Here is the entire fragment:

> *Reif sind . . .*
> *Reif sind, in feuer Getaucht, gekochet*
> *Die Frücht und auf der Erde geprüfet und ein Gesetz ist*
> *Das alles hineingeht, Schlangen gleich,*
> *Prophetisch, träumend auf*
> *Den Hügeln des Himmels. Und vieles*
> *Wie auf den Schultern eine*
> *Last von Scheitern ist*
> *Zu behalten. Aber bös sind*
> *Die Pfade. Nemlich unrecht*
> *Wie Rosse, gehn die gefangenen*
> *Element' und alten*
> *Geseze der Erd. Und immer*
> *Ins Ungebundende gehet eine Sehnsucht. Vieles aber ist*

Zu behalten. Und Noth die Treue.
Vorwärts aber und rükwärts wollen wir
Nicht sehn. Uns wiegen lassen, wie
Auf schwankem Kahne der See.[18]

The fruits are ripe . . .

The fruits are ripe, dipped in fire, cooked
And tested here on earth, and it is a law,
Prophetic, that all things pass
Like snakes, dreaming on
The hills of heaven.
And as
A load of logs upon
The shoulders, there is much
To bear in mind. But the paths
Are evil. For like horses
The captive elements
And ancient laws
Of the earth go astray. Yet always
The longing to reach beyond bounds. But much
To be retained. And loyalty a must.
But we shall not look forward
Or back. Let ourselves rock, as
On a boat, lapped by the waves.

Against the background of the post-Kantian (Hölderlinian, romantic, Wittgensteinian-Cavellian) conception of mind and language, it is fairly straightforward to parse much of this fragment. Our lives are lived out amid already afforded ways of culture—ripe fruits—that are themselves formed somehow by both natural processes (growth and ripening) and self-conscious agency (dipping and cooking). Present human action and speech are further natural-agentive refigurings (ripenings and cookings) of these affordances. They have no pure, self-present origin in either nature alone or culture alone but instead arise both naturally and culturally out of already past interplays.

Both prior cultural affordances and present actions pass away or go under (*hineingeht*), into the earth like snakes, or into oblivion. There is no possibility of present immortality for us, in and through our actions in culture.

It is chastening to recognize this. This recognition is a burden (*Last*) to be borne or kept (*zu behalten*).[19] Though the burden is heavy, holding it fosters humility.

We cannot, however, simply stand and hold the burden. There are paths—ways of culture—on which we are always already in motion. Only to stand and wait, quietistically, is also to act, as long as one bears conceptual consciousness and the possibility of attitudes toward the world. To go on these paths—to take up and modify one cultural affordance rather than another—is to move in a specific cultural direction. This has its costs, in ignoring both others outside one's specific cultural orbit and aspects of oneself that might engage with those others. A life of universal, reciprocal freedom and acknowledgment is not to be attained from within individual modifications of culturally afforded specific patterns of action. Playing the cello, organizing for better housing, working in a soup kitchen, participating in communion, raising one's children, telling jokes, comforting the sick, seeking and offering forgiveness—none of these activities is free from partiality; none is a sure and straight road toward human freedom: toward community and independence, love and selfhood. Hence the paths are "evil." That is to say (*nemlich*), they go astray, or are not right, or are unsuitable (*unrecht*), like horses we cannot control. What we have managed to build and accomplish on these paths (the captive elements) fails to match or express the deeper necessities and possibilities of freedom (the ancient laws of earth). Or our accomplishments are informed by the ancient law of their partiality, their one-sidedness that will lead them to go under. There is no perfect remembrance and enactment of freedom along these paths of culture.

Yet still we wish for our lives in culture to be straightened, informed wholly by what is eternal, so that they are rationally transparent and in good order, to ourselves and to others. We wish to act on standing good reasons that can be endorsed reflectively by everyone, no matter what: "always the longing to reach beyond bounds." In this too there is much to be retained, held: the facts of human desire for rational transparency and of the limits in fulfilling that desire that lie along its tangled, crossed paths. These facts now present themselves as facts of conceptual consciousness as such, as facts of our lives with thought and language as we inherit and extend them. We must retain, hold, both the fact of our partiality and the fact of our standing desire to overcome it.

In this condition, it will be necessary to trust certain ways of culture as the best, the most sure vehicles for the expression and cultivation of freedom that one has to hand (*Und Noth die Treue*). One should not step back from cultural engagements—from cello playing, political organizing, feeding the poor, telling jokes—into an empty, skeptical-solipsistic rejection of the value of anything that is present. Yet we cannot quite help doing this sometimes, in our awareness of the rational one-sidedness of any cultural affordances and present actions.

In this necessity and impossibility of trust of the common lies the difficulty and accuracy of the fragment's final three lines. What does the *wollen* at the end of the fifteenth line mean? The translator offers "shall," and this captures one sense of *wollen*: to be about to do something or to be on the point of doing it. This reading captures a sense of resoluteness in acceptance of the common, of what is already culturally afforded, as at least of partial value: We shall let ourselves be rocked by it, carried by it out of our skeptical resistances. It is unavoidable. Yet *wollen* also carries an even stronger sense of wanting, willing, or wishing. We want to let ourselves be carried by culture, want not to look forward or backward but instead to abandon ourselves to the common, or even to allow ourselves to be swept away by an unusual destiny in a blue sea of August: anything to move out of mere onlooking, alone. This sounds less honorable, as the skeptical voice has always intimated. Perhaps we should rather owe loyalty also to the fact of our desire to reach beyond bounds, to our possibilities of judging and refiguring the present. Though we want not to look forward and back and want instead only to drift over the infinite of the sea, we must also hold and retain our desire to go down into the infinite, to hold our present ways to account.

So which is it, and what are we to trust—the ways of culture as they present themselves to us in their partial value or our powers of assessment and refiguration, of looking forward and backward and accepting and pursuing agentive control? It is Hölderlin's special and difficult expression of the post-Kantian sense of our mindedness to have posed these alternatives in the very same words, thus letting us see the appeal of each mode of trust as we swerve between the sense of each reading. It is this enactment of our mindedness, I want to say, to which our immigrancy in mind and language and culture comes. But, if this is right, then that is not something for anyone simply to say.

7

Criticism and the Risk of the Self

Stanley Cavell's Modernism and Elizabeth Bishop's

Both Stanley Cavell's sense of being a modern subject and his practice of modernism in philosophy have a number of interrelated roots, including at least his cultural-biographical circumstances, his philosophical conception of the ontology of being a human subject, and his response to certain precursor performances of subjectivity within culture, including to some poets. Matters of ontology to one side, much the same is true of Elizabeth Bishop's modernist poetics and modernist poetry. According to Bret Millier's intellectual biography, Bishop lived with a continuous sense of not inhabiting time comfortably, and Millier suggests that this sense on her part is due at least in part to her wish to please her lost parents.[1] (Her father died when Bishop was eight months old; her mother was institutionalized when Bishop was five). There is something about a wish to please lost parents in Stanley Cavell, too, as his 2010 philosophical memoir *Little Did I Know* makes clear. Such senses of loss and wishes to please may not, however, be merely personal or idiosyncratic. After all, all of us, or most of us, will also sooner or later be children of absent parents, and just about all of us have senses of unresolved relations with our parents in any case. What is more interesting and important is how Cavell and Bishop respond in exemplary ways to their broader cultural-historical, ontological, and artistic situations that both inflected by and inflect the personal—how they register these situations and work them through in exemplary ways. It is what can be done in response to features of a shared situation that is of greatest interest.

I

In a key passage from his 2006 *Philosophy the Day After Tomorrow*, Cavell raises explicitly a question that announces the nature of his interest in philosophy. "What if," he writes,

Anticipations of Freedom. Richard Eldridge, Oxford University Press. © Richard Eldridge 2026.
DOI: 10.1093/9780197841785.003.0011

when what we used, remarkably, to call the inner man [the subject, say, of biological hunger, and other needs that are unproblematically present to consciousness] is satisfied, my impressions of the world and of myself and others in it do not return to interest and amuse me, and I am left philosophically blank to most of the necessaries of my life? (PDAT, 2)

Philosophy, then, as Cavell practices it, is to address and, if possible, overcome this condition of blankness. It is to make one's impressions of the world, of oneself, and of others matters of interest and amusement rather than (we may suppose) things just to be suffered and allowed to pass by.

The underlying thought here must be that modern life threatens to cast human subjects, or at least Stanley Cavell, into a condition of blankness and lack of interest in it. Why might this be so? More specifically, what perception of his, possibly our, condition is it to which Cavell is giving voice, and what are the functions, risks, and successes of this effort at giving voice to a condition? Can raising and responding to Cavell's what-if question somehow lead us out of blankness and into a sunlight of fuller interest in life?

To raise this what-if question is already to move beyond the orbit of Hume's turn to avocations to still his despair. Playing backgammon may amuse me, but it is unlikely to address my philosophical blankness to the necessaries of my life, leaving me, as Hume recommended, overcome by them, rather than animated within them. Can I, Cavell is asking, become interested in my life—in my world, in myself, and in others—in an animated way? Can I affirm my life and its necessaries, and, if so, how? A perfectionist impulse that is opposed to the settlements of distraction and simple consumption lies at the heart of these questions.

From his earliest essays to the present, Cavell has argued that an enabling response to these questions is not to be wrung out of abstract reasoning that takes mathematical proof as its model of progress. Instead, a response that yields animation—if it is available at all—must come from finding oneself perplexed, stopped by something, and then coming to take an awakening interest in what has thus perplexed and stopped one. (Cavell's sense of getting underway to take an interest or a renewed interest in life through first being stopped by something and then, somehow, going on is remarkably similar to the Wordsworthian topos of the halted traveler.) This thought—that one may pursue and sometimes find a certain animation centrally by being stopped by something and then by working through the perplexing material that has brought one to a halt—is distinctively expressed in Cavell's 1965 essay

"Aesthetic Problems of Modern Philosophy." A guiding idea of that essay is that the activities of philosophy, criticism, and (modern) art-making are importantly like one another. More specifically, in each activity, a human subject finds it difficult, but unavoidable, to try to make sense of the material encountered. Trying to make sense of this material, or to find one's way of going on with it, carries a risk of fraudulence. One cannot know in advance that the effort will come off well, and one may be taken in by something that fails to reward attention and to support animation. But there is also a chance that things will go well, that the material will repay one's trust in attending to its perplexities.

All this is clearest in the encounter with difficult modern art, where the guiding sureties of tradition and genre are lost or attenuated. In criticism of the modern work of art, one undertakes to give articulate voice to the sources in the work of what has stopped, perplexed, and attracted one, in the hope that one's responses to the work will be stabilized, confirmed, and shared, at least by some. Absent such stabilizing, confirming, and sharing, my responses may be mad, may isolate me from others and from myself. Stopped and perplexed and attracted by the work, I cannot *not* speak, if I am to find my way at all, in anything other than departure and dullness. My ability to take an active and apt interest in the new is at stake. Hence the enterprise of the criticism of modern art, as Cavell sees it, is radically distinct from both non-critical literary history and mere ranking alone, without the articulation of one's responses.

The striking further twist is then that both modernist art-making and modernist philosophy stand in the same relation to modern life and its halting perplexities as the elucidatory-perceptualist critic stands to the difficult work of modernist art. What if my impressions of the world and of myself and others in it do not return to interest and amuse me, and I am left philosophically blank to most of the necessaries of my life? That is the problem of modern life to which the modernist artist and the modernist philosopher alike respond, in ways that are usefully modeled by the responsive activities of the modernist critic of the arts.

It is worth noting the distinct pressure that this picture of the activity of the modernist philosopher places on business as usual in academic philosophy. The working through of perplexing material in both modernist art and modernist criticism is strongly contingently initiated and at least in part somatically driven. One is stopped as a modernist critic or artist or philosopher by something surprising, unforeseen, rather than being only abstractly engaged by an eternal question posed from nowhere. And one has felt something bodily, some mixture of attraction, alertness, apprehension, engagement, difficulty, and repulsion. Suddenly, a contingently appearing work or incident plus a felt, somatic response constitute the material to be worked through. The idea that modernist critical and artistic working-through provide apt models for philosophical activity in response to modern life here clearly cuts against the dominant academic model of the achievement of impersonal authority in philosophy via distantiation and abstractive-subsumptive rationality. Yet in modernist philosophy a kind of impersonal authority, arising out of the somatic encounter, is nonetheless pursued: the authority of exemplarity in the articulation of response instead of the authority of abstraction.

Cavell registers this point by noting that philosophy, or philosophy as he pursues it, may have something to learn from art. In *Philosophy the Day After Tomorrow*, he describes his approach as involving an

> emphasis I place on the criticism, or reading, of individual works of art. I think of this emphasis as letting a work of art have a voice in what philosophy says about it, and I regard that attention as a way of testing whether the time is past in which taking seriously the philosophical bearing of a particular work of art can be a measure of the seriousness of philosophy.... The work of such criticism is to reveal its object as having yet to have its due effect. (PDAT, 10, 11)

To say this is to say that the philosopher, or Cavell as a modernist philosopher, is, like the modernist artist and modernist critic, to be the one through whom something happens. Somatically, the critic or artist or philosopher is moved, halted by something. Then impersonality and exemplariness are achieved—if they are achieved—not abstractively, but through articulating the sources of one's responses, in such a way that others can enter into them, so that the initiating work or incident comes to have its due effect, and so that these responses are stabilized and redeemed from madness. Through critical articulation of response, one may come fully to say and mean what one has felt and valued.

But the question with which we began is why Cavell turns to this kind of philosophy, why he raises the question "What if I am left philosophically blank to the necessaries of my life?" which blankness can then be met, he judges, only by this kind of critical-aesthetic philosophizing. What may have brought Cavell to such straits of worrying about blankness and thence to his critical-aesthetic turn within philosophizing? We can locate in Cavell's writing three distinct, but also interrelated, registers of an answer to this question.

The first register is cultural-biographical. Doing his graduate work and then his first teaching in the late 1940s and then throughout the 1950s, Cavell seems, like some others, to have been struck and blocked by an institutional greyness or complacency in American life. This was, after all, the post-war Eisenhower 1950s, the era of Daniel Bell's end of ideology thesis and the time before the civil rights movement, the sexual revolution, the Vietnam War, and feminism. To be sure, there were prominent undercurrents of discontent coupled with a sense that things could be otherwise: Beat and Modernist poetry (especially Wallace Stevens), jazz, Abstract Expressionist painting, film noir, and the bodily graces of Cary Grant and Fred Astaire. But these are, it seems, exactly the halting, perplexing works that attracted Cavell's interest and spoke to his sensibility. Above all, though coming to prominence in his published work only fairly recently, Cavell's experience of Freud was focal for him in articulating for him his discontents in the face of a stultified culture. During "several months to myself in New York" after college, Cavell tells us, "Freud's *Introductory Lectures on Psychoanalysis* . . . proved to be the first book of ideas I read with the hypnotic attention and identification that reading novels had from an early age produced in me" (CW, 282). This hypnotic attention and identification that Freud solicited from Cavell had centrally to do with Freud's depiction of the psychoanalytic process as embodying an awakening *from* dullness, lack of attentiveness to life, and failure to speak and mean in one's own voice *to* alertness, self-consciousness, and fullness of meaning in one's own voice. "The sufferer," as Cavell puts it,

> has to be, as Freud characteristically puts the matter, awakened . . . [from] feeling himself a prisoner of his circumstances. This sense of imprisonment, of the need for liberation, is critical both for Wittgensteinian philosophizing and for Emersonian perfectionist aspiration. I have sometimes called it the crisis from which the wish for philosophy and for a morally comprehensible life begins. (CW, 284)

Images of awakening, rebirth, conversion, and liberation, of dancing, singing, leaving the cave, and turning around, are everywhere in Cavell's work, early and late. The figures who have most interested him—Wittgenstein, Austin, Emerson, Plato, Marx, Rousseau, Luther, and all the rest—are those who have, in dull or decadent times, articulated routes of liberation into which Cavell felt he could in some measure enter. But biographically, so far as I can tell, Freud came first, and specifically the experience of Freud, itself also nurtured by jazz and Modernist poetry, against the background of the 1950s. "The figure of Freud has shadowed my work in philosophy," Cavell tells us, "from the time I first published an essay about Wittgenstein, more than forty years ago" (PDAT, 213). (Cavell is referring to the "The Availability of Wittgenstein's Later Philosophy," published in *The Philosophical Review* in 1962.)

The second register of answer to the question about the source of Cavell's fear of blankness and his sense that critical-aesthetic philosophizing might fruitfully respond to it is, for want of a better word, ontological. Cavell, that is to say, argues that it is inherent to the life of a subject as such that that life is subject to interruptions and disappointments. It suffers from a kind of standing immigrancy, in being marked by reflectiveness and in being ungrounded in any continuously available origin that might smoothly yield continuing orientation. Instead, the life of a subject, the life of a point of view haver and claim-maker, arises through the fragile inheritance of language, which alone makes a discursively structured point of view possible. Hence, in arising in fragility, in such a way that standing orientation is unavailable, "human existence, with its gift of language, chronically presents itself as a melancholy, disappointing business" (PDAT, 115). We are inherently prone to empty repetition, and so to cliché, rather than to animated inheritance. (Parenthetically, one might profitably compare this passage with Walter Benjamin's sense in his 'Language' essay that we suffer from disappointment in virtue of the fact that we overname things, or overspecify what things are for and how they might interest us, thus blocking ourselves from fullness of expressive life with them.)[2] In "Excerpts from Memory" (later incorporated into *Little Did I Know*) Cavell notes that a "frozen . . . power of surprise . . . negates the essence of human speech,"[3] which is to say that speech inherently and always lives in part by having the continual power to surprise us, unfrozen. Or, as the point is put in the "Excursus on Wittgenstein's Vision of Language" in *The Claim of Reason*, the general terms of a language are necessarily both stable enough to enable us, over time, to sort things and get a 'take' on them, but also tolerant of new usages (CR, 168–90). No take on things in relation to our interests is final. Hence we too, as speaking and thinking subjects, live only insofar as we, too, are open to surprises. In the terms Cavell draws out of Thoreau, the self as watchman, critically assessing progress, is always in critical tension with the self as workman, undertaking projects, with no final settlement in view. (SW, 107–8). Cavell registers the thought that new takes on things in relation to our interests may always and at any moment be prompted within our experience in what he calls "a recurrent surmise that whatever happens—whatever is eventful enough for speech—is from the beginning accidental, as if a human life is inherently interrupted, things chronically occurring at unripe times, in the wrong tempo, comically or poignantly."[4] To deny the openness of the life of a human subject as such to interruption, accident, mischance, comedy, and poignancy is reactively to try to wreak vengeance on life and the ordinary, a reactive tendency that is all too prevalent in scientific-theoretical philosophy. As Nietzsche mordantly puts it, "You ask me which of the philosophers' traits are really idiosyncrasies? For example, their lack of historical sense, their hatred of the very idea of becoming, their Egypticism. They think that they show their *respect* for a subject when they de-historicize it, *sub specie aeterni*—when they turn it into a mummy."[5] Or in Cavell's formulation, such a denial of interruption is manifest in "philosophy's chronic tendency to violence, violence principally toward the ordinary, measured in its treatment of ordinary language, against letting it speak, having decided in time out of mind that it is vague and misleading, to say the least" (PDAT, 231). The way out of or beyond interruption, stasis, perplexity, and failure to notice and mean is then not that of eternalized theory, but rather that of the handling of words, as Emerson and Thoreau and Wittgenstein do, in a kind of philosophy without philosophy. Call this the way of poetry, or of philosophy that has become literature but still knows itself, in letting language speak, in taking up the fragile inheritance of language productively so as to formulate, and so to find, circumstances of interest.

The third register of answer is, again for want of a better word, performative. It takes the biographical and the ontological to be inflections of one another, each life being both distinctly individually led *and* the life of a human subject in general, subject to its plights. What is personally biographical and what is ontological are always intertwined. Or, in Cavell's formulation, "each life is exemplary of all, a parable of each" (PP, 11). More important, this answer is oriented toward futurity. It expresses a sense that—whatever the initiations of plight are, biographical or ontological as may be—something can be done. A step can be taken; more fullness of felt meaning and of voice can be achieved. In *Philosophy the Day After Tomorrow* Cavell remarks that

"George Eliot as it were, after Emerson, envisions the democratization of perfectionism, asks for each the right to seek a step toward an unattained possibility of the self, toward a world closer to the heart's desire" (PDAT, 131). Here Cavell is, among other things, expressing his sense of possessing a future-oriented possibility of self, a satisfaction of the heart's desire, that could be achieved expressively, in fullness of voice. The experience of Austin, both as a teacher and a writer, fused performatively for Cavell the attractions of jazz, musical composition, Freudian liberation, modernist poetry, and philosophy. No wonder this experience knocked him off his horse. When one has the sense that performative achievement of this kind is possible, but as yet unattained, then the cultural-biographical sense of conditions of cultural greyness and the ontological sense of immigrancy are held together productively in direction toward futurity.

To gather together these three threads of answer—the cultural-biographical, the ontological, and the performative—we can say first that for Cavell the modern subject is ontologically capable of reflection and self-criticism, is given over to these as possibilities in virtue of the development of point of view via the inheritance of language with its flexibility in expressing interests in things. Second, this inherent possibility of reflectiveness is increasingly foregrounded in modernity, as subjects in growing up are forced to build lives increasingly out of skill and will within a framework of highly differentiated social roles. The modern social economy demands some form of skill-development, and this calls for long periods of detachment, internalization, and preparation, before getting on with the work, where modes of work are themselves divided up into spheres that are increasingly opaque to one another. Detachment and internalization in turn put pressures on community and intimacy, as the agent undertaking preparatively to plot or find its social fate stands in some measure apart from full immersion in family, tradition, or life routine. But, third, it is possible for something to be done. Certain modern works of art, especially modern poetry, show a fullness of meaning that is all at once felt, gestural, and discursive and that blends distinctiveness of individual somatic stance with accomplished craft. Psychoanalysis holds out the hope of similarly liberating achievements, and the fact of the heart's as yet unsatisfied desire can motivate the taking up of these expressive possibilities. Getting the hang of a position can happen, even without absolute, guiding sureties, just as the audience of a modern work can come to 'get' it or the pupil can come to get it 'for himself'. Or, as Cavell puts it,

You never know. I mean, you never know when someone will learn the posture, as for themselves, that will make sense of a field of movement, it may be writing, or dancing, or passing a ball, or sitting at a keyboard, or free associating. So the sense of paradox expresses our not understanding how such learning happens. (IQO, 115–16)

A similar sense of current fallenness into greyness and roteness, not to mention injustice and exploitativeness, and generally a failure of human freedom, which fallenness happens at once, ambiguously, both historically and ontologically, and which fallenness may, paradoxically, beyond the force of formulae, be answered to by a gesture or by a moment of perception and expression carried out by a pupil, is found in the writings of another prominent Jewish modernist of the twentieth century, Walter Benjamin. Here is what Benjamin has to say about what might happen under the conditions of human reflectiveness and of modern life, so as to forward human freedom, in relation to the ordinary:

This divine power [of movement toward greater fullness of life] is attested not only by religious tradition but is also found in present-day life in at least one sanctioned manifestation. The educative power, which in its perfected form stands outside the law, is one of its manifestations. These are defined, therefore, not by miracles directly performed by God but by the expiating moment in them that strikes without bloodshed, and, finally, by the absence of all lawmaking.[6]

This expiating moment cannot be extorted by bloodshed. Behaviorist rewards and punishments are inadequate to bring anyone to see for himself what might be done. Nor do rules suffice; something beyond lawmaking and rule-formulation must figure in seeing the sense of the rule and of how to go on with it now. But a miracle can happen, and it can happen within the everyday, if we but open our eyes and take seriously certain exemplary possibilities of expression that are to be found around us.

II

No matter what mixture of biographical, ontological, and performative considerations is active in Cavell's experience of modern life and sense of possibilities of address to it, there is likely to be some suspicion about whether Cavell's sensibility is worth following. Within philosophy, resistance is likely to arise from Cavell's relative lack of interest in abstraction and in the solving of standard problems: his lack of interest, that is, in bringing a particular area of debate to an end by, say, proving that the will is free or that the mind is really nothing but the brain or that utilitarianism gives the one correct account of our obligations. Within literary studies, Cavell is likely to be charged with too much interest in his own possibilities of experience from a personal point of view and too little sense of the political. He might, it may be urged, take more interest in how subjectivity is shaped by political realities that must be understood in their own right, somehow or other, as having force for possibilities of experience. Just how idiosyncratic, then, might Cavell's explorations of modern experience be?

There is no way to answer this question with any precision. Different subjects will have different experiences and different senses of how possibilities of blankness and animation present themselves within them. But one way to understand Cavell's sense of modern experience as not exclusively idiosyncratic is to set it against accounts of experience that do not arise directly in relation to philosophy as an academic discipline. Like Cavell, certain contemporary poets in coming to terms with and for their experience show a strong sense of being surprised and stopped by something, followed by getting underway again with a renewed and deepened sense of interest in life. Poets in whose work this plot-figure appears present themselves as ones in and through whom, exemplarily, something happens: fuller interest is taken in life.

Among contemporary poets, this plot-figure appears in an especially clear and persuasive form, in ways that may be surprising, in the work of Elizabeth Bishop. Bishop is often classed primarily as a follower of Marianne Moore and as a kind of soft-edged Objectivist or as an "apolitical modernist."[7] (This is Betsy Erkkila's term, where Erkkila goes on to defend Bishop against typical condescension by pointing out how her work "problematizes the binarisms—literature/politics, formalism/social consciousness, modernism/leftism, high culture/popular culture, subjectivity/objectivity, private/public, male/female—that have characteristically governed our reading and writing of modernist literary history."[8]) Take Bishop's concern for formal craft, her interest in the description of objects, and what David Kalstone calls her "personal, even quirky, . . . offhand way of speaking,"[9] and it becomes, apparently, all too easy to see Bishop's work as somehow unpolitical and delicate, in comparison with the sexual declamations of Ginsberg, the high modernism of Eliot, and the overt confessionalisms of Lowell, Sexton, Plath, and Berryman.

Things perhaps, have begun to change by the centennial year of Bishop's birth. In the March 24, 2011 issue of *The New York Review of Books*, April Bernard calls Elizabeth Bishop "one of the great artists of the twentieth century; her poems now tower over the landscape alongside those of Eliot and Stevens."[10] Bernard goes on to note how in Bishop's writing "modesty and mastery went hand in hand; good humor was the useful conveyance of profound and often shattering wisdom. . . . Any reader, scholar, or editor of Bishop's work is likely to find himself feeling like a friend, in part because of the warmth of her voice and the intimacy of her insights."[11] This is accurate characterization and high praise, though it also carries perhaps still a trace of the older condescension. At any rate, such characterizations do not yet do the work of telling us either what Bishop's profound and often shattering wisdom is or how, exactly, it is achieved in her poems.

Similarly, Dana Gioia, a one-time Harvard student of Bishop's, in reviewing recent editions of Bishop's poetry and prose, remarks that

> Elizabeth Bishop stands as the most highly regarded American poet of the second half of the twentieth century. She is admired in every critical camp—from feminists to formalists—who agree on little else. Her work also attracts a wide general readership. Taught and studied in high schools and universities, Bishop is, for the time being at least, the most popular woman poet in American literature after Emily Dickinson. . . . [Her] quiet perfection is hard to express without making it sound like a Swiss time-piece. Bishop simply wrote so well that she never needed to raise her voice for emphases or effect.[12]

Again, this is true but faintly condescending, and again the work of really reading Bishop's poetry does not quite take place.

How, then, can we begin to attend to the productive work that the re-cording subject is doing in finding words for its perceptual and reflective experience? Bonnie Costello usefully identifies two dominant tropes that are persistently in interplay with each other within Bishop's descriptive po-etry: "the desire for mastery and the dangers and illusions to which such desire is prone."[13] Bishop's "eye perceives but also resists . . . natural diver-sity,"[14] as she attempts both to take in what is objectively 'out there' and also to render its meaning, in and for reflection, in such a way that her authority in response and speech is established and stabilized. Or as Neil Besner puts it, in the Brazilian poems especially, the "observations become, not simply ends in themselves, but occasions for reflections from and in the doubting interior eye that is so important to Bishop."[15]

Among Bishop's Brazilian poems, "Arrival at Santos" occupies a special place, in standing as both the final poem in her 1956 *A Cold Spring* and the first poem in her 1965 *Questions of Travel*. So positioned, it may be taken to have been, for Bishop, exemplary in demonstrating the particular powers of her kind of descriptive-reflective poetry. It describes her first arrival in Brazil, on November 26, 1951, supported by a traveling fellowship from Bryn Mawr College, for a planned two-week visit that turned into a fifteen-year residence:

Arrival at Santos

Here is a coast; here is a harbor;
here, after a meager diet of horizon, is some scenery:
impractically shaped and—who knows?—self-pitying mountains,
sad and harsh beneath their frivolous greenery,

with a little church on top of one. And warehouses,
some of them painted a feeble pink, or blue,
and some tall, uncertain palms. Oh, tourist,
is this how this country is going to answer you

and your immodest demands for a different world,
and a better life, and complete comprehension
of both at last, and immediately,
after eighteen days of suspension?

Finish your breakfast. The tender is coming,
a strange and ancient craft, flying a strange and brilliant rag.
So that's the flag. I never saw it before.
I somehow never thought of there *being* a flag,

but of course there was, all along. And coins, I presume,
and paper money; they remain to be seen.
And gingerly now we climb down the ladder backward,
myself and a fellow passenger named Miss Breen,

descending into the midst of twenty-six freighters
waiting to be loaded with green coffee beans.
Please, boy, do be more careful with that boat hook!
Watch out! Oh! It has caught Miss Breen's

skirt! There! Miss Breen is about seventy,
a retired police lieutenant, six feet tall,
with beautiful bright blue eyes and a kind expression.
Her home, when she is at home, is in Glens Fall

s, New York. There. We are settled.
The customs officials will speak English, we hope,
and leave us our bourbon and cigarettes.
Ports are necessities, like postage stamps, or soap,

but they seldom seem to care what impression they make,
or, like this, only attempt, since it does not matter,
the unassertive colors of soap, or postage stamps—
wasting away like the former, slipping the way the latter

do when we mail the letters we wrote on the boat,
either because the glue here is very inferior
or because of the heat. We leave Santos at once;
we are driving to the interior.[16]

The poem begins with almost excessive casualness, joining the most general objects of perception (coast, harbor) with a singsong rhythm of childhood. (Several commentators have noted that the opening line echoes the
"here is a church, here is a steeple" of the childhood hand play.) That the
diet of horizon provided by the steamer prior to its arrival has been meager
already introduces, however, an attitude on the part of the perceiving subject. Though it is perhaps better than the blankness of only sea and sky, there
is only "some scenery" that is more than a bit too cozy, with its greenery-
covered mountains, its pastel dots of warehouses, and its uncertain palms, to
provide an experience of the sublime. The rehearsal of unenthralling details
is marked by what Kim Fortuny aptly calls "a teasing lyrical undercurrent
that surfaces in waves of self-mockery."[17] The tone is further carried and
reinforced by the rhyming of the second and fourth lines of each quatrain,

framing the casual diction and the irregular line lengths. As the speaker's eye moves downward and toward the foreground, from mountaintops to warehouses, to palms, an interruptive, self-mocking question intrudes. Bishop, or the speaking Bishop persona (there is no particular reason to draw this distinction for this poem), finds herself not to be really looking at what is there, but rather imposing her own expectations on the scene, only to have them disappointed. (Compare Wordsworth on crossing the Alps in Book VI of *The Prelude*.) She finds herself to be, as Costello puts it, all too typically, one of the "exiles from a dominant culture who nevertheless bring with them that culture's archaic values and preconceptions."[18] The suspense (suspension) and anticipation of the journey are blocked, rather than fulfilled, by the relative mundaneness of the first sights, compared to what was expected.

And that will not do. Bishop admonishes herself to get about her business ("finish your breakfast"), instead of imposing expectations that lead to disappointment. And now a set of genuine surprises come anyway—the surprises against a background of initial disappointment and self-admonishment that must have led to the force of the memory and thence to its being worked out in a poem. A tender flying "a strange and brilliant rag" appears, where the flag is an artifactual signifier of cultural difference. What will then display itself to be genuinely encountered is not just the disappointing landscape that should be different, but isn't different enough, but further and more powerfully the fact of other cultures, as indicated in flags, coins, and paper money that are all unfamiliar.

Though it expresses Bishop's commitment to the fully visual description of encountered strangeness, the phrase "a strange and brilliant rag" is also not far from being also a name for poetry, so that noticing it with surprise amounts to asking, "What is it, poetry, doing there?" And "Who am I, the poet as 'the tender' who is, or is practicing 'a strange and ancient craft'?" That is, both the nature and value of poetry—its occasioning circumstances, its negotiations of contingency and significance, its effects and uses—and the nature of the poet are the topics that are all but continuously on the mind of the authorial persona throughout the poem.

Yet the thought that poetry may be startled into being by an encounter with difference is not one into which the speaker is able or allowed to settle. A second, interruptive surprise comes: the boat hook catching the elderly Miss Breen's skirt as she is descending the ladder into the tender. Here there is not only otherness, but also genuine danger for a woman of roughly seventy, primarily of a very nasty tumble that could do great harm, and also, perhaps, of a half-implied risk of sexual assault (skirt lifted by boat hook). Either one would be horrible, though perhaps also horrifically entrancing. Here it is worth noting, too, as Brett Millier reminds us, that Miss Breen, at 70, is the retired warden of the Women's Jail in Detroit and that she is, unabashedly, gay, so that she represents for Elizabeth Bishop "a vision of an accomplished and successful lesbian life, not at all secretive or ashamed, at a time when she was herself at a major transition, a moment of courageous 'growth and redirection' unprecedented in her life."[19]

But no: "There. We are settled." There will be negotiations with customs officials and a passage through the port. The port, seemingly like all ports, has failed to signify anything, perhaps for want of effort or as a result of modesty of effort, in attempting only "the unassertive colors of soap, or postage stamps." Postage stamps, or at least Brazilian ones, slip away—that is fail to deliver a message, to signify. This thought, incorporated into a poem of present experience, alludes to and condenses a later letter of March 3, 1952, to Marianne Moore: "As you may have noticed, [the stamps] come almost without glue on them. The mail-boxes are never collected so one has to go to the Post Office; and there are glue-machines which are frequently incapacitated by their own glue so that one gives up and goes to the woman who runs a stamping-machine, even if the stamps are much nicer."[20] Here the unassertive port and the slipping stamps function metaphorically as images of letters ("slipping the way the latter/letters do," "when we mail the letters we wrote on the boat"), hence indicating the lack of finality of language in securing a moral or message. The significances of arrival and of experience are not to be captured once and for all. Ports and stamps and poems alike "only attempt . . . the unassertive colors of soap"; they do not offer any didactic messages, and they repose on no doctrine that secures their significance. They lack enough glue to make them stick.

Instead, something further will and does happen: "We leave Santos at once; /we are driving to the interior." Yet despite their fragility, both poet and poem are here something in and through which something has happened, is happening. The present perfect "are driving into" implies both a getting underway from the past and a projection into the future. An experience on the part of the subject at time T_m (which calls up antecedents at T_a to T_l in memory) is being worked into a sense of being a continuing subject, moving into T_n to T_z, with a sense of identity achieved exactly through this negotiation of temporality. As Costello summarizes Bishop's sense in the Brazil poems of the situation of experiencing consciousness,

> no supreme fiction, no ultimate metaphor, overrides the local force of metonymy. Bishop represents consciousness struggling to establish meaningful order in the moving plethora of facts, struggling to read fact before it slips away from its names. Simply bearing witness to the world's variety remains a positive value within the [Brazil] poems as significance advances and retreats.[21]

Brett Millier similarly usefully notes that "Bishop's habitual manipulation of perspectives in her observations—both poetic and personal—is another symptom of [her] war [with time] . . ., a preoccupation with unhappy compromise, a desire to give up, submit, cease, resist,"[22] but here a desire that has been given voice and motivated survival and movement, an overcoming of submission and withdrawal.

Technically, this survival through and across temporality is achieved in Bishop's astonishing modulations of inner and outer. That is, a typical Romantic lyric will begin with a moment of perception of a perplexing external object, scene, or event. Call this moment OUT1. It will be followed by a set of internal memories and reflections that are called up by the perception, as the thinking consciousness attempts to come to terms with perplexities. Call this moment IN. It will then be followed by a return to perception, embodying a reacceptance of the world and of life in it. Call this OUT2. While there are echoes of this structure in "Arrival at Santos"—it begins with OUT1, modulates into IN, and ends with a present tense observation or anticipation of what we are doing: OUT2, it is in fact more complicated than this. OUT1 in lines 1–7 is followed by IN1 in lines 7–14, beginning with "Oh, tourist." Then comes OUT2 ("Finish your breakfast. The tender is coming."); IN2 ("I never saw it before"); OUT3 ("And gingerly now we climb down"); IN3 ("Miss Breen is about seventy"); OUT 4 ("There. We are settled."); IN 4 ("The customs officials will speak English, we hope"); and OUT 5 ("We leave Santos at once"). Consciousness is moving continuously from observation to reflection and back again, sustaining itself and building its thought and stance in this very movement.

In the poem as we have it that incorporates this movement, something has happened, without final order rooted in doctrine. As Bonnie Costello puts it, the "compensations of heightened sensation, imaginative play, [and] historical and personal awareness . . . constitute a positive alternative"[23] to finality of message. And something further will happen, is happening: "we are driving to the interior," where the struggle to establish meaningful order will again bump up against the plethora of fact, and the precipitate of that struggle, Bishop's poetry, will come forth.

III

Modernist poetry and philosophy and criticism can always be dismissed as escapist or as emptily subjective or as entertainment indexed to certain self-anointed advanced classes. (People can say anything.) History can be read either as flat or as a thing of good enough compromises or a scene of large forces that crush subjectivity, and not so much a thing of alternating blanknesses and surprising engagements. It might seem that we should betake ourselves to the serious matters of experimental science, political negotiation, or simply getting on with survival. And no doubt sometimes we should. But what would human life really be like for us, if we gave up struggling to establish significance in the moving plethora of fact. I characterized Cavell as seeking stabilization, confirmation, and the sharing of experience in and through the articulation of responses to changing moments of perplexity. A seeking of all this that amounts to a stabilization, confirmation, and sharing is just what we find in "Arrival at Santos." Autobiographically, ontologically, and performatively, I cannot do other than to join my expression of hope for greater possibilities of interest and engagement in life to the thoughts, perceptions, and expressions of Benjamin and Freud and modernist poetry, of Stanley Cavell and of Elizabeth Bishop.

8

"This Most Human Predicament"

Cavell on Language, Intention, and Desire in Shakespeare

In the second paragraph of "The Avoidance of Love," the earliest of his essays on Shakespeare, Cavell asks, "What has discouraged attention from investigations of character?" in Shakespeare criticism of the mid-twentieth century. "What . . . has [instead] specifically motivated an absorbing attention to words?," as in the criticism of William Empson and G. Wilson Knight. The answer that Cavell offers is that it is "the merest assumption," foisted off on us "by some philosophy or other, that [literary] characters are not people, [and] that what can be known about people cannot be known about characters" (DK, 40).[1] Cavell then goes on to challenge this assumption by noting that it is at the very least quite natural "to account for the behavior of characters" by applying "to them [psychological] predicates, like 'is in pain,' 'is ironic,' 'is jealous,' and 'is thinking of . . .'" (DK, 40).

In one sense, then, Cavell is committed instead to treating characters as or as importantly like real people. This might well raise the worry that criticism based on this commitment is slack, inattentive, and emptily impressionistic relative to the real work of the plays, as if the practitioner of this criticism has somehow forgotten that plays are made materially out of words. If we are left only with the thoughts, say, that Hamlet is melancholy, Coriolanus is angry, or Othello is jealous, this worry might well be justified. Kenneth Burke, for example, charges the character criticism or "portraiture" practiced by A. C. Bradley and Samuel Johnston with just this kind of empty impressionism.

> The risk in "portraiture" of the Bradleyan sort (and Samuel Johnson has done it admirably too, also with reference to Othello) is that the critic ends where he should begin. . . . Let the critic be as impressionistic as he wants, if he but realize that his impressions are the beginning of his task as a critic, not the end of it. Indeed, the richer his impressions the better, if he goes on to show how the author produced them. But the great risk in "conclusive"

Anticipations of Freedom. Richard Eldridge, Oxford University Press. © Richard Eldridge 2026.
DOI: 10.1093/9780197841785.003.0012

statements about a work is that they give us the feeling of conclusions when the real work of analysis is still before us.[2]

Here, for Burke, the real work of analysis must consist not simply in having impressions of characters as types, but further in close attention to the specific words that Shakespeare or any other dramatist has used to make the characters the distinct, situated individuals they are.

As Cavell rightly remarks on behalf of Coleridge and Bradley, however, and in turn also on behalf of the linguistic criticism of Empson and Wilson Knight, the assumption that interest in characters competes with interest in their specific words should surely be rejected.

> Can Coleridge or Bradley really be understood as interested in characters *rather than* in the words of the play; or are the writings of Empson or G. Wilson Knight well used in saying that they are interested in what is happening in the words *rather than* what is happening in the speakers of the words? . . . The most curious feature of the shift and conflict between character criticism and verbal analysis is that it should have taken place at all. How could any serious critic ever have forgotten that to care about specific characters is to care about the utterly specific words they say when and as they say them; or that we care about the utterly specific words of a play because certain men and women are having to give voice to them? Yet apparently both frequently happen. My purpose here is not to urge that in reading Shakespeare's plays one put words back into the characters speaking them, and replace characters from our possession back into their words. The point is rather to learn something about what prevents these commendable activities from taking place. (DK, 39, 41)

As Cavell's engagements with Shakespeare develop throughout the essays that compose *Disowning Knowledge*, it emerges that the sorts of things that prevent these commendable activities include a materialist metaphysics (according to which the only real thing composing a play is a pattern of ink on paper and the only thing composing an action is a bodily motion with an inner material cause) plus a kind of self-protective fear of engagement on the parts of readers, who might find their metaphysical and moral commitments challenged by the thought that some characters in dramas make available exemplarily valuable or horrific possibilities of action as such. As readers, that is, we tend to protect ourselves by covertly assuming models of reality, knowledge, and self that may be insupportable and that express an overriding commitment to the value of control, as achievable by detached internal intelligence facing off against inert, mere material nature. (Here the metaphysics and the fear may be internally related: fear of exposure to moral criticism of oneself by the text may motivate the pursuit of control over it, and commitment to detached control may help to suppress fear of exposure.) The work of challenging both materialist metaphysics and self-protective fears via readings of Shakespeare's plays then both requires and centers on the commendable activities of putting the words back into the characters speaking them and replacing characters from our (too-knowing) possession back into their self-possession in, by, and through their words, so that characters and words together might teach us about the plights of mind and circumstance in which they occur. Or as Cavell puts it in the *Coriolanus* essay in his most direct methodological remark,

> I might characterize my intention in spelling out what I call these fantasies [of Coriolanus] as an attempt to get at the origin of words, not the origin of their meaning exactly but of their production, of the value they have when and where they occur. I have characterized something like this ambition of criticism variously over the years, and related it to what I understand as the characteristic procedure of ordinary language philosophy. (DK, 156)

From the very beginning of his career, Cavell's understanding of the characteristic procedure of ordinary language philosophy involved less a commitment to demotic ordinary speech as such, as a norm for all speech situations, than a psychoanalytically inflected commitment to figuring out why *anyone* might utter *exactly these words* within *a very specific speech situation*. This commitment on Cavell's part has evident affinities with any dramatist's commitment to, and with Shakespeare's genius for, getting exactly right the words that a genuinely human character within certain straits of circumstance, character, passion, and verbal talent would say when.[3]

That ordinary language must be both available as a vehicle for communication and for meaningful interaction among subjects, yet also open to change and never fully under the control of any individual subject, is a dominant theme of *The Claim of Reason*, especially of chapter 7, "Excursus on Wittgenstein's Vision of Language." Language must be, as Cavell puts it there, both stable enough to permit successful communicative and expressive use *and* tolerant of change. Nothing—no putative universal or fixed convention—can function as *the* meaning of a word, such that if one just knew *that* exact entity or fixed fact associated with the word, then one could be absolutely assured of the conditions of its correct application and thus immunized against even the possibility of making a mistake. Or as Cavell picks up the thought in *Disowning Knowledge*:

> Words recur in foretellable contexts; there could be no words otherwise; and no intentions otherwise, none beyond the, let me say, natural expression of instinct; nothing would be an expression of desire, or ambition, or the making of a promise, or the acceptance of a prophecy. Unpredictable recurrence is not a sign of language's ambiguity but is a fact of language as such, that there are words. (DK, 231–2)

This ontological fact about language—that it is both stable and tolerant, and that linguistic meaning depends on nothing more or less than human subjects continuing well enough and intelligibly enough to invest their recognitions, interests, and passions in what is mostly ordinarily done with words, even while change in usage is possible—then has immediate consequences for the life of human subjects as such. One becomes a distinctively human subject—or enters into the role of a discursive, deliberating, reflective, subject, as opposed to being simply an empirically identifiable biological human being—over time, through training, by imitatively taking up the possibilities of communication and expression that come to dawn on the infant as manifest in the behaviors of grownups. Grownups being what they are, and relations with them on the part of infants being what they are, the development of a sense of what it is correct to say when is bound up with conflicting demands made on the infant and with the infant's desperate wish to please parents and others who make these conflicting demands. Adventure and a sense of dawning cognitive, communicative, and expressive power are crossed for the infant with anxiety and frustration, as an ego develops caught between libidinal impulses and superego commands and prohibitions that are internalizations of the demands of others.[4] Apart from all anxieties, frustrations, and risks, all bound up with considerations of correctness in action and speech, there would be no articulated desires and no uses of language, but only instinctively prompted bodily motions of eye, mouth, and limb.

One natural reaction to the agon of entry into language and into the life of a human subject is a wish to know absolutely and to have absolute control of the conditions of linguistic-discursive-judgmental performance and of the actions that follow from judgment. This wish is the source of philosophy's repeated and repeatedly frustrated attempts to make contact with absolute givens that determine correct judgment. Plato's talk of abstract forms, Aristotle's of forms immanent in nature, Aquinas's of divine Providence, Descartes's of clear and distinct perceptions, Hegel's of the Absolute, and Marx's of species-being are all ways of giving expression to this natural wish that remains unappeasable within the ambit of ordinary experience. They promise, but in fact fail to yield, understanding of and resonance with something as a source of absolute assurance and orientation in one's life as a subject. Alternatively, one might accept one's complete powerlessness and ability to judge and act according to reason by embracing Humean skepticism and naturalism. Here one is promised freedom from responsibility for orientations and relationships, but with the implausible cost of being able to do nothing, as if all one's bodily motions and utterances were necessarily no more actively formed or alterable than is the turning green of leaves when chlorophyll production diminishes with falling temperatures. Exculpation under causal forces both replaces justification and deflates action into a mere event in nature.

Both these flawed strategies for coping with the agon of the inheritance of language are absolutist, in resting on an all-or-nothing assumption. Either we are, or can become, absolute masters, or we are absolute victims. But this all-or-nothing assumption is the very thought that should be rejected. We are, instead, always at stake and at risk in judgment and in action (even if sometimes, happily, the stakes are low and easily met). We cannot stand on self-enclosed, internalized intentions (formed either under contact with absolutes or passively under conventions); we always mean more in what we say and do than we can fully control, and we are always responsible for coming to reasonable enough terms with that fact. That we must mean what we say is both a description of commitments enacted in judgment and action that outrun our foresight *and* a normative demand to take responsibility for our commitments as best we can with our finite foresight and finite accomplished powers.[5] "Intension [—a meaning-entity grasped and enclosed within the subject—] is not a substitute for intention [or what is always expressed and at stake in action]," as Cavell puts in "Must We Mean What We Say?" (MWM, 29); we should reject the thought that "if intention counts for anything in meaning, it counts for everything" (DK, 240). Or, in a wonderful question that occurs in the collection *In Quest of the Ordinary*, "Is W. C.

Fields our only alternative to Humpty Dumpty?" (IQO, 117).[6] The standing fact of our lives with language as human subjects, as *Disowning Knowledge* puts it, is that

> you always tell more and tell less than you know. Wittgenstein's *Investigations* draws this most human predicament into philosophy, forever returning to philosophy's ambivalence, let me call it, as between wanting to tell more than words can say and wanting to evade telling altogether—an ambivalence epitomized in the wish to speak "outside language games," a wish for language to do, the mind to be) everything and nothing. Here I think again of Emerson's wonderful saying in which he detects the breath of virtue and vice that our character "emits" at every moment, words so to speak always before and beyond themselves, essentially and unpredictably recurrent, say rhythmic, fuller of meaning than can be exhausted. (DK, 201)

Within this most human predicament, character and one's uses of language in judgments, together with the actions that express them, are each other's obverse and reverse, each being and meaning what they are only in relation to each other. Burdened by multiple, conflicting demands, coming from other subjects, freighted with anxieties, and haunted by fantasies, yet in possession of some possibilities of agency and expression, our words—anyone's words—must at some level reveal our complex lives as subjects.[7] (All this applies all at once to Shakespeare, his characters, and his readers, including, of course, Cavell and us.)

This most human predicament is arguably felt to be more pressing in modernity, from say roughly the early fourteenth century in Italy (Petrarch) onward, as emerging transportation networks, developing urbanization, and improved technologies of production (themselves all resting on skill development in pursuit of genuine human interests) begin to make less repetitively local and more diverse and skill-based social identities available.[8] But it is also arguably an ontological predicament that attaches to human life with language as such, with economic scarcities and facts of coercive power sometimes acting to inhibit the emergence of a felt sense of this predicament. A sense of human life as open to exercises of creative power and conversion of interest is certainly evident as early as in the Platonic texts and in early Christianity, as well as in modernity.

For those caught within this predicament who have both a strong sense of it and possess substantial imaginative power and self-discipline, so that they might inaugurate new possibilities of life, there is a natural tendency to experience what Cavell elsewhere calls the uncanniness of the ordinary: a sense that

> the everyday is ordinary because, after all, it is our habit, or habitat; but since that very inhabitation is from time to time perceptible to us—we who have constructed it—as extraordinary [sometimes in its decadence and resistance to full expressions of creative individuality]—, we conceive that some place elsewhere, or this place otherwise constructed, must be what is ordinary to us, must be what romantics—of course including both E. T. and Nicholas Nickleby's alter ego Smike—call "home." (IQO, 9)

Within the grip of this sense, there is then for those with visionary power a standing tendency to deny the significance of the fallen ordinary as it stands in favor of the pursuit of a reformed, different, more meaningful ordinary. Both the skeptic's repudiations of ordinary knowledge and the systematizing philosopher's turn to a world of forms or the will of God or a world of absolutized mathematical physics are disciplined efforts to deny the significance of the ordinary.

The systematizing philosopher's efforts at radically new intelligibility founder, however,[9] and there is, by Cavell's lights, no intellectual way out of this condition: the truth of skepticism—its correct perception that meaningfulness is not as fully present and lived as it is felt it ought to be; its "expression of an awareness that presentness was threatened, gone" (DK, 95)—is "that while criteria provide conditions of (shared) speech, they do not provide an answer to skeptical doubt" (DK, 205–6). From within either the skeptical or the systematizing impulse,[10] "acknowledging that the world exists, that you know for yourself that it is yours, is not so clear a process" (DK, 203). Skepticism—more honestly and directly so than its systematizing double and rival—is "an intellectualization of some prior intimation" of lost or absent meaningfulness (DK, 206). It is "an expression of the human wish to escape the bounds or bonds of the human, if not from above then from below, . . . the human craving for, and horror of, the inhuman, of limitlessness, of monstrousness" (DK, 229). It is "a power that all who possess language possess and may desire: to dissociate oneself, excommunicate oneself from the community, in whose agreement, mutual attunement, words exist," for the sake of a better one, or, failing that, for the sake of intactness, privacy, and (fantasized) invulnerability. Skeptics at times are we all.

Shakespearean tragedy is then "an interpretation of what skepticism is an interpretation of": our human predicament, that we live within "the human fatedness to significance, . . . victims of intelligibility," both its fact and its limits (DK, 5, 95).[11] Hence Cavell's character criticism is not an impressionistic encounter with singular eccentricities or, as it were, denizens of possible worlds. It is instead a criticism of human character, fated always to partial significance, as it appears within an individual within a particular set of highly straitened circumstances, ambitions, power, and desire. Lear's skeptical impulse is toward withdrawal and hiddenness, an "attempt to avoid recognition, the shame of exposure, the threat of self-revelation" (DK, 58). Coriolanus's takes the form of "disgust with the world, . . . a vision of communication as contamination, the discovery that human existence is inherently undistinguished" (DK, 12). Macbeth's seeks "deeds done in the doing without consequence, when surcease is success, [in name of] a wish for there to be no human action, no separation of consequence from intention, no gratification of desire, no showing of one's hand in what happens . . .—a wish to escape the human (DK, 233). Othello's takes the form of murderous jealousy driven by a wish to preserve his intactness, apartness, and invulnerability to the claims of ordinary love.

Happily, however, we are not fully fated to follow these figures in their shames, disgusts, and murderous rages. In his sunniest book, *Pursuits of Happiness*, Cavell describes how some couples, through a combination of luck, wit, readiness to have fun, and acceptance of chastenings, may "trace the progress from narcissism and incestuous privacy to objectivity and the acknowledgment of otherness as the path and goal of human happiness" (PH, 102).[12] Skills in managing this progress, are, however, fragile, and we live "between avoidance and acknowledgment," and so open to being caught to various degrees within both the tragic skepticisms of Lear, Coriolanus, Macbeth, and Othello and the happinesses in joint purposiveness without a purpose of Cary Grant and Katherine Hepburn, Cary Grant and Irene Dunne, and Clark Gable and Claudette Colbert (or the characters that their bodies incarnate on film). This betweenness—our human predicament, our fatedness to (limited) intelligibility and to fantasies of overcoming or escaping it—then entails its continual expression in our lives and its continual expression and rescrutinizing in the art that engages with our lives. "Apart from the wish for selfhood," as always to be more fitly achieved, Cavell writes, "hence the always simultaneous granting of otherness, I do not understand the value of art. Apart from this wish and its achievement, art is exhibition" (WV, 22). *Disowning Knowledge* is Cavell's account of Shakespeare's art, and its tracking of major forms of the accomplishment of selfhood under the tragic but all too human conditions of domination by a wish for absolute orientation, assurance, and control.

The trouble, then, with criticism that focuses either only on characters or only on words (as material tokens on pages of types) is that it threatens to deny or miss the specific dramas of avoidance and acknowledgment that are enacted in the plays and hence to deny or suppress the standing affinities and entanglements between those dramas and the uncontrollable dramas of our own lives. It is all too natural to practice these denials. The wish for control of both one's life and of one's encounters with an unruly, commanding work that challenges one, or even calls one out of self-satisfaction and self-stupefaction, is both strong and unappeasable. But that is no reason for succumbing to this wish full stop and claiming absolute critical mastery over a work, especially over Shakespeare's plays (or, alternatively, for dismissing them as mere fictions, mere entertainments), when we might instead learn to read ourselves, our wishes, our ambitions, and our dramas by reading them or having them read us.

9

How Movies Think

Cavell on Film as a Medium of Art

The main title of this chapter, "How Movies Think," claims that some movies manage to address some of the deepest and most important problems of human life—problems of selfhood, of meaning in experience, and of social conflict, among many others—in ways that are specific to the medium of moving photographic images. The subtitle then implies that Stanley Cavell's work on movies is particularly pertinent to this topic. While a number of philosophers—for example, Stephen Mulhall on the *Alien* and *Mission Impossible* movies,[1] Paisley Livingston on Ingmar Bergman,[2] and Thomas Wartenberg[3] on a range of films––have looked seriously and productively at philosophical thinking in and through films, Cavell's work remains larger in scope, more articulate about the ontology of film as a photographic art, and more attentive to how images are used artistically to address problems of human life in innovative ways than these other studies.[4] Yet Cavell's large argument about the powers of film as art to engage productively with important issues about human life remains little understood. In particular, he is sometimes dismissed as a naive realist about the ontology of film, and his critical readings of films are often both misunderstood as overwhelmingly plot-oriented and left unconnected to his more general remarks about film as photographic art.[5]

One important point to begin with is that Cavell's thought about movies is not directly concerned with all things that are rightly called movies: not with *Shrek*, *The Little Mermaid*, or otherwise digitally produced or drawn movies, and not so much with movies where special effects, matte paintings, chromakey composition, and the like are predominant features of the way images are presented; that is, not with movies as spectacle. Of course the borderlines here are very rough, with lots of overlaps; nowadays, almost all photographically produced commercial movies incorporate some special effects, matte paintings, and so forth. The questions concern rather what is central to the production of the movie as a whole and how the significance of the images

Anticipations of Freedom. Richard Eldridge, Oxford University Press. © Richard Eldridge 2026.
DOI: 10.1093/9780197841785.003.0013

is achieved. Cavell's thought is concerned principally with centrally photo-graphically based movies, that is, movies wherein the exposure of film stock[6] to light rays emanating from things and persons that are of our world is central to the significance and interest of the movie as an artistic achievement. Certain makers of photographic movies have discovered how to use moving photographically produced images as a medium of art, and it is the nature of that discovery and of those artistic achievements that are of central interest to Cavell.

To say this, however, is not to say that Cavell regards film as an essentially documentary or reproductive medium; it is not to say that he favors a simple-minded Bazinian view of film as against Eisenstein's emphasis on montage and other directorial decisions. In fact, Bazin's views, on which Cavell draws extensively, are substantially more complex than any naive realism, and Bazin explicitly incorporates in his theory the significance of both director's decisions and symbolic meaning.[7] Bazin does argue that film (like photography) to some extent involves "a mechanical reproduction in which man plays no part."[8] But Bazin's point here is just to emphasize where decisions are made and how photography and film differ from painting. Unlike painting (and ignoring cropping and other darkroom editing), once the camera is aimed, the film stock chosen, and the aperture and the shutter speed are set, then the film stock receives and registers light rays reflected from its subject matter automatically, without the intervention at that point of the human hand. The film stock registers at that point what the camera has been aimed at. Film then adds to this mechanical capturing of subject matter the capturing of motion, thus solving "the problem of movement."[9] These two points—mechanical reproduction (subsequent to photographers' decisions) plus solving the problem of movement—then have the consequence that film "completely satisf[ies] our appetite for illusion."[10]

Crucially, for Bazin this is a psychological fact about our experience of film. The psychological concern to capture or render likeness is one of the two tendencies that have given shape to all plastic art, according to Bazin. The other is the aesthetic-symbolic tendency to express the meanings of things. Once freed from the psychological "obsession with likeness," the plastic arts, and film in particular, were able to turn to the essentially aesthetic ambition of art: "namely the expression of a spiritual reality wherein the symbol transcended the model," so as to achieve "the preservation of life by a representation of life."[11] This latter, aesthetic aim—"the primordial function of art"—is already partly, but only partly, achieved in mummies buried along with corn and terracotta statuettes, or in cave paintings that present "a magic identity substitute for the living animal [in order to] ensure a successful hunt."[12] According to Bazin, "the great artists, of course, have always been able to combine the two tendencies"[13] that give shape to all art: the psychological tendency to duplicate reality and the aesthetic tendency to represent continuing meaningful life symbolically, where the symbol is itself also a focus of interest and experience. The point of Bazin's emphasis on photography's and then film's automatic satisfaction of the psychological need for the duplication of reality—an automatism that is operative, Bazin admits, only after the photographer's "selection of the object to be photographed [. . .] and the purpose he has in mind"—is that photography and then film are able "to present [the object in a situation, an aspect of the world] in all its virginal purity to my attention and consequently to my love."[14]

In presenting the object by means of "a kind of decal or transfer," the photographic and filmed image takes on "the irrational power to bear away our faith,"[15] specifically the power to make visually palpable and to sustain a faith that the world continues beyond or without us as a locus of life where things mean something. This power will be effectively achieved, however, only when the photographic duplication of reality is coupled with the aesthetic-symbolic-expressive rendering of things as meaningful to human subjects. In film, according to Bazin,[16] this is better accomplished stylistically by means of "invisible montage," which involves "the creation of a sense or meaning not objectively contained in the images themselves but derived exclusively from their juxtaposition," in contrast with either "intellectual montage" or "montage attraction," where the meaning is only intellectually or associatively generated by the director-editor, rather than being derived from the juxtaposed images themselves, that is, by following the meanings of the things that are photographed.[17] That is, in invisible montage the meaning is derived not only from formal or perceptible features of the image, but also from (a) what the image is an image of (the real subject in the world that the photographic image captures and presents), and (b) the realistic, subject matter based arrangement of photographic images of things as an action is followed. This is a critical, stylistic judgment on Bazin's part about the conditions of artistic success in filmmaking. Bazin names Griffith, Flaherty, and in general the directors of first-generation Hollywood "talkies" influenced by the need to follow a moving singer or dancer as among the early masters of invisible montage or what we have come to know as traditional or dramatic or continuity editing. Eisenstein and Kuleshov, despite some powerful moments, are by contrast criticized as less artistically successful practitioners of intellectual or associative montage. Bazin further lists seven genres of American film that use dramatic editing and became prominent in the period from roughly 1927 (the first sound-synchronized feature film) to 1940: (1) American comedy, (2) the burlesque film (e.g., the Marx Brothers), (3) the dance and vaudeville film (Astaire-Rogers, the Ziegfeld Follies), (4) the crime and gangster film, (5) psychological and social dramas, (6) horror or fantasy films, and (7) Westerns.[18] In each case, Bazin is struck by "a complete harmony of image and sound" and by the effectiveness of "analytic" or "dramatic" editing in contrast with the expressionist-symbolist "ambition of [associative] montage."[19] Bazin further notes that *Citizen Kane* (1941) achieves a distinctly realist use of depth of focus, wherein the audience is required to scan a large, focused image and to choose where to direct its attention, thus mimicking the necessity of our scanning and focusing in ordinary viewing of the world.[20]

Cavell roughly assumes all this from Bazin. Like Bazin he offers critical judgments about artistic successes and failures that are achieved within the medium of film, and like Bazin he celebrates the spectacular successes of traditional editing in largely Hollywood films between roughly 1930 and 1950. He has written about almost all the categories Bazin lists: American comedy as the comedy of remarriage in *Pursuits of Happiness*, the Marx Brothers,[21] Astaire's *The Band Wagon* (dir. Vincente Minnelli, 1953),[22] and psychological and social dramas in his treatment of the melodramas of the unknown woman in *Contesting Tears*, with incidental remarks about Westerns and gangster movies throughout *The World Viewed*.

Following Bazin, Cavell argues that movies *screen* reality; they present persons and things on film—not images of things only, that is not what Cavell calls *likenesses* as in realist painting (WV, 17)—but things and persons themselves, albeit not in their direct quiddity in our space and time, but rather *on film*. Presentation of things on film is quite compatible with—in fact it requires—that they be presented from a point of view, with the camera placed somewhere by the director, with lighting, focus, and close-up all decided by those who are making the film rather than by the things themselves. As William Rothman and Marian Keane aptly note, Cavell's view "is that there is an inescapable element of mechanism or automatism in the making of photographs, not that there is nothing but mechanism or automatism in their making."[23] This view, moreover, does not require that the persons presented be other than fictional characters. But it does require that the fictional characters presented be embodied in the visible screen presence of a real person, a photographed human being.

Photographs, as opposed to visual images produced otherwise, present, as Cavell puts it, "the real world without existence. [...] The camera [...] crops a portion from an indefinitely larger field" (WV, 24). This is a phenomenological remark about the experience of photographed things on film, about how that experience is produced, and about the kind of significance some experiences of this kind have had. As Stephen Mulhall notes, Cavell offers us "a partial elucidation of what seeing a photograph of an object [and therein also of movies composed of photographs of objects] amounts to."[24] "A painting is a world; a photograph is of the world. [...] The altering frame is the image of perfect attention" (WV, 24, 25). The world "inhabited by figures we have met or may well meet in other circumstances" (either as types or as singular individuals photographed in other films) presents itself to me as viewer "automatically, [...] magically, [...] without my having to do anything [...], [thus] satisfying the wish for the world recreated in its own image" (WV, 35, 39). Cavell remarks in a note to *The World Viewed*, "There may be possibilities open for the great sound and visual cinema of the future.[25] But in the meantime the movies have been what they have been" (WV, 232n8).

Cavell, then, is interested in what some photographically produced movies have been. More particularly, he is interested in the feats of art that have been achieved in certain photographically produced movies by way of effective dramatic editing of moving photographically produced images. The home movies that my parents shot of my childhood antics contain images that share a photographic basis with, say, *Bringing Up Baby*. Both present things of our world on screen. But that there is a difference in quality of achievement amounting to a difference in kind scarcely needs comment. Likewise, Cavell notes that there are such things as experimental films (Chris Marker, Stan Brakhage) and cartoons (WV, 142–3). While these may achieve their own forms of success, that success will not be achieved by means of sustained, narrative *photographic* attention to the motions of real subjects. In Rothman and Keane's useful phrase, Cavell is concerned to elucidate and respond to "the astonishing capacities for meaningfulness that movies have discovered within the singular conditions of their medium"[26] of photographically produced presentations of things on film.

In achieving their astonishing meaningfulness, photographically produced movies have established themselves as a medium of art. That movies are a medium of art is *not* a matter of their physical basis alone. It rather requires what Panofsky called "the exploitation of the unique and specific possibilities of the new media" (cited, WV, 30). "The aesthetic possibilities of a medium are not givens"; instead they are created by "giving significance to specific possibilities of photographic presentation via framing, lighting, mise-en-scène, cutting, editing, and so on" (WV, 31, 32; see also WV, 145). These movies explore the deepest problems of human selfhood: for example, intimacy and its failure, heroism, the special beauty of some natural scenes and some persons, the odd beauty and visual interest of nearly anything in certain lights (what one might call the beauty of the world as a whole in its smallest details), and how people look at and respond to one another. Movies do this in and through photographic attention to the smallest nuances of look, glance, presence, and tone. For example, conveyances, fashions, gaits, stances, and faces may be "lovingly studied" by film (WV, 43). Cavell notes that some directors use the camera "to let the world happen, to let its parts draw attention to themselves according to their natural weight" (WV, 25), listing Dreyer, Renoir, and Antonioni, among others; since *The World Viewed*, we can add Malick and Herzog and Mendes.

Extending this thought just slightly, we can say that some directors also use the camera to let the being of the person happen, specifically to let the star in character manifest itself for us on film. Howard Hawks and Leo McCarey are masters of this. The frontispiece to *Pursuits of Happiness* is a still of Cary Grant from McCarey's *The Awful Truth*, accompanied by Cavell's remark, "This man, in words of Emerson's, carries the holiday in his eye; he is fit to stand the gaze of millions" (WV, frontispiece). It is important that in the moment in the movie that is stopped in this still photograph the Cary Grant character, Jerry, is taking a delighted interest in something he has just arranged that is about to happen in front of him: his estranged wife Lucy (Irene Dunne), a trained art singer, jitterbugging with her new "country" admirer Dan (Ralph Bellamy), a jitterbug champion. Here Jerry is taking an interest in this specific woman in this specific situation, and it shows.

Art, according to Cavell, explores in its various material media how taking an interest in one's life is possible. "Apart from the wish for selfhood (hence the always simultaneous granting of otherness as well), I do not understand the value of art" (WV, 22), Cavell writes. To say that we wish for selfhood is to say that we often live with a sense of selfhood unachieved, in silent melancholy or quiet desperation, caught within conformities—grammars, routines, repertoires—that are not ours, not alive for us, not animations for us or of us. Yet it is possible to overcome such melancholy conformities and to "consent to our present state as something we desire, or anyway desire more than we desire change" (CR, 465), as, for example, the Marx Brothers do in their gloriously manic undoing of *Il Trovatore* in *A Night at the Opera* or as the remarrying pairs of the films considered in *Pursuits of Happiness* do. By having powers of reflection, activity, and will, we are as human persons fated to take an interest in our experience or to fail to. Photographic movies as art investigate photographically (through the photographing centrally of persons, since 1927 of speaking persons) how interest in experience may be either achieved or lost. This is why Cavell remarks that "American film at its best participates in [the] Western cultural ambition of self-thought or self-invention" (CT, 72). (Other art media take up this topic of human interest in experience in their own distinctive ways: in opera, for example, "the intervening or supervening of music into the world [is] revelatory of a realm of significance that either transcends our ordinary realm of experience or reveals it under transfiguration," Cavell notes [PP, 142]).

An astonishing thing about movies—certain dramatically edited, photographically produced narrative movies between 1930 and 1960—is that they absorb us into their perfect attentions to their subjects and into their discoveries of significances in things without any distinctions "between high and low audiences, and between their high and low instances, [...] without having assumed the burden of seriousness" (WV, 14, 15). This is to say that (mostly) Hollywood movies constituted for a period of time a modern art that was not yet *modernist*. In them, significance was achieved as if naturally, without paroxysms of authorial self-display and in a way that was open to being readily experienced by all, free of "modernism's perplexities of consciousness, its absolute condemnation to seriousness" (WV, 118).

When one views a photographically produced movie, then—when things go well; when "the integrity of a given work [...] make[s] out the significance of a given possibility (WV, 142)—the plot that is forwarded through the words and photographic images is experienced as necessary, mythical. An artistically successful sequence of automatic world projections is a means, as Rothman and Keane put it, of "magically satisfying our wish to view, unseen, the world re-created in its own image."[27] This means that we see the world obeying its own logic, with everything—every glance, every posture,

every thing presenting itself, every word—happening by immanent necessity, without me being present to the events. To be sure, this happens only
when things go well. It is a criterion of art to achieve satisfyingly felt necessity
in the internal relation of its compositional elements: in music, each note
requiring every other; in painting, each patch of pigment requiring every
other; in poetry, each word requiring every other, or at least our feeling continuously that this is so. In movies, however, since the material medium is
the world itself—things and persons themselves—presented on film, this felt
necessity seems to be of the whole world or at least whatever is in this filmed
portion of it, as though *its* meaning were being presented. Again, following
Rothman and Keane, "the projected world is, we might say, the past *mythically.*"[28] This is, I take it, a way of saying, as Aristotle says, that in a successful
dramatic presentation, events that are possible or probable are presented
as necessary. They are presented *as* the working out of the necessities of
achieving or failing to achieve humanity's *telos*, where the achievement or
failure happens as a result of character and in and through action in a situation. The universal—for Cavell, concrete, free human life, or achieved
interest in experience, plus the kind of difference characters in actions in
situations make to either achieving it or missing it—is presented in the particular, in just this sequence of human subjects in action. This is true in photographic movies, too, in virtue of their having what Cavell calls "narration
itself, whose tense is past" (WV, 26). But in film narration, unlike drama on
the stage, the necessities include everything in the photographed world, and
the *telos* that is typically in question is interest in experience, which means
interest in the experience of at least some others too. Again the crucial passage about art from *The World Viewed*: "Apart from the wish for selfhood
(hence the always simultaneous granting of otherness as well), I do not understand the value of art" (WV, 22).

That the pursuit of this *telos* is presented mythically—in the past tense,
and with everything a matter of necessity, at least when the movie is very
good and has succeeded in establishing its particular narratively sequenced
moving images as art—explains why Cavell has focused primarily on the two
genres that have most occupied his attentions and on why the second is the
inversion of the first. In the comedies of remarriage considered in *Pursuits
of Happiness*, we see, as William Rothman puts it, "a marriage between a
woman and a man that also 'marries' the realities of the day and the dreams
of the night, the public and the private, and city and country."[29] In Cavell's
words, this amounts to "a new step in the creation of the human" (PH, 140),

"as if the sexual and the social are to legitimize one another" (PH, 31), where "the acceptance of human relatedness [manifests itself as] the acceptance of repetition" (PH, 241). "It is a matter of a new reception of your own experience" (PH, 240), where the pair "find happiness alone, unsponsored, in one another, out of their capacities for improvising a world, beyond ceremony" (PH, 239). Soul and body, self and other, self and experience and world, are all put together again, each a vehicle for each, out of nothing other than the full immanent logic of embodied relationship, realized in posture, word, tone, and look, all captured on film. "Redemption by happiness does not depend on something that is yet to happen [but] on a faith in something that is always happening, day by day" (PH, 131).

In the melodrama of the unknown woman, by contrast, "a woman achieves existence (or fails to), or establishes her right to existence (or fails to), apart from (or beyond satisfaction by) marriage (of a certain kind) [. . .] where something in her language must be as traumatic in her case as the conversation of marriage is for her comedic sisters—perhaps it will be an aria of divorce, from husband, lover, mother, or child" (CT, 87–8). And so we see Stella Dallas turning away from the window at which she has witnessed her daughter's wedding from outside, walking toward us in the rain, alone, eyes shining and looking up, half-haunted, half-satisfied at being on her own and at having successfully let her daughter go, possessed of a power for interest in experience and for relationship that has shaped, for her, in her material situation, only a life apart.

In both the comedy of remarriage and the melodrama of the unknown woman, photographic narrative film's investigation of every visible nuance of the pursuit of interest in experience—including every visible manifestation of thought and feeling, and including communication by posture, glance, style, tone, and look—focuses in particular, according to Cavell, on the specific body of the actor. In general, Cavell finds, "the actor is the subject of the camera" (PP, 137). The body is taken as "a field of betrayal"[30] to the camera and thence to the viewer (and to any character in the movie who has eyes to see). The screen performer "is the subject of study, and a study not his own" (WV, 28), where "the only thing that really matters [is] that the subject be allowed to reveal itself" (WV, 127). "The distinction between actor and character is broken up on the screen" (WV, 175), so that we talk of the Humphrey Bogart movie, the Clint Eastwood movie, the Katherine Hepburn movie, the Barbara Stanwyck movie, and so on, with the sense that the same person is being studied and revealed across roles in different films. Character as type—the mythical figure of the star or, alternatively, the special presence of the character actor—is "established by the individual and total physiognomy (of face, of figure, of gait, of temperament) of the human beings taking part in the drama" (WV, 175). Throughout *The World Viewed*, Cavell worries that such figures—Cary Grant and Clark Gable, Katherine Hepburn and Barbara Stanwyck—may no longer be present for us, for a variety of reasons. Technically the shift to color, especially 1950s and 1960s Technicolor, diminished the felt realism of the camera's scrutiny of the embodied subject. In addition, by about 1960 movies began to split into "high" self-conscious art movies, where attention is called to the innovativeness of freeze frame or angle of shot rather than to what the shot studies, as opposed to "low" commercial movies. "Sudden storms of flash insets and freeze frames and slow-motions and telescopic-lens shots and fast cuts and negative printing and blurred focusings" began to compete with and jostle against traditional dramatic editing (WV, 122); the now "high" modernist film began to compete with and jostle against "mere" Hollywood entertainment. (These were emergent tendencies, not absolutes. Cavell notes that Truffaut's *Jules and Jim* [1962] is a masterpiece in combining distinctive authorial presence with traditional editing [WV, 137–42].)

In an important article written in 1979,[31] David Bordwell contrasts along Cavellian lines the emergence of a distinctive style of art cinema (Fellini, *La Strada* [1954], Bergman, *Wild Strawberries* [1957], *Smiles of a Summer Night* [1957], Truffaut, *The 400 Blows* [1959]) that involves "narrative irresolution" and a "loosening" of cause-effect logic" in contrast with "classical narrative cinema."[32] Art cinema combines psychological realism, where the action has a "drifting, episodic quality" and "the characters [. . .] lack defined desires and goals" and "act for inconsistent reasons," with marked "authorial expressivity" involving "stylistic signatures" and "recurrent violations of classical norms," as in unusual camera angles, pronounced camera movement, editing, and lighting.[33] Beyond the distinctive art film in the use of experimental techniques, the hyper-avant-garde film involves what Noël Carroll calls "images to be viewed at an analytic remove, like specimens under a microscope."[34] Indulging in "intense didacticism"[35] and displaying "professional coolness, expertise with systems and technologies and controlled experimentalism,"[36] avant-garde filmmakers such as Hollis Frampton, Ernie Gehr, and Michael Snow abandoned all content, especially narrative and visual metaphoric content, in favor of an effort "to make the viewer aware of certain generic features of film perception," such as flickering light as such, thence leaving viewers "little to attend to save the process of attending."[37] Yet—or so Carroll argues in 1985—such an effort "appears either to have exhausted itself or ground to a halt."[38] "The time has come again [...] to make images that are expressive and aesthetic, to make narratives and psychodramas, political and personal, that reflect first and foremost on life and the world rather than primarily on the medium and the sign."[39] Yet how is photographic-narrative reflection on life and the world possible, if the world of human subjects photographed seems drained of significance and a matter of empty successiveness?

Once upon a time, the movies had inherited their conventions of visual presentation and emplotment as if naturally. Techniques of dramatic editing were simply taken on initially (and then developed) from following the action of song or dance; plots, character types, and comedic bits were taken on initially (and then developed) from vaudeville. But that time, with all its aching joys and dizzy raptures, is past. Worse yet, these lapses in the availability of traditional technique (plus compensatory upsurges in "personal" authorial style) have happened, Cavell notes, "within the last decade"—1960–70—insofar as and *because* "conviction in the movies" originating myths and geniuses—in the public world of men, the private company of women, the secret isolation of the dandy—has been lost or baffled" (WV, 60). That is, meaning experienced by subjects within those roles is no longer available within the culture to be studied photographically and narratively. Instead, under the pressures of intensifying commodity culture and assertive individualism (with all their virtues and vices), experience tends more strongly to become merely my experience, something consumed by me, not a matter of relationships to persons and objects in my world in which I might take an interest. Interest becomes subjectivized into merely felt response—a kind of tingle within—and there is nothing meaningful about experience and relationship left for the camera to investigate. Something in the culture and making itself manifest in the new, quasi-modernist techniques of film construction, Cavell reports, "broke my natural relation to movies" (WV, xxix).

At the same time, by the mid-1970s (*Jaws*, 1975; *Star Wars*, 1977) producers of special effects movies became all too accomplished at furnishing subjective tingles by means of the blandishments of spectacle. Movie-going is now frequently premised, some art and revival houses apart, on the lure of the materials of the summer blockbuster—explosions or chases or special effects—rather than the photographic-narrative investigation of the significance of the real. In public culture as a whole, there is all too little trust in personal life, in social life, or even in nature. To the extent that experience has now become significantly subjectivized and cultural life drained of meaning, one may begin to worry whether Cavell's talk of human freedom, interest in experience, and the reciprocal achievement of full selfhood is anything other than merely idiosyncratic, generally empty, quasi-religious nostalgia or sentimentalism. Can such ideas any longer matter for us? And how, if at all, might movies productively take them up?

I have felt the force of these questions, and I continue to feel it. There is much to be worried about in contemporary life. There is, for me, at least a question about whether any recent actor has had or has the kind of authority and presence that Barbara Stanwyck and Cary Grant have and sometimes have with and for one another. Perhaps it provides some ground for hope that for many Grant and Stanwyck still have this authority and presence today. Three further grounds of hope for photographic narrative art are (a) the facts, noted by Bordwell (echoing Bazin and Cavell) that some major directors (Hitchcock, Truffaut, Ford) have already managed to blend distinctive authorial signatures with traditional techniques of narration,[40] and (b) the development since the early 2000s of long-form serial narrative on cable television (*The Sopranos*, 1999–2007; *The Wire*, 2002–8; *Friday Night Lights*, 2006–11; *Breaking Bad*, 2008–13), where the demands of blockbuster financing exert less pressure than on feature films. Finally, (c), the conditions of social life and of filmic art outside the United States often differ significantly from the social conditions and filmic practices of the United States and Hollywood.[41] Filmmakers from other traditions may discover new plot arcs and ways of focusing on filmed objects and persons that give to their films distinctive presences that are different from, though related to, what Hollywood once achieved. To fill in this last point, it will help to look briefly at one contemporary movie that under current social conditions does have something like the authority and presence of the movies Cavell has studied at length: Michael Verhoeven's 1990 *The Nasty Girl* (*Das schreckliche Mädchen*), starring Lena Stolze.

This film has a number of features of the melodrama of the unknown woman. Among other things, a marriage is broken, and the movie ends with a woman left outside a society that has shown itself unable to house her distinctive intelligence and eros. I can neither summarize the entire plot here nor dwell on how the camera studies Lena Stolze in the role visually. But just to suggest that movies as art can still investigate what Cavell takes them to investigate, let me point to the following:

1. The movie opens with a shot that establishes the mythical character of the story: a shot of a classical statue, accompanied by a text from the *Nibelungenlied* about tales of heroes in ancient times.

2. The movie repeatedly displays an artful relation to documentary reality, as some opening shots introduce the character of Sonja as though she were appearing in a television documentary about her life. Throughout, several scenes are shot either in black and white (often those focusing on hypocrisies on the part of authorities) or with obviously artificial, projected backgrounds, as though to insist on both the presence of the camera and what the camera studies. (The plot of the movie is loosely based on incidents in the life of an actual German woman.) These techniques remind us in the course of viewing that the film is an authorially constructed object, yet they do so without significantly interrupting the overall flow of traditional narration.

3. The camera, director, and writer dwell on the protagonist Sonja's distinctive spirit or eros, shown first in her resistance to convention in the names of nature and embodied activity, as in throwing the Friday fish dinner into the river, dancing, and whistling. Sonja's difficulty is that she expects and demands that society and her energy inform and express one another. As a child, she had had an instinctive faith that this would be so, centering on the life of her family. (Early on, her mother, a teacher of religion, is shown teaching, while pregnant with Sonja, the story of Jesus throwing the moneychangers out of the temple. Later a five-year-old Sonja is shown beaming with pride as her father reads the Scripture lesson during a worship service.) As a child, her energy is cathected to routine and to the way things are done. She is unable to participate in making fun of a teacher, and she invariably prepares her lessons well and gives the right answers. Notably, however, she also likes to dance to rock-and-roll.

4. Sonja's instinctive insistence that her social world make sense—in particular that her energies of spirit and common social routines should inform one another—enables her at about fourteen to write a prizewinning essay on "Freedom in Europe," in which she celebrates modern European life, despite some initial hints that the world has its hypocrisies. (Taking the advice of a librarian, she passes by the fact that a military junta in Greece is part of Europe by writing "Greece is the cradle of democracy.")

5. When a second essay competition is announced, about two years later, Sonja chooses the theme "My Hometown during the Third Reich," expecting to write a story of heroic resistance fighters. She comes, however, despite opposition from archival authorities, gradually to suspect that current leading figures in the town were collaborators who denounced Jews.

6. Without proof, however, Sonja is unable to complete her essay. She instead finishes secondary school and marries her physics teacher, Martin, with whom she has fallen in love. They move in next door to her parents and have two daughters, Rebecca and Sarah, while Martin continues teaching in the school.

7. Despite her happiness in marriage and motherhood, Sonja is unable to forget about what she had begun to discover and about what it was like actively to discover important truths. "But sometimes I had the feeling that I had failed [daß ich gescheitert bin]; that I wasn't there anymore [daß ich gar nicht mehr da bin]," she remarks. She enrolls in university to study history and to carry on her research into her hometown.

8. As this research develops, Sonja is forced to file lawsuits for the release of documents. Even without a lawyer or any support from the town, she wins each case. As the townspeople become increasingly aware of her work, she repeatedly receives telephone threats, her cat is murdered and nailed to her front door, her apartment and that of her parents are firebombed, and she is beaten by thugs.

9. The movie focuses closely on the question of how, in such circumstances, anyone can go on at all, or whether anyone should continue with such a project. In a crucial scene, Sonja looks at a photograph of Father Schulze—a priest who had denounced Nazi policies and, contrary to law, preached in the camps, prior to his execution. As she holds the photograph, its glass cracked from the bombing, she thinks, in a past-tense voice-over that has the sound of Wittgenstein or Beckett, "I thought: no, enough; I can't go on; I'll stop. [. . .] No, I'll continue."

10. The breakup of Sonja and Martin's marriage is presented as a figure of the failure of social life to satisfy the demands of spirit. Though Sonja genuinely loves Martin and he loves her, Martin nonetheless shows himself unable to stand with her in her integrity. He fails to

find happiness in her adventure, but instead leaves for Munich, settling for mere ordinariness rather than adventure and a (potentially)
redeemed ordinariness.

11. The movie ends, shockingly, with Sonja left outside the
    conventionalized social sphere, all but alone with her demands, intel-
    ligence, and ego. When her book is at last published, it receives very
    favorable reviews in leading German newspapers outside her home-
    town. She is then awarded honorary doctorates from the universities
    of Vienna, Stockholm, and Paris. At last, the townspeople once again
    begin to regard her as their "dear Sonja." Her book appears in the shop
    window of the pharmacist who had earlier refused to sell her eardrops
    for her daughter. The town officials commission a bust of her, by a
    sculptor who has already done Steffi Graf and Princess Stephanie, to
    be placed in the town hall. At the unveiling ceremony, however, Sonja
    abruptly screams no, she will not let them do this to her, not partici-
    pate in their shit. She slaps her mother, grabs her younger daughter,
    and runs desperately to the "tree of life"—a shrine tree on the top of a
    hill outside town.

Nearly the last words of Cavell's *The World Viewed* are: "The knowledge of
the self as it is always takes place in the betrayal of the self as it was. That is the
form of self-revelation until the self is wholly won. Until then, until there is a
world in which each can be won, our loyalty to ourselves is in doubt, and our
loyalty to others is in partialness" (WV, 160). *The Nasty Girl* tracks, I would
say, the immanent logic of such a world—our world—as Sonja finds herself
forced by the world to betray her past self and its achievements—specifically,
to stand on her apartness, repudiating an acceptance by others that strikes
her as all too contrived. She knows that this is not—not yet—a world for her
powers, a world in which she can be interested in her own experience, yet
she is unable to give up the demand that this should be so, and she persists in
recognizing and claiming her powers, in ways we follow and honor visually,
despite continuing hypocrisies and conflicts. She is, if not quite an unknown
woman, at least a woman outside, but in possession of human powers and
capacities for interest that this movie investigates, in tracking their partial
exercise and frustration, so that this movie achieves a full narrative photographic presentation of a subject in the world.

That a movie, that *this* movie, does this, in ways that compel continuous
conviction in its words and images and in their development, from moment

to moment to moment, shows, perhaps, that an aspiration to fullness of self-hood, interest in experience, and lived freedom are not quite yet dead for us, not quite as empty as all that, and not quite unfilmable, even if not wholly and unambiguously achievable either. This is something about movies to be grateful for: that the creation of the human is still possible for us and still draws us, as that creation is sometimes presented in artfully ordered moving images.

10

Imagining Life Together

Psychosexual Intimacy, Social Roles, and Contemporary Comedies of Remarriage

It is a deep organizing theme of *Pursuits of Happiness* that the seven films it analyzes, made between 1934 and 1949, somehow manage to show how the psychosexual and the social might, despite difficulties, nonetheless ratify one another. Private intimacy and the occupying of public social roles as husband and wife might be compatible with or even ultimately require one another. The achievements of the (re-)marriages of the principal pairs are shown both to require mysterious, witty intimacy that is incomprehensible to outsiders and yet also to win social approval. The individuals that form the principal pairs themselves come to understand that their (re-)marriage is necessary, so that they arrive at allegiance to a public institution as compellingly apt for them, and in turn their commitment and allegiance are approved by their external audiences (including us) even when these audiences do not fully understand or share in their intimacies. One measure of a just society is then the extent to which it makes room for anyone to enter into relations of this kind and the extent to which its citizens at least stand in analogous conversational relations to each other. The films propose jointly, as Cavell puts it, "a criterion for the success or happiness of a society, namely that it is happy to the extent that it permits conversations of this character, or a moral equivalent of them, between its citizens" and a criterion for private happiness: "the pair is attractive, their wishes are human, their happiness would make us happy" (PH, 32).

In the contemporary world, however, such proposals are likely to seem to many to be fantastic, escapist, and irrelevant: the empty consolations of art in its appeal to fantasy and in its detachment from the serious business of life. What, then, in the world might have happened that at least constitutes a commonly enough perceived threat to the very possibility of sustained and sustainable intimacy, psychosexual and social, within the institution of marriage? And can that threat be answered, or at least addressed? Or are both

Anticipations of Freedom. Richard Eldridge, Oxford University Press. © Richard Eldridge 2026.
DOI: 10.1093/9780197841785.003.0014

(re-)marriage à la Cavell and the movies that urge it as an ideal and a criterion of personal and civic happiness instead consigned to the dustbin of history and the realm of empty, irrelevant fantasy?

One way to approach these difficult questions is to note that Cavell's thinking about remarriage comedies is from the beginning thoroughly historical and critical: an engagement with on the ground, evolving conditions of psychosexual and social life, not the specification of an abstract Platonic ideal. In general, Cavell holds that philosophy, including his own thinking and the thinking he finds in the films, "aims to disquiet the foundations of our lives" as they stand, "and this on the basis of no expert knowledge" of a kind that might be acquired by the specially intelligent through consulting a domain of fixed, abstract ideals (PH, 9). Instead, in philosophy and in life, one must begin from one's attractions and aversions as they first present themselves, often inchoately, and then "let the object or the work of your interest teach you how to consider it" (PH, 10). Cavell calls this a piece of advice about how to think that is simultaneously theoretical and practical (PH, 10), thus emphasizing that philosophizing requires a turning of both thought and activity in relation to present conditions. Attentiveness to the present and to one's inextricably cognitive-emotional-erotic-attitudinal registerings of it is all. It is a matter of "checking one's experience," that is, "of consulting one's experience and of subjecting it to examination, and beyond these of momentarily *stopping*, turning yourself away from whatever your preoccupation and turning your experience away from its expected, habitual track, to find itself, its own track: coming to attention" (PH, 12).

This fact about Cavell's critical-philosophical practice is frequently missed by those who complain that Cavell has failed to offer an adequate definition, in the form of atemporal necessary and sufficient conditions, for the genre of the comedy of remarriage. Edwin Curley finds that Cavell's "conception of the genre of the comedy of remarriage is highly arbitrary, both in its inclusions and exclusions. . . . We have so little theorizing about the concept [of compensating features that link genre members], and so few examples of its use to guide us, that, in the absence of an official pronouncement by Cavell, we can hardly tell whether a film belongs to the genre or not."[1] Noël Carroll objects both that Cavell's conception of genre is too weak in focusing only on a shared myth or plot, so that it is open to counterexamples, and vague to the point of arbitrariness in failing to specify what counts as a compensation.[2] The underlying assumption that drives the objections of both Curley and Carroll is that philosophy *should* provide clear, necessarily true statements of necessary and sufficient conditions that (more or less) inform clear identification in the absence of detailed critical readings.

While this is certainly a common enough demand in philosophy, it is at odds with Cavell's conception of philosophy—a conception that is also exemplified in the improvisatory work of the principal pairs of the comedies as they get to know themselves and each other through their interactions. For Cavell and for his principal pairs, arriving at critical self-understanding is instead centrally a matter of getting clearer about one's experience, about what is going on *in it*, from a point of initial obscurities of attraction and aversion. It is a core modernist trope of Cavell's writing that we suffer not from mistaken definitions, but from failures of attentiveness to our experiences, as if were sleepwalking within the dominant ethical universal, so that we might and should awaken ourselves within and from where we are. The typical *sine qua nons* of philosophy, detachment and critical neutrality, are foreign to Cavell's spirit and enterprise. Curley concedes that "If the function of criticism is to alter permanently our perception of a work of art, to show that it can bear the weight of detailed analysis and discussion, that it illuminates our deepest human concerns, then Cavell has written criticism of the highest order."[3] Despite the praise, however, there is an implicit sneer here that Cavell has written only criticism, not philosophy, and excellent criticism only if we accept further (unargued?) assumptions about the nature of criticism.

Cavell is clear that the account he gives of the genre of the comedy of remarriage as defined by myth and mutually compensating features is not intended either to substitute for or to foreclose critical reading (of the kind the principal pairs do of themselves and each other). "There is," he remarks, "nothing one is tempted to call *the* features of a genre which all its members have in common. First, nothing would count as a feature until an act of criticism defines it as such. (Otherwise, it would always have been obvious that, for instance, the subject of remarriage was a feature, indeed a leading feature, of a genre.)" (PH, 28). Settling exactly which films are members of the genre and which are not is not the point. "Films other than the ones I give readings of belong to the genre of remarriage; six or seven of them are cited along the way" (PH, 2). These include *Together Again* (Charles Vidor, 1944), *Woman of the Year* (George Stevens, 1952), *Pat and Mike* (George Cukor, 1952), and one might add *That Uncertain Feeling* (1941), *The Palm Beach Story* (Preston Sturges, 1942), *My Favorite Wife* (Garson Kanin, 1940), *Love Crazy* (Jack Conway, 1941),[4] as well as the later *Kramer vs. Kramer* (Robert Benton, 1979), *An Unmarried Woman* (Paul Mazursky, 1978), *Starting Over*

(Alan J. Pakula, 1979), and *Crazy Stupid Love* (Glenn Ficarra and John Requa, 2011). "But," Cavell adds, "I take the seven featured here to be definitive of the genre, the best of the genre, worthy successors of the great comedies of the Hollywood silent era" (PH, 2). What counts as a worthy successor is a matter of which films fully invite and sustain absorbed thought and interest, in particular in relation to the issue of the nature and value of a certain kind of marriage. Cavell takes the films he reads in *Pursuits of Happiness* (as well as, perhaps, his readings of them) to be "exercises in explicitness" about features that matter *to* the argument about remarriage and that "reflect upon one another, looping back and forth among the members" and "striving toward a state of absolute explicitness, of expressive saturation" (PH, 30). That state might be unattainable, since the social circumstances within which marriage exists as an institution change, so that more argument is called for, and since the material-aesthetic medium of film is syntactically and semantically dense[5] in a way that cuts against the kind of explicitness that is achievable in language. The pursuit of permanent clarity about marriage might be a fool's Platonic errand. Or marriage as an institution might simply wither away or take on a shape that is unrecognizable in relation to current conceptions. But as long as that does not happen, what matters for membership in the genre for any particular film is whether or not an argument about marriage is being productively advanced in it, whether a particular film engages "the inner agenda of a culture" (PH, 17).

The important issue, then, is not absoluteness and tidiness about the borderlines of the genre of the comedy of remarriage, but rather whether any contemporary film productively takes up the argument about the nature and value of a certain kind of marriage (and a certain kind of democratic society) that was pursued exemplarily in the seven films that are the subjects of *Pursuits of Happiness*. Whether it is possible for a film productively to take up this argument is not only a matter of the inventiveness of writers, producers, and directors, but also a matter of whether there is an argument to be made and an audience for it. With respect to the nature and value of marriage of a certain kind, these are matters of social fact. Cavell answers "the question why it was only in 1934, and in America of all places that the Shakespearean structure [of romance comedy] surfaced again" in the form of the comedy of remarriage by noting that 1934 was "a date at which a phase of human history, namely, a phase of feminism, and requirements of a genre inheriting a remarriage structure from Shakespeare, and the nature of film's transformation of its human subjects ... met together on the issue of the new creation of a woman" (PH, 19–20). Cavell cites the feminist theorist Alice S. Rossi's claim that "the generation that followed the activist generation of suffragists may have been consolidating feminist ideas into the private stuff of their lives and seeking new outlets for the expression of the values that prompted their mothers' public [suffragist] behavior," himself adding that there is "no 'may have been' about it."[6] Given the historical circumstances, women and men found themselves in a new form of "the struggle . . . for the reciprocity or equality of consciousness between a woman and a man, . . . a struggle for mutual freedom" (PH, 17, 18). When women have at last achieved publicly acknowledged, formally equal political citizenship in winning the right to vote, then the pressing issues are: where can the energies of the struggle for full equality and reciprocity, economic and domestic as well as formal and political, now go, and what are the modes and fates of undertaking to re-deploy these energies? Even more broadly, the issue is how to achieve "a proposed marriage or balance between Western culture's two forces of authority: Hellenism [as] *spontaneity of consciousness* [and] Hebraism [as] *strictness of conscience*, so that American mankind can refind its objects, its dedication to a more perfect union, toward the perfect human community, its right to the pursuit of happiness" (PH, 158–9).[7] This issue will not be on the table in the same way in all times and places, and it is evidently not on the table between men and women in the United States in the same way after 1949 as it was earlier. Cavell is clear that the genre of the remarriage comedy can continue and its guiding myth of the mutual ratification of the psycho-sexual and the democratic-social can be productively revised only "if the issue is still living" (PH, 33).

So is this large issue all at once of recognitive reciprocity between women and men, of the balance of spontaneity and conscience, and of the mutual ratification of the psychosexual and the democratic social still living? If not, or not in exactly the same way, why not? What about American life and about the lives and hopes of men and women changed? And do the changes leave room for anything *like* a contemporary version of the comedy of remarriage that addresses these issues?

Writing in 2005 on *Mr. and Mrs. Smith* (Douglas Liman, 2005), Cavell remarks that "surely the genre cannot command the cultural prominence it once enjoyed."[8] He notes the perception, forwarded by the film, that "the world itself has become inhospitable to the imagination of marriage as con-tinuously ratified in remarriage, no longer willing to entertain the possibility of joining duty and inclination. . . . More generally the film shows the present world's inhospitability to the comedy of remarriage in its [the world's? the film's? the film's reflecting the world's?] active negating of the significance of words and of work,"[9] as though all deep psychosocial satisfactions have become somehow privatized and not somehow expressible and ratifiable in public life. As a possible reason for this unhappy condition, he adduces the thought "that, somehow paradoxically, given the increase of freedom among the young beginning in the Sixties, shrinking again in recent years, it is harder to imagine a somewhat older pair, especially a male of the pair, say a decade past college age, risking all for love."[10] We can fill in this somewhat cryptic thought by noting that part of the relevant freedom is the ability to enjoy sexual experience significantly unencumbered by worries about pregnancy, in light of the general availability of largely effective birth control. Second, especially among the college-educated classes but also in general, the median age of marriage has significantly increased over the past seven decades, from 20 to 22 for women and 22.4 to 26.1 for men between 1890 and 1960, to 28.1 for women and 30.4 for men at present.[11] Among the many causes of this development, we might point to increasing economic uncertainty as the United States lost its international manufacturing hegemony, increasing demands from the workplace for formal education that requires time and energy, and increasing life expectancy, so that child-rearing comes to occupy a smaller percentage of one's adult years, as well as the more ready availability and acceptance of sex outside marriage. Whatever their underlying causes are, however, the rise in median age of marriage and widely available birth control are surely both effects and causes of psychological changes in how people think about relationships. Instead of being something expected (and generally approved) at a relatively early stage of life, marriage becomes from the beginning something of a compromise between more fully formed and mature adults who are each individually seeking satisfactions of which they have had some experience. Marriage is now commonly thought to be "hard work," with its burdens of care imposed as costs (albeit, it is hoped, worthwhile ones) on those who enter into it, rather than a mysterious, continuously transformative experience, offering a promise of things not seen. The very idea of transformative experience comes to seem less than credible, as the demands of economic credentialization come to dominate adolescent development. In *The Upswing*, their comprehensive survey of economics, politics, society, and culture from 1890 to the present, Robert Putnam and Shaylyn Romney Garrett uncover a general upsurge of what they call "expressive individualism," beginning sometime in the early to mid-1960s. As a result of what they call "the Sixties Earthquake," "beliefs, values, and norms" centering around solidarity, mutual responsibility, and equality were displaced by ones centering around personal liberation and individual happiness.[12] Ideologically, many people come to take economic, instrumental rationality—the efficient satisfaction of preferences and desires one takes oneself to have—as the default or sole form of practical rationality, at the expense of conceptions of rationality that have to do with justice, mutual recognition, and mutual citizenship. Identification with any social role—familial, gendered, economic, religious, or political—comes to seem more provisional in comparison with the strength of more labile individual interest.

On the level of couple formation, for some considerable historical stretch of time—perhaps the late 1700s for some and developing and spreading until the mid-1960s—companionate love or what we, drawing on Aristotle, might call an erotic friendship of virtue, was a significant possibility and aspiration. In this relationship, as Andrea C. Westlund puts it, "companion lovers are united in the ongoing process of forging a shared practical perspective—a perspective on what's to be done and why, on what is worth caring about, on what is valuable or important or choiceworthy and what is not—in short, a perspective on how to live (and, in particular, on how to live together)."[13] But when expressive individualism and economic rationality come to the fore and relatively formed individuals already know what they want, then the very idea of committing oneself to the process of forging and developing a shared perspective comes to seem unintelligible. Trust and faith in participating in a process that will involve change begin to lapse.[14]

Even in 1934–49 in the worlds of the comedies of remarriage, the overcoming of individual, instrumental rationality in favor of discovery of and submission to the demands and possibilities of transfigurative reciprocity required the existence of a space apart from daily life—the Shakespearean green world identified in *Pursuits of Happiness* primarily as Connecticut, sometimes as on the road—where a pair might happenstantially find themselves and so find each other (and their surprising, unacknowledged deeper needs for each other). In such spaces out of the ordinary, mutual improvisation could be called for and its value could be suddenly made manifest, as in the playacting for the detectives scene in *It Happened One Night*. Nowadays, however, such spaces seem less available. Adults carry more of their formed identities with them into unusual spaces, and the result of a camera following a couple cast into a forest or onto a desert island is likely to read more like a piece of theatricalized reality TV than as an occasion for transfigurative intimacy.

Given all this—the freedom to find sexual experience elsewhere, the necessity of spending time and energy on technical preparation for the workplace, the rise in the median age of marriage, the development of expressive individualism, the increasing strength of individual instrumental rationality, and the disappearance of spaces for mutual improvisation—it is then little surprise that Cavell concludes, again, that "the world itself has become inhospitable to the imagination of marriage as continuously ratified in remarriage," with *Mr. and Mrs. Smith* counting as much as "satire of remarriage" as a continuation of it.[15]

> The satiric value of the pair's being in the business of assassination gives their work an air of fantastic anti-work, dedicating themselves to destructiveness, work that is necessarily uncelebrated, socially unacknowledgeable. The object of the satire is nicely ambiguous. Is this a further mimesis of modern marriage, whose true basis is necessarily a secret from society, so that while the family is thought to secure the bond of the social, the privacy of the marriage at its origin is ... a standing threat to the way society is? Or is the satire directed at remarriage comedy's internal relation to utopian ideas, what Tracy Lord's fiancé George, at the denouement of *The Philadelphia Story*, contemptuously calls "you and your sophisticated ideas"?[16]

Yet, despite the worry about the inhospitability of the world to marriage as daily remarriage, Cavell's assessment of *Mr. and Mrs. Smith* is not entirely one-sided or bleak. It may be a mimesis—a continuation—of modern marriage and its possibilities of intimacy as well as a satire of utopian fantasy. "The film recurrently takes its bearings *from, or away from*, the classical remarriage comedies"[17]: it is unclear exactly which. And if, at least in part, it takes its bearings from them, then the film is somehow still exploring a living issue. Here an interesting point of comparison with *Mr. and Mrs. Smith* is *Ocean's Eleven* (Steven Soderbergh, 2001). Where *Mr. and Mrs. Smith* is more or less a comedy of remarriage crossed with a buddy flick (was *Lethal Weapon* [Richard Donner, 1986] a model for Mr. and Mrs. Smith's wisecracking?), *Ocean's Eleven* is a comedy of remarriage crossed with a heist flick. While the heist caper is in the foreground, it is also crucial to the plot and to the film's appeal that Danny Ocean (George Clooney) is arranging the heist in order to unmask the mercenariness of Terry Benedict (Andy Garcia) and to show his ex-wife, Tess (Julia Roberts), that he, not Terry, is still the one with whom, for her, (re-)marriage makes sense. He makes her laugh.

As in *Mr. and Mrs. Smith*, however, we are not shown any process of the mutual transformation of the couple through conversation. Danny from the beginning is fully committed to Tess and to recovering her, albeit that he hides this from his fellows—Rusty [Brad Pitt] has his suspicions—and from us. The pair share relatively little screen time, and the crucial transformation in Tess's perception occurs not directly in conversation with Danny, but instead through her watching a security camera capture, arranged by Danny, of Terry agreeing to an offer of $165 million in exchange for Tess. The fitness of Danny to win Tess is established more by his general poise and charm (George Clooney at his most self-deprecatingly attractive, frequently in interaction with Rusty [Brad Pitt]), contrasted with Terry's cold instrumentalism, than by anything he does with Tess. All the action takes place in Las Vegas, in connection with the heist, away from the ordinary worlds of work and life (as in *Mr. and Mrs. Smith*, where assassination is no ordinary occupation) but not in the green world of Connecticut. Yet both films succeed in presenting the accomplishment of remarriage, despite their limits in displaying conversational action, and through their genre crossings both films find places (foreign assassination sites, Las Vegas) or modes of action (mutual assassination, the heist) apart from the ordinary within which this accomplishment is possible. Each of them at least encourages the thought, central to the comedy of remarriage, that "what this pair does together is less important than the fact that they do whatever it is together, that they know how to spend time together, even that they would rather waste time together than do anything else—except that no time they are together could be wasted" (PH, 88).

To this strain of guarded optimism, we can add the thought that the canonical comedies of remarriage still work for many audiences in soliciting their enjoyments, their identifications, and their thought. Echoes of these enjoyments, identifications, and lines of thought are to be found in their less canonical successors. At the same time, given the shape of the public world and its ideology of instrumentalist individualism, many will have trouble trusting their enjoyments and identifications as having any cognitive significance. As Nietzsche mordantly remarks in criticizing utilitarianism, when we focus only on means to subjectively individual or broadly ameliorative social ends, then we become "unknown to ourselves, we knowers,"[18] in being suspicious of trust and transformation, and hence likely to will the shapes of our lives half-heartedly, as a kind of compromise. And of course promises of transformation can be hollow and coercive, especially so when they are associated with coercive authorities and highly parameterized social roles. Sometimes art's dramatic closures and happily-ever-afters continue, rightly, to call forth mistrust, given any realistic understanding of the demands and complexities of social, economic, political, and sexual life over time.

Beyond its costs, increasing individualism has also yielded the benefits of increasing fluidities both in gender identities and in possibilities of relationship as well as increasing approval of these fluidities. Non-heterosexual comedies of remarriage are at least a live possibility, even if non-heterosexual relationships and marriages also face the same pressures of economic and social circumstances as heterosexual ones. *The Kids Are All Right* (Lisa Cholodenko, 2010) is an interesting case, both complicated and enriched by the presence of children.

But can art, and art in the form of comedies of remarriage, also nonetheless sometimes make a difference?[19] Is trust in transformation within the world and in the powers of art to inform it still possible? Early in his career, in the fraught era of the Vietnam War and the Civil Rights movement, where chaos seemed everywhere, Cavell wrote that what we might hope for, from art and from life, is "not the re-assembly of community, but personal relationship unsponsored by that community; not the overcoming of our isolation, but the sharing of that isolation—not to save the world out of love, but to save love for the world, until it is responsive again" (MWM, 212). Full community may be too much to ask for, given relentless individualism and given the value and the sheer facts of difference. Political liberalism and competition have their points. Yet there remain the surprising transfigurations of attention that are afforded by art, by humor, by sports, by music, and by personal intimacies in daily life, among other things. To keep the significance of these intimacies alive and the dream of them relevant to how we live, there is little that is more pertinent than the canonical comedies of remarriage and their less canonical successors, together with thought and talk about them.

11

Modernity, Skepticism, and Meaning in *The World Viewed*

A running motif of *The World Viewed* is that sometime in the early to mid-1960s film lost its one-time combination of universal appeal and seriousness. Like the other arts, it has fragmented into a mannerist, coterie modernism, on the one hand, and clichéd entertainments, on the other. Cavell opens the book with the question, "What broke my natural relation to movies?" (WV, xix), and expressions of a sense of loss recur throughout. "Our sudden storms of flash insets and freeze frames and slow-motions and telescopic-lens shots and fast cuts and negative printing and blurred focusings," Cavell tells us, "are responses to an altered sense of film, a sense that film has brought itself into question and must be questioned" (WV, 122–3). The sense of a "loss of connection, [a] loss of conviction in the film's capacity to carry the world's presence as [or in the form of] a new theatricalizing of its images," is, he suggests, "a response to the draining from the original myths of film of their power to hold our conviction in film's characters" (WV, 131). Film now suffers from a "growing doubt of its ability to allow the world to exhibit itself" and, as a result, it "instead . . . take[s] over the task of exhibition, against its nature" (WV, 132). "The genres and types and individualities that have constituted the media of movies"—Chaplin, Keaton, Bogart, Grant, and Gable among the men; Hepburn, Russell, Garbo, Stanwyck, and Bette Davis, among the women—"are now gone or old. When they and their particular locales are gone, Hollywood is ended" (WV, 68–9). Perhaps the deepest reason for these developments is an asserted social fact: "We no longer grant, or take it for granted, that men doing the work of the world together are working for the world's good, or that if they are working for the world's harm they can be stopped" (WV, 62). We have lost our grips on both a shape of heroism in life and on types and individualities that might embody it. "I hope I am not alone," Cavell avows, "in simply being unable to recall the names or faces

Anticipations of Freedom. Richard Eldridge, Oxford University Press. © Richard Eldridge 2026.
DOI: 10.1093/9780197841785.003.0015

or presences of so many of the men and women who have come to people American movies over the past five or ten years" (WV, 70).

Here, unsurprisingly, *The World Viewed*, published in 1971, in certain respects shows some marks of its age, while also being in other respects prescient. Clint Eastwood, Robert Redford, and Jack Nicholson were already well-established stars by 1971, and Robert de Niro and Harrison Ford came to prominence soon after. Among women, Jane Fonda had won the Academy Award for best actress, and she would soon be followed by Jodie Foster and Sissy Spacek. The Hollywood star system shows little sign of abating: consider Julia Roberts, George Clooney, Brad Pitt, Robert Downey, Scarlett Johansson, Bradley Cooper, and Jennifer Lawrence, among others. Instead of generally being marked by modernist techniques of construction that call attention to the filmic surface, most mainstream, commercial Hollywood movies have remained generally realist—in Deleuzian terms more a matter of the movement image than the time image, or in Bazinian terms more a matter of continuity editing than of montage.

Writing in 2002, David Bordwell argues that

> today's films generally adhere to the principles of classical filmmaking. Exposition and character development are handled in much the ways they would have been before 1960. Flashbacks and ellipses continue to be momentarily teasing and retrospectively coherent. . . . In particular, the ways in which today's films represent space overwhelmingly adhere to the premises of "classical continuity." Establishing and reestablishing shots situate the actors in the locale. An axis of action governs the actors' orientations and eyelines, and the shots, however different in angle, are taken from one side of that axis. The actors' movements are matched across cuts, and as the scene develops the shots get closer to the performers, carrying us to the heart of the drama.[1]

At the same time, however, Bordwell also notes the prominence—surely even more marked since 2002—of "endless remakes and sequels, gross-out comedies, overwhelming special effects, and gigantic explosions with the hero hurtling at the camera just ahead of a fireball" that some have argued collectively constitute an essentially post-classical "cinema of narrative incoherence and stylistic fragmentation."[2] Bordwell's way of making sense of these two prominent modes of film style is to propose that what has taken place is an *intensification* of established techniques. Intensified continuity is traditional continuity amped up, raised to a higher pitch of emphasis. It is the dominant style of American mass-audience films today. . . . Faster cutting rate[s], . . . bipolar extremes of lens lengths, and . . . reliance on tight singles are the most pervasive features of intensified continuity: virtually every contemporary mainstream film will exhibit them. . . . Intensified continuity has [also] become a touchstone for the popular cinema of other countries.[3]

What goes largely missing in Bordwell's analysis, however, is an account of whether these interlocking, tendencies of stylistic development are artistically effective. (Bordwell's interests are here primarily historical and taxonomic rather than critical and aesthetic.) He points to "the perceived demands of television presentation" and "video-based production tools," including "tape-based editing," and the use of light-weight cranes and aerial drones, along with the influence of "some great set-pieces of film-history" such as "the Odessa Steps sequence [in *Battleship Potemkin*], the shower assault in *Psycho*, [and] the opening and closing carnage of *The Wild Bunch*" as possible influences on contemporary film construction techniques.[4] Bordwell does note that one broad result of these stylistic tendencies is "an aesthetic of broad but forceful effects" that produce a sense of "the mannerism of today's cinema, [which] asks its spectators . . . to revel in still more flamboyant displays of technique. . . . Techniques which 1940s directors reserved for moments of shock and suspense are the stuff of normal scenes today."[5] Yet he does not consider whether these stylistic developments make for effective film art. Apart from observations about which directors most prominently or most effectively use particular techniques, Bordwell offers not a single aesthetic, evaluative judgment about either any individual films or the artistic achievements enabled by contemporary developments in style as a whole.

Overall, a principal aesthetic result of the prominent use of techniques of intensified continuity, especially when coupled with increasing use of CGI, where photographic exploration of individualized faces, gaits, and landscapes is impossible, has been what Willam Rothman and Marian Keane call the manifestation in big-budget, commercial film of "film's growing doubt of its ability to allow the world to exhibit itself."[6] In intensified continuity film construction, filmmakers, both responding to and shaping audience expectations and technical possibilities alike, seem no longer to take an interest in the camera's possibility of discovering meaning in following more prosaic actions, conversations, demeanors, and scenes of experience.

Meanwhile, mostly outside Hollywood, and mostly outside the United States, photographic exploration of the world coupled with a largely realist plot and continuity editing has yielded some important artistic achievements, even while some of the impulses toward big-budget, blockbuster filmmaking are also in place internationally (as in CGI-heavy Chinese *wuxia* films such as *Kung Fu Hustle* or Indian CGI-heavy sci-fi epics such as *Kalki 2898 AD*). Here I am thinking of Abbas Kiarostami's *Koker Trilogy*, Alfonso Cuarón's *Roma*, and Pedro Almodóvar's *Pain and Glory*. (*Roma* and *Pain and Glory* were shot digitally, not using filmstock, but nonetheless photographically.) Though these films contradict Cavell's worry that serious film has collapsed into esoteric modernisms and trivial entertainments, it is also noteworthy that the instances and forms of heroism on which they focus photographically and by using continuity editing are not found in the United States and do not involve the figures of the Western hero, the detective, or the leading man or woman in a heterosexual romance with traditional gender roles.[7] These striking artistic successes each in one way or another reanimate in one way or another the Romantic trope of recovering a meaningful relation to a rural-agricultural past from within otherwise contested and disorganized modern urban and commercial life. Cavell's deeper worry that we in the industrial-commercial West, where agricultural life is now less the product of manual labor, have somehow lost our grips on social roles worth inhabiting and on ways of working for the world's good may be well placed.

Why this deeper worry matters to Cavell, apart from any merely personal nostalgia, and why it should matter to us, is a function of how photographically produced, realist, continuity-edited films once successfully answered— for both high critical and mass audiences simultaneously—to a wish to find meaning in the world or to find the world good enough to live in. The depth and generality of the worry about meaning to which popular American movies once upon a time answered, according to Cavell, is evident in a pair of remarks he offers about the condition of selfhood in modernity—that is, the condition of human beings with distinctive powers of reflection, comparison, and responsiveness to reasons. Such beings, Cavell finds, live with

the human wish, intensifying in the West since the Reformation, to escape subjectivity and metaphysical isolation—a wish for the power to reach this

world, having for so long tried, at last hopelessly, to manifest fidelity to another. (WV, 21)

This is to say that once upon a time—perhaps roughly between the Council
of Nicea in 325 CE and Luther's posting of the *Ninety-five Theses* in 1517—at
least many human beings lived with and according to a sense of how best to
exercise their distinctively human powers: namely by responding to God's
grace and providence, thence acting on earth so as to prepare for an after-
life. Arguably this thought misascribes a simple unity to medieval thought
and life, which was in fact more polyglot, polytheological, and polypractical
than the image of lived unity under a Christian script suggests. In *The Cheese
and the Worms*,[8] for example, Carlo Ginzburg memorably traces syncre-
tistic complexities of peasant life and thought in northern Italy from 1532
to 1539. Yet the case he analyzes occurs after 1517 (though there are surely
similar cases earlier); the central figure, Menocchio, argued that his cosmo-
logical and theological beliefs were consistent with Christianity; and the religious authorities, who sent him off only with a warning to change his ways,
seem not to have been particularly shaken by Menocchio's professions. In
general, that most or many people in the West took Christian religious authority seriously for a millennium or so, and that advanced intellectuals
thought and argued within the framework of Christianity about the correct
uses of human powers, taking that overall framework for granted, seems beyond reasonable doubt. Pierre Hadot aptly argues that Christian medieval
philosophy from Augustine through at least the tenth century CE inherited
and continued the ancient practice of *philosophia* as spiritual exercises,
centering on reflective training in right practices. Only in the late medieval period in the thirteenth and fourteenth centuries CE, as philosophy
became the handmaiden of abstract theology, did intellectual activity shift
away from being *praxis*-centered and toward *theoria*—a development on
which the seal was finally put by Descartes and the rise of modern scientific
theory.[9]

For a variety of interrelated reasons, including at least urbanization,
increased technological powers, wider trading practices, and human
interests in each of these things, the medieval Christian theological-practical
consensus broke down. In Cavell's terms, manifesting fidelity to another
world via working, waiting, praying, and acts of charity no longer made
as much practical sense as doing other things. But this meant that the central routes for the actualization of distinctively human powers of reflection,

comparison, and responsiveness to reasons were no longer clear in practice. Shakespeare's tragedies, above all *Hamlet* (1599–1601) with its governing crisis of broken paternal, political, and religious authority, memorably register this development, as does Descartes in the 1640s, with his turn away from what he sneeringly calls "letters" and "the schools" and toward intellectual meditation and intellect-guided scientific theory.[10] Our sense of our possession of distinctive human powers to be put to use in practice has come apart from the ways of the world. As Robert B. Pippin aptly remarks, "There is . . . throughout [Cavell's] film books and articles . . . an inherent and sometimes explicit theory of Western modernity, and what such modernization means for us, does to us, psychologically. It largely calls us away from ourselves, makes us forget what we somehow know, encourages a kind of willed thoughtlessness,"[11] as we are left adrift and without orientation in practice.[12]

Or as Cavell himself puts it, "At some point the unhinging of our consciousness from the world interposed our subjectivity between us and our presentness to the world. Then our subjectivity became what is present to us, individuality became isolation" (WV, 22). Having fallen out of engagement with immediately credible, religiously conceived practices of meaning-making, human beings are now left with a sense of their powers and point of view as internal to them and as having problematic, unclear worldly vehicles of expression and ratification, if any. As Cavell remarks in *Disowning Knowledge*, "The issue is no longer, or not alone, as with earlier skepticism, how to conduct oneself best in an uncertain world; the issue suggested is how to live at all in a groundless world. Our skepticism is now a function of our illimitable desire" (DK, 3). Both epistemological skepticism and its realist antagonist double are the registering in reflection of this social fact: the first seeking self-certainty within and in freedom from all entanglements with an unsatisfying public practical world, the second by seeking connection to a world that it begins by taking as lost.

In *The Claim of Reason*, Cavell traces a sense of the unhinging of consciousness from the world to

an experience which I described as one of being sealed off from the world, within the round of one's own experiences, as one of looking at the world as one object ("outside of us"). . . . It is as though, deprived of the ordinary forms of life in which that connection is, and is alone, secured, he [the skeptic together with his realist antagonist and double] is trying to reestablish it in his immediate consciousness, then and there. (CR, 238)

The suggestion I am now adding or making more explicit is that this experience of feeling oneself to be sealed off from the world arises when ordinary forms of life are no longer evidently serving as vehicles for the expression and ratification of distinctively human powers. When that happens, both objects and other people become, as it were, dead for us, and we feel ourselves to be sealed within the circle of what we now take to be private, inner experiences. This feeling has, perhaps, a particular prominence in the modern period, with its losses of paternal, political, and religious authority, and it is perhaps experienced more frequently and intensely by reflective intellectuals than by those forced by the press of circumstances into daily labor and care. No wonder, too, that this feeling is most intensely experienced by adolescents, who have not yet found their ways into satisfying practices, social, sexual, and economic. But it might happen to anyone at any time, so that there is a kind of truth of skepticism as something other than what Richard Rorty jocularly dismisses as a set of "temporary, historically conditioned little frenzies."[13] What Cavell calls "the attempt to convert the human condition, the condition of humanity, into an intellectual difficulty, a riddle" (CR, 493), may happen to anyone when practices as vehicles of distinctive human powers have foundered or seem unavailable. And once this attempt is made—once the problem of skepticism about both the external world and other minds, posed from within an experience of being sealed off, has been raised—then there is no route back to the world or to others through intellectual argument. Acknowledgment of the value of some forms of practice and relationship into which one has somehow stumbled, against the grain of one's self-centered, intellect-driven will and choices, is the only way out. This is the major line of argument in Cavell's *Pursuits of Happiness*, clearest in the case of *It Happened One Night*.

For Cavell, then, it is not intellectual argument, but rather doing something and accepting something in an original way (the old ways having lost their power)—a blend of action, acknowledgment, and art—that is of central importance for the achievement of selfhood.

> . . . Apart from the wish for selfhood (hence the always simultaneous granting of otherness as well), I do not understand the value of art. Apart from this wish and its achievement, art is exhibition. (WV, 22)

The exemplarily successful artist is for Cavell the principal vehicle for the original, intelligible manifestation and ratification of the powers of subjectivity in the world, thus overcoming isolation and a sense of human powers frozen within. This is a major line of thinking, too, in Cavell's "Aesthetic Problems of Modern Philosophy," where we are told that "the problem of the critic, as of the artist, is not to discount his subjectivity but to include it; not to overcome it in agreement, but to master it in exemplary ways"—to show that the trick of the embodiment of subjectivity in worldly practices in original and ratifiable ways can be done. Showing that, Cavell adds, is the source of "our gratitude" for art (MWM, 94).

Mannerism, or otherwise foregrounding technique and point of view over the original and ratifiable rendering of lived content within worldly practice, will not succeed at this trick. In calling attention to the aesthetic surface and to the idiosyncratic point of view that produced it, rather than inviting the audience into a working-through of shared lived experience, it amounts to "the sealing of the self's fate by theatricalizing it" (WV, 22). An idiosyncratic performance of isolated subjectivity displaces exemplary responsiveness to and within the world.

Nor is the attempt to enact pure impersonality (if that is even possible) a solution. Consider 'purely' realistic video footage produced photograph-ically via a convenience store surveillance monitor. While it will accurately capture the spatiotemporal locations of objects and people from a fixed viewpoint across specific times without evident stylization, it will scarcely (except by an extraordinary accident) capture enactments of subjectivity that make human powers of meaning-making newly evident in distinctive performances. Meaning cannot be discerned in action in the world—either in the actions of characters or in the actions of artists—when there are no ar-tistically presented characters (fictional or historical) bound to emplotment and where actions are free of significant expressive content.

In place of either literalism or modernist, hyper-self-conscious directo-rial display, what is needed is a form of address to "the wish to act without performing, . . . allow[ing] the self to exhibit itself without the self's interven-tion" (WV, 159). This can happen on film when the camera tracks actors who seem fully to incarnate their characters, who seem less, as Cavell puts it, to work themselves into a role, as a stage actor does, than to take their roles upon themselves, incarnating the character in themselves as a subject of the camera's study, especially in close-ups or medium-range shots (WV, 27–8). Sometimes, at least, the human subjects of the camera's photographic study can seem "to act without performing, to allow action all and only the significance of its specific traces" (WV, 153), as, for example, in the particular look on Cary Grant/Jerry

Warriner's face as he seats himself to enjoy the fancy dancing of Lucy/Irene Dunne with Dan Leeson/Ralph Bellamy (*The Awful Truth*, 1937), or in John Wayne's gait, or in Greta Garbo's laugh. It is crucial to how films make meaning that it is equally natural to talk of the actor's doings as of the character's and that we sometimes identify films as Katherine Hepburn or Humphrey Bogart films. Finding meaning in actions unfreighted or less freighted by theatrical experience as well as in sheer looks, gaits, or bearings can happen and has happened, when moviemakers have found appropriate subjects (individual and thematic) and trusted the ability of the camera to take them in from the world, as they are in the world. And for things really to go well—for the power of film as a medium and form of art fully to address the plights of isolated subjectivities and the possibilities of finding meaning in the world—both of these things have to happen: the filmmaker's willed, emplotted, and stylized forms of photographic attention answering to the human subject's filmable specificities of look, manner, and action, and vice versa.

In the absence of this achievement of filmic art, or like achievements in the other arts where they are possible, or like achievements in the rest of life, which is often saturated with dull routine in the industrial-commercial world, we run the risk, Cavell suggests, of "forfeiting [our] ... humanity ... to taste, to appetite, to irony, to boredom, to incitement, to halfhearted skepticism, to halfhearted belief, to scorn of an unknown past, to the mercy of an unchecked future" (WV, 123)—to anything that might fill up the empty space left by meaning-making unachieved.

Movies offered a special possibility of making meaning artistically and against the grain of the rest of life by combining a photographic basis with the projection and screening of the things of the world in motion, especially human beings. "Movies from their beginning," Cavell writes, "avoided (I do not say answered) modernism's perplexities of consciousness, its absolute condemnation to seriousness. Media based upon successions of automatic world projections do not, for example, have to establish presentness to and of the world: the world is there" (WV, 118), on the screen. "They do not have to deny or confront their audiences: they [their audiences] are screened" (WV, 118), so that there is no possibility or risk of either pandering in live performance or (mostly, when things go well enough) of impelling the audience to ask why they are there at all in front of this object, why it is somehow special. The audience is just there to see the world screened, and they see an instance of a film, not an object. Movies are, as Cavell puts it, "not exhibited (or performed), but distributed and screened and viewed" (WV, 122).

For a major stretch of film's history as a form of art, say from Griffith (ignoring the difficulties of *Birth of a Nation*) and Chaplin to Billy Wilder and Elia Kazan, people—high audiences and low alike—just did watch the screened world, without falling much into modernist agonies of self-consciousness about their presence in viewing sparked by modernist agonies of the filmic surface. This fact was neither inevitable nor necessary. It rests, rather, on a discovery of how to use sequences of automatic world projections narratively in ways that are immediately compelling, a discovery enabled but not simply caused by the photographic basis of the movies. Cavell is right that his—and our—relation to movies no longer has this kind of naturalness so readily. But given that this relation of natural absorption in successions of automatic world projections was prominent for so long, it makes sense to ask how the discovery was made: what filmic techniques it involved (photography, including close-ups; continuity editing; the uses of individualities or stars and of types drawn from vaudeville and common life). "My business," Cavell tells us, "is to think out the causes of my consciousness of films as it stands" (WV, 12), both in its history of natural absorption and in its present, more troubled relation to its objects. So *The World Viewed*, while it has much to say about the photographic basis of film as such, is oriented fundamentally around the experience of film and around the discoveries and decisions made by filmmakers in manipulating that photographic basis that produced that natural absorption. That is to say, *The World Viewed* is ultimately a work of phenomenology, asking what has gone on in the experience of film at its best and what has now become of that experience. Here, as Rothman and Keane put it, *The World Viewed* carries out an "investigation of its author's subjectivity," where "coming to know what films are—what film is—is inseparable from self-knowledge."[14] Like ordinary language philosophy, this phenomenological self-investigation can inform our attentions to our experiences and make them more fully meaningful to us. We can remember films we have seen through Cavell's writing about them and thus come to heightened appreciations of both these films themselves and the experiences they present. "The memoir [Cavell] . . . has composed," Rothman and Keane observe, "is an account of the conditions that were satisfied by movies and moviegoing for all who enjoyed the relation to movies he enjoyed."[15] At its deepest level, Cavell's thought about this experience is that film, when it works, presents "a world complete without me which is [also] present to me" and that it "affirm[s] that the world is coherent without me" (WV, 160), which is to say that it—both nature and how people dwell, live, and work within it—is not irredeemably hostile to subjectivity, subjectivity not irredeemably isolated and interiorized. Meaningful action in the world is possible after all. There, both on the screen and in the real world, in Astaire's dancing, Grant's carriage, Stanwyck's wit, and Hepburn's verve, as well as in the guided camera's attentions to such things, is meaning-making taking place, subjectivity overcoming isolation, there in the world to be seen.

II

Is film now central and pre-eminent among the modern arts in showing, for many, that the achievement of selfhood, albeit with limits, is significantly possible in the contemporary world? Was it ever thus central and pre-eminent? First, we should not scant whatever achievements of selfhood—whatever satisfying actualizations and ratifications of distinctively human powers—are available elsewhere, in other forms of practice. Surely for many, for most, family life and, say, sports or games or friendship are more important and more readily available and more continuously satisfying in ways that are not purely hedonic than the experience of movies. At the same time, there is often enough a need for successfully stylized, original individuality within these other practices, to the extent, at least, that these practices have themselves become routinized, commercialized, and dominated by instrumental reason, in such a way that their lives as vehicles of the actualization of distinctively human powers are threatened, qualified, or undermined. One might then need and find in art models of originality in attentiveness, style, and bearing that can be brought to bear within the rest of life, *mutatis mutandis.*[16] Recall Jean-Paul Belmondo/Michel in *Breathless* (1960) testing his imitations of Bogart in front of a mirror.

Second, I share Cavell's sense that movies from roughly 1915 or 1920 to roughly 1960 or 1965 or 1975 offered absorbing models for the achievement of selfhood that were powerful for both mass audiences and reflective intellectuals. Following Cavell, I have suggested that readiness for absorption in the types and individualities of these films broke down not only in response to incursions of modernist and then mannerist technique, but also and more deeply because we have lost our grips on the sorts of social roles worth inhabiting that those types and individualities incarnated.[17] Finally, I have pointed to some films made outside the Hollywood system that successfully solicit and reward absorbed viewing by reactivating a central

Romantic trope: Kiarostami, Cuarón, and Almodóvar. But what about contemporary Hollywood films? While there are some valuable entertainments, I nonetheless have difficulty yielding to and being rewarded by Hollywood movies in ways that I once did in relation to the films of Capra, Hawks, Ford, and Hitchcock. The closest analogues to those experiences that are provided by recent films are for me *Moonrise Kingdom* (2012) and *Little Women* (2019).[18] *Moonrise Kingdom*, however, while beautifully shot and supported by a beautiful score, both remains in the registers of fantasy and childhood and is perhaps too ready to call attention to its contrivances of design.

Little Women is a more interesting case. The film is brilliant in revising the ending of the narrative, showing Jo—the soon-to-be author we are following—acceding to a publisher's pressure to marry off her heroine—Jo in the autobiographical novel she is writing—to Professor Baehr in return for retaining the book's copyright and for a greater percentage of the book's profits, then cutting back to the actual Jo, still unmarried, now a bestselling author, and happily running a school. As the film's director and writer Greta Gerwig explains,

> Part of what I wanted to do was 150 years later give her [Jo] an ending she [Alcott] might have liked. I thought if we can't do this now then we've really made no progress and we should all hang our heads (laughs). But the structure truly came out of wanting to introduce this layer of authorship everywhere in it, how we author our lives even if we're not writers and how we kind of tell and retell the story of how we become who we are.[19]

Notably, this ending distinctively refigures or finds an available social role that is satisfying, original, and ratifiable, with the deliberately unmarried woman happy and admired in life and with work as a teacher and writer displacing the figure of the married woman. (Or does the figure of the married woman—the Jo of the published novel—still somehow linger in our imaginations, too?) It is an exemplary instance of using the camera to track a new type of individuality, with her subjectivity well housed in worldly practice. It takes the value of contextually situated and contextually specific self-authorship seriously as achievable in the world.

Can this exemplary instance within contemporary Hollywood practice be taken up and productively varied and developed by further filmmakers? Will the deliberately unmarried woman-as-author become a type? Will Saoirse Ronan, the primary human subject of the camera's study, become a filmic individuality, a star, so that we talk of Saoirse Ronan films in the way we once talked of Katherine Hepburn films? Time will tell, as filmmakers do their work and as audiences respond with absorption or fail to. Given the politics of the moment, however, there is good reason to wonder whether we will be able to recover a shared, livable sense that human beings "doing the work of the world together are working for the world's good, or that if they are working for the world's harm they may be stopped" (WV, 62). With regard to routes of meaningful practice available to occupants of social roles, we seem at present to have some trouble with the thought there is *a* world that we share and that is such that any commitments enacted within it might win general allegiance. (Notably, *Little Women* is set in the Civil War and post-Civil War New England past.) We might, however, in the meantime of our uncertain present, nonetheless trust the achievements of some classical Hollywood films, of Kiarostami, Cuarón, Almodóvar and some others outside the Hollywood system, of some television series, and of Gerwig, as we wait to see what time will tell about our possibilities of meaningful life and art.

12

Cavell as Halted Traveler

The Experience of Music

Early on in *Here and There*, in the Prologue entitled "A Site for Philosophy" and originally delivered as an address on "the place of visual art" at Harvard and, more broadly, in the university in general, Cavell observes that, as he sees things, "there is an internal relation between philosophy and sites or spaces that is mostly unthematized in philosophy" (HT, 14, 16). This lack of attention to specific sites (and experiences in them) that Cavell notes is at least clòse to non-accidental in relation to more or less typical conceptions of philosophy. All but constitutively, philosophy seeks timeless answers to timeless questions: what are knowledge and justification?; what is the fundamental nature of reality?; what is justice?; what is virtue? These are typically taken to be questions that might be raised by anyone at any time, and satisfactory answers must take the form of necessary truths, invariable across all contingencies of time, place, culture, or history. In challenging this typical conception of philosophy, then, Cavell has evidently set himself a monumental task of calling philosophy back to its true nature as a kind of open-ended, specifically situated criticism of important commitments that have somehow fallen into question for someone in a particular time and place. His effort must be to awaken philosophy and philosophers, or anyone who might seek justification for a fundamental commitment, from an enchanting dream or nightmare (or both) of absolute authority, freed of anything personal, local, or contingent.

If the relation between philosophy and occasioning sites that Cavell proposes is generally unthematized in philosophy, however, it is far from unthematized elsewhere. As Geoffrey Hartman has shown at length, the *topos* of the halted traveler—arrested in a specific spot of time and place and thereby given over to thought—is central to Wordsworth's poetry.[1] As Hartman puts it, Wordsworth's poetry is typically precipitated (though not yet completed, since completion requires "emotion recollected in tranquility"[2]) when "what others might have passed by produces a strong

Anticipations of Freedom. Richard Eldridge, Oxford University Press. © Richard Eldridge 2026.
DOI: 10.1093/9780197841785.003.0016

emotional response in him."[3] The strong responses in question are not simply materially caused by the scene of experience, but instead are the joint product of the scene and the poet's attentive mind, "which actively desires the inauguration of a totally new epoch"[4] or new joint habits of thought, feeling, and activity wherein things will at last make sense and significant reconciliation with others and with oneself is possible. These responses typically alternate between wild hope in a prospective, transfigurative apocalypse, promised by a sublime, fearful moment of experience, but haunted, too, by a sense of its unshareability, hence a sense also of its risk of madness, and calm rebinding to the earth and to what is common, or what Hartman calls *akedah*: "a soul," as Hartman puts it, "has to renaturalize itself"[5] in order to lead a life on earth with others in time, as opposed to escaping into empyrean but potentially empty liberation.[6] The body of Wordsworth's poetry as a whole and in particular *The Prelude* presents "no argument [for a settled conclusion] but a vacillation between doubt and faith."[7] In seeking justified reconciliation with and within a radically new form of earthly life, Wordsworth "carried the Puritan quest for evidences of election into the most ordinary emotional contexts"[8] and gave expression to the experience of that quest as unconcluded rather than resolving it under any settled doctrine.

Cavell gives frequent expression to a similar desire or ambition for radical transfiguration, both individual and cultural, alternating with a competing desire for settlement with and within the common. The genius of Austin's practice of ordinary language philosophy, as Cavell saw it, was to answer to both desires, as one could speak (and hear) freely and intelligibly, in redemptive escape from conceptual confusion, while also remaining within the sways of the common. The limitation of that practice was its ultimate failure to move beyond particular ranges and construals of examples (mistakes vs. accidents; succumbing to temptation vs. losing control of oneself) in a way that quieted the desire for systematic theory. The great discovery of *The Claim of Reason* is that rehearsing criteria of identity does not settle questions of existence, so that *if* questions of existence (of the world, of the minds of others) have to be raised (from within a prior experience of alienation), *then* they cannot be settled by the procedures of ordinary language philosophy: the skeptic is equally a master of ordinary language, and *if you have to ask* whether the occluded side of an object is *really, absolutely there beyond all possible doubt*, then the honest answer is that you don't know, not absolutely. "The human creature's basis in the world as a whole, its relation to the world, is not that of knowing, anyway not what we think of as knowing"

(CR, 241), and if trust in the world and in others in it is lost (perhaps partly through one's misbegotten but natural and motivated directions of desire, ambition, and effort), then it is by no means clear how it can be recovered. The force of appeals to the ordinary is inadequate to undo fundamental distortions of ambition and desire.

In *Here and There*, Cavell expresses a joint sense of a continuing desire for philosophy—that is, for its putative achievement of timeless and impersonal authority—and of the impossibility of satisfying this desire, insofar as one remains always belated and self-opaque in coming to one's words, which are in shifting circulation within the common. "The arrogance of philosophy is to show that I can speak universally, for everyone. The confidence of psychoanalysis is to show that I do not so much as speak for myself" (HT, 145). Here Cavell finds himself, and (many or most modern) human subjects as such, fated to live between and with both this arrogance (in undertaking to speak for everyone) and this confidence (in psychoanalytic doubt).

How, then, might this fate be lived with aptly? In a central leitmotif that runs throughout both *Here and There* and his work as a whole, Cavell finds some materials for an answer in the experience of music, which offers something like the satisfaction of the ambition of philosophy for full, grounded, confidence in and cathexis to activities under commitments, coupled with a registration of finitude and incompleteness. As Cavell remarks in a crucial passage about the course of his life with philosophy:

> While I have written very little explicitly about music over the ensuing decades [since . . .] I graduated with a major in music from the University of California at Berkeley [in 1946, . . .] I have known for most of that time that something I have demanded from philosophy was an understanding precisely of what I had sought in music, and in the understanding of music, of what demanded that reclamation of experience, of the capacity for being moved, which called out for, and sustained, an accounting as lucid as the music I loved. (HT, 260)

This crucial passage is difficult both conceptually and grammatically, and it is worth some extended paraphrase. Cavell had sought something in music. Evidently enough, he had frequently enough found it, had found his experience in general reclaimed (from dullness, lack of meaningful presence) by the experience and understanding of music as a temporally unfolding order that moved him and that engaged both his intellect and his ear (and his body) in what he was doing (playing or listening). Initially, at least, this experience, while entrancing, was also obscure—as though Cavell himself were a Wordsworthian halted traveler, stopped in his otherwise wandering through life by an overwhelming experience of unfolding sound that in its suddenness and force demanded that it be reflected on, tested, and worked through. "What," Cavell must have asked himself, "has just happened to me? What does it mean? Is it trustworthy? Is it repeatable and shareable? Or am I mad or otherwise the victim of an unintelligible fit of transport?"[9] He turned to philosophy in hopes of carrying out this working-through and of finding a language for this experience and assessing its value. In seeking that understanding of music, he hoped further to understand what in life otherwise—a matter of idleness, drift, and lack of orientation (such as he may have experienced in breaking off from the formal study of music at Juilliard in New York in 1947)—demanded the compensations and redemptions that musical experience afforded. "What is (my) life, such that it needs music in order for me to bear it?" And the account of this would, itself, have to be as lucid—that is, as convincing, continuously absorbing, and moving—as the experience of music itself. Hence the philosophical account of music would have to have something like distinctively musical structure. To sum up schematically:

1. Cavell sought and found in music (both playing it and understanding it) an overwhelming but obscure and fearful experience of transfigurative, engaged, absorption and meaningfulness.
2. He turned to philosophy in order to work through, understand, and assess this experience.
3. In doing so, he remained in the grip of the thought that the account he sought must be as entrancing and nonartificial—as lucid—as the experience of music itself, must, in effect, itself be musical.[10]

In short, Cavell takes music to provide "a figure of the mind in its most perfected relation to itself, or to its wishes for itself" (HT, 260–1), and philosophy is to parse that figure conceptually, but without dominating it, that is, while itself repeating, echoing, or participating in that figure.

An obvious question to ask is *how* music works as a figure of the mind in its most perfected relation to itself. (Answering this will require the philosophico-musical parsing of that figure.) In the essay "An Understanding with Music," the title of which implies all of understanding music (what it is, how it works, why we have it), coming to terms with one's experience of it (how it affects one, working through that arresting experience), and doing all this in a musical way, Cavell comments on a passage from Lévi-Strauss' *Introduction to a Science of Mythology*, volume four, as cited by the French music theorist Michel Poizat in his book *The Angel's Cry*. Here is the passage from Lévi-Strauss:

> There would be no music if language had not preceded it and if music did not continue to depend on it, as it were, through a privative connection. Music is language without meaning: this being so, it is understandable that the listener, who is first and foremost a subject with the gift of speech, should feel himself irresistibly compelled to make up for the absent sense, just as someone who has lost a limb imagines that he still possesses it through the sensations present in the stump. (HT, 251)

Cavell then further cites Poizat's own comment on this passage: "Is it perhaps this primordial act of separation that opera speaks of, letting us know that it is paid for with suffering? And is it perhaps in the nostalgia for a paradisiacal unity of preseparation that the opera lover's ecstasy resides?" (HT, 251, citing Poizat).

What guides Cavell's attention here is the more or less psychoanalytic idea that the experience of music provides the individuated subject (the subject with the gift of speech) with a kind of reminder of or reconnection to a lost unity, insofar as the listening or playing subject is caught up in and cathected to the musical development, together with the critical sense (registered in the development's drive toward its final cadence, where it will break off) that one remains nonetheless a finite, individuated subject. Cavell remarks in particular that:

> Poizat's hypothesis of a primordial connection relies elsewhere than evidence [from human prehistory] for its conviction, presumably upon a more or less unspoken theory of the psychic development of singing as stretching between speech and the cry, under the demand for pleasure and for an enjoyment beyond pleasure, linked with the identification of this beyond in moments across the history of opera. (HT, 251)

This suggests that singing, or the hearing of singing in certain high moments in opera, both responds to and satisfies that demand for an enjoyment beyond pleasure in a specifically bounded way. In doing so, it makes available to the singer or hearer a partially reparative all but re-connection to what Julia Kristeva has identified as the semiotic: the register of experience that is prior to ego individuation and that is marked by bodily emotional involvement and responsiveness to a maternal (not quite) other, where discursive structure is absent and where rhythm and melodic contour predominate and support diffuse *jouissance*, as opposed to the pleasurable satisfaction of a discretely articulated desire.[11] This register of experience is prior to the symbolic, understood as the register of experience of the now individuated, discursively structured ego, with its now distinct plans, goals, and specified pleasures. That something like this partially reparative experience is what Cavell has in mind as afforded by music is evident in his going on to observe that Poizat's account of "the cry as the epitome of opera's expressiveness, the final anguish that transcends both language and music to reach an expression of pure voice," recalls Nietzsche's account in *The Birth of Tragedy* of "the cry as the suffering of individuation, that is of finite existence, of which music allows the expression, as if we should, without such expression, suffocate from our words, buried alive" (HT, 252). Here the thought is that without the cry that expresses the suffering of individuation—the cry that resummons pre-individuative libidinal energies and investments that are cathected to rhythm and melody—our words threaten to become not ours, less than fully felt and meant, or things that suffocate us under the demands of conformity.[12] In moving into song, with words, but remaining shaped as a melodic contour of passion, an operatic aria simultaneously recovers and liberates original libidinal energies and registers of experience, while also re-enacting and compensating for their loss via conventionalization and submission to language and authority. In this way, it functions as a vehicle for becoming more present as a distinctive individual both to oneself and to others in one's words and life. It brings remnants of originary libidinal pre-ego identity into the ambit of conventionalized expression. This is the source of its redemptive power. And the same thing is true of purely instrumental melodic and harmonic development. Or, as Cavell puts it, "one might see the possibility of understanding without [compositional, linguistic] meaning," in cathexis to a melodic contour of passion or to other forms of musical development that gesture toward but exceed linguistic meaning—Lévi- Strauss' "privative connection"—"as redemptive, like losing one's chains" (HT, 253),[13] in an experience of what one might call meaning for the subject beyond (linguistic) meaning. "We could say that the instance of music defeats the idea of a certain *theory* of meaning, the one Wittgenstein seeks to defeat as expressed in the opening paragraph of *Philosophical Investigations*, according to which every word has a meaning which is the object it refers to" (HT, 253). Wittgenstein himself once remarked "[i]t is impossible for me to say in my book one word about all that music has meant to me in my life. How then can I hope to be understood?"[14]

Notably, however, cathexis to musical development—feeling one's powers of thought and feeling wedded to the course and cadencing of the music—provides no possibility of full, enduring escape from self-doubt and the feelings of being hostage to conventions and sealed within one's privacy. Any piece of music with hearable development[15] comes to an end, its final cadence achieved. After that, the rest is silence, at least until a new piece occupies one's attention. In the intervals that constitute the bulk of anyone's life, one will again be within the orbits of language and discursively structured experience and activity, and one will again face whatever problems of distance and difference from others and of personally felt inexpressiveness and isolation that made the experience of music so absorbing and redemptive. Can that experience, in its particular guided raptures, be trusted? Which, if any, others share it? What significance, if any, does it have for the rest of life, apart from being a bounded compensation? Nor is this kind of cathexis to development that affords a distinct, intense mode of experience limited to music. Cavell wonders how it is that the arts in general "show, or remind us, or expand our horizons, so that we see, or remember, or learn what truly matters to us?—as though without them we build our knowledge of our place in the world on the basis of sensory deprivation, starving our desires" (HT, 277). There is sometimes, as in lyric poetry, or in richly attentive conversation, or in following the development of a movie, what Cavell calls "the music of [. . .] the dense contexts in which speech makes its specific sense" (HT, 277). Theoretically minded, arts- and music-scanting philosophers in pursuit of a guiding *doxa* arrived at and sustained on the basis of deductive argument, are, Cavell claims, characteristically deaf to and unable to enter into this kind of music of and in speech. Or as Cavell puts the thought that he finds in Wittgenstein: "Wittgenstein takes philosophers, succumbing to the temptation to metaphysics or false transcendence or skepticism, to torture human speech, to madden human encounter, unable or unwilling to imagine, to participate in" that kind of musical speech and mutual sense-making (HT, 277). One way out of this self-torture is then specifically to trust works of music and art along with intimate conversational life and experiences of them—to open oneself to their development, rather than standing on formulas that restrict significance to literalness—however one might manage that trust and however much these works and experiences remain bounded and their affordances remain less than fully sustainable.

Yet here too, trust proves less than perfectly sustainable, and when uncritical it verges on idolatry, which will not do as a mode of meaningful, individual life with others. One must also think and feel for oneself, actively engaging with what one encounters. As Cavell comments on Allan Bloom's dogmatic and thus misbegotten defense of the authority of classical texts:

> [T]he *distrust* of reading—[that is, of the authority of "mere letters," in comparison with the serious work of science and of "analyzing and solving problems"]—is half of the philosophical spirit. A devotion to thinking by reading—however great the books in question—will not count, in my corner of things, as a philosophical devotion, unless it knows at each moment how to distrust reading. (HT, 212)

It is ongoing interaction with others and with works of the various arts, involving both joint sense-making and critical engagement, both similarity and difference, both community and isolation, that is the genuine vehicle of fuller, more active life for a human subject.[16]

Achieving this fuller life is more a matter of imagination and investment as open-ended skills whose fit exercises blend responsiveness (taking seriously the commitments and feelings of others) and originality (having the courage of one's affections and aversions) than it is of living according to formula or rule. For Cavell, at least, there remains, always, "the unappeasable human dissatisfaction with each of its dispensations, the condition I called human restlessness" (HT, 285), as we find ourselves always moving into new regions of doubt and experience and self-assertion, whatever temporary absorptions we have achieved. Hence our lives remain marked by both "the torment in human restlessness [. . .] and [. . .] the dream of peace," as we remain in the grip both "of an urge to misunderstand" (and to mark out one's own way, leaving the work of music, or the work of art, or the metaphor or the other behind, going one's own way) and of the possibility "of understanding as knowing how to go on" (with them) (HT, 282).

In Book II of *The Prelude*, Wordsworth comes to articulate his sense that with the death of his mother just before his eighth birthday "The props of my affections were removed / [. . .] I was left alone / Seeking the visible world nor knowing why"[17] in continuing experiences of an ongoing lack of direction and investment in meaningful activity that might enable him to sustain a sense of the worth of his own life in a world with others. This sense of a lack of direction or orientation sharpened in him as a young adult into the sense that he might be "Unprofitably traveling toward the grave, / Like a false steward who hath much received /And renders nothing back,"[18] with his human powers of meaning-making and significant action blocked or stultified. Thus are we all, sooner or later, betimes cast into the world.

Yet Wordsworth retained a sense of the possibility of, and sometimes took himself to have achieved, "that peace / which passeth understanding," involving "the consciousness / Of [who one] is, habitually infused / Through every image and through every thought [. . .]: / Hence endless occupation for the Soul, / Discursive or intuitive / Hence cheerfulness for acts of daily life / Emotions which best foresight need not fear / Most worthy then of trust when most intense,"[19] as he found himself as a halted traveler first undergoing alternating moments of intense, calming absorption (*akedah*, the beautiful) and intense, unsettling disturbance (*apocalypse*, the sublime, the fearful) and then later working them through, articulating them—locating and assessing their places in his life—in reflection and in writing. As I have elsewhere put it, "[o]ur humanity, Wordsworth's example suggests, is lived out within [and amidst] these [experiences and] articulations, between the sublimities of partial transcendence into individual vision and the beauties of partial community in shared valuations and engagements."[20] Cavell's life and writing—his ongoing experiences of being stopped in various ways by works of music and art (and by others)—and his ongoing reflections on them confirm this suggestion. There are, always, occasioning circumstances for renewed reflection, "events of a life that turn its dedication toward philosophy" (PP, vii) *as* reflective criticism that courts transcendence and yet always founders—none of them more powerful for Cavell than the experience of music.

13

Cavell and Day for Night

I

Throughout his work on film Stanley Cavell is concerned with the relation between the ontology and construction techniques of photographically produced movies, on the one hand, and their uses within modern life, on the other. He focuses on how creative uses of photographically produced and projected moving images might help to further freer and more meaningful life. In doing so, he joins an ontology and technic of photographic movies to an account of human freedom, arguing that movies have been the major form of art in the twentieth century precisely by interrogating possibilities of free life. By focusing his critical attention on singular objects—giving readings of films that attract his interest rather than offering a systematic theory—he manages to avoid both dangerously authoritarian political utopianism and relapse into quietism and concentration only on the details of film construction.

In doing all this, Cavell works within a recognizably Hegelian tradition, according to which media of art become historically salient insofar as major works within them successfully exploit their distinctive material potentials technically and imaginatively in response to conditions of material and cultural life. Where for Hegel symbolic architecture, classical Greek sculpture, and post-medieval painting, music, and dramatic poetry were successively the most important forms of art for their epochs, for Cavell movies are the pre-eminent form of art of the twentieth century, uniquely suited in their material bases and technical possibilities to scrutinize possibilities of freedom for us.[1] Yet Cavell develops his argument without any Hegelian closure claims about the end of history or our arrival at final and complete self-understanding. The open form of critical-interrogative attention to life in Cavell's philosophical writing echoes and is enriched by the open forms of critical-interrogative attention to the works of art, especially films, that attract his interest.

Anticipations of Freedom. Richard Eldridge, Oxford University Press. © Richard Eldridge 2026.
DOI: 10.1093/9780197841785.003.0017

Cavell's distinctive mode of attention to film is rooted in his experience and practice of ordinary language philosophy. The central argument of his early essay "Aesthetic Problems of Modern Philosophy" is that traditional philosophy, in search of eternally true definitional formulas that specify essences, has collapsed into defensive and inattentive formula-mongering and that we would do better to try to find words for our difficult experiences—to try *to come to terms with them*—than either to look to a Platonic heaven above or to lapse into cynicism and despair. Undertaking this task of attention and articulation is exactly what Cavell takes to be the practice of ordinary language philosophy, a practice that he further analogizes to the practices of art criticism and of art.

> All the philosopher, this kind of philosopher, can do is to express, as fully as he can, his world, and attract our undivided attention to our own. . . . The problem of the critic, as of the artist [and the ordinary language philosopher], is not to discount his subjectivity, but to include it; not to overcome it in agreement, but to master it in exemplary ways. . . . [This achievement] is, with perhaps a slight shift of accent, what we hear recorded in the philosopher's claims about "what we say." (MWM, 96, 94)

Unsurprisingly, a direct echo of this characterization of ordinary language philosophy appears in the opening pages of *The World Viewed*, where Cavell characterizes his approach to the study of film. In choosing movies as the topic of a seminar in aesthetics, Cavell writes,

> [the] pedagogical advantages looked promising: everybody would have had memorable experiences of movies, conversation naturally developed around them, and the absence of an established canon of criticism would mean that we would be forced back upon a faithfulness to nothing but our experience and a wish to communicate it. (WV, xx)

In *The World Viewed*, and throughout Cavell's subsequent film analyses, the aim of faithfulness to one's experience and to becoming articulate about it is the uncovering or re-establishing of interest in that experience, thus overcoming boredom, isolation, and drift. For modern human beings in general, Cavell holds, art is [a] way of questioning [one's experience] without forfeiting it—to taste, to appetite, to irony, to boredom, to incitement, to halfhearted skepticism, to halfhearted belief, to scorn of an unknown past, to the mercy of an unchecked future. (WV, 123)

In the wake of the collapse of finding earthly life meaningful as a form of preparation for life eternal, modern human beings are prone, Cavell argues, to exactly these multiple forms of the forfeiting of experience to which art and especially photographically produced film then answer.

So far as photography satisfied a wish, it satisfied . . . the human wish, intensifying in the West since the Reformation, to escape subjectivity and metaphysical isolation—a wish for the power to reach this world, having for so long tried, at last hopelessly, to manifest fidelity to another. . . . At some point the unhinging of our consciousness from the world interposed our subjectivity between us and our presentness to the world. Then our subjectivity became what is present to us, individuality became isolation. (WV, 21, 22)[2]

Modernist painting at its best responded to this condition by avoiding all representation; it "overcame it by abstraction, abstracting us from the recognitions and entanglements and complicities and privileged appeals and protests which distracted us from one another and from the world we have constructed" (WV, 117), through the presentation of nonetheless fully meaningful, convincingly present objects that eased the burdens of subjectivity through absorption.

The ways of photography and film are different. In photographs and films, the world itself *is* present. "The reality in a photograph is present to me while I am not present to it" (WV, 23)[3] so that any burdens of response and complicity are lifted, since response is impossible. When the objects, scenes, and persons and their doings that have been photographically captured support continuing conviction in their meaningfulness as they unfold themselves on screen, what I can find is that "the world is coherent without me" (WV, 160)[4] and hence, at least partially and potentially, good enough to live in.

Of course not all movies achieve this presentation. The episodic or the mannerist or the sheerly flat are enemies of filmic art. Defeating them and achieving coherence will require appropriate framing, editing, emplotment, and so on, as well as the presentation of characters about whom we feel that they are "doing the work of the world together [and] for the world's good, or that if they are working for the world's harm they can be stopped" (WV, 62). Once upon a time, Cavell holds, perhaps in the wakes of the heroisms of the Depression and the Second World War, and via the reworking of the characterological conventions of romantic comedy and of the Western, it was easier to have this feeling than it is now.

Nor is there any wide political redemption in view. In one of the two genres that Cavell later takes up, the melodrama of the unknown woman, "a woman achieves existence (or fails to), or establishes her right to existence (or fails to), apart from or beyond satisfaction by marriage (of a certain kind)," where this achievement within apartness registers the standing fact "that our ordinary language and its representation of the world *can* be philosophically repudiated and that it is essential to our inheritance and mutual possession of language that this should be so" (CT 88, 89). Neither language nor other forms of shared practice are such that they could or should happily and continuously house everyone. Individuality will have its claims, sometimes against the ways of the world, and the truth of skepticism is that human beings will often enough be opaque to one another in practice if not in principle.[5] Even within the sunnier genre of the remarriage comedy, the happiness achieved by the couple comes essentially pairwise, as they achieve "purposefulness without purpose" (PH, 89)[6] in improvisation and acknowledgment, with each other but not with the world at large. This achievement retains political significance. It functions as a model for and a provocation to the achievement of "a more perfect union, . . . a perfected human community" (PH, 159) that nonetheless forever eludes full accomplishment. Uptake on this provocation is registered, for example, in the older married couple's uncomprehending approval (itself a metonym for the audience's) of the marriage of Ellie and Peter at the end of It Happened One Night, but political revolution is not forthcoming. The pursuit and promise of happiness in free and meaningful life remain open, but less than wholly fulfilled.

II

Cavell's analysis of the powers of photographic film is rich and balanced in blending ontological, axiological, technical, political, and critical considerations. It avoids both the Scylla of utopianism and the Charybdis of quietism. But is it still relevant to contemporary film experience and contemporary life? Writing in 1971, Cavell expresses more than a little doubt about whether photographic film can any longer hold and shape wide and serious attention. He reports his sense of a "loss of connection, [the] loss of conviction in . . . film's capacity to carry the world's presence," arising from a felt "draining from the original myths of film of their power to hold our conviction in film's characters" (WV, 131). The conventions of the Western (stoicism, male heroism, the legitimacy of displacing and slaughtering indigenous peoples) and of romantic comedy (dominant heterosexuality, authority coded masculine, allure coded feminine) have come to seem at best questionable and at worst despotic. In more recent years the technical conditions of film-viewing have changed, as films are frequently streamed on monitors or even cell phones to individuals or small groups rather than projected on giant screens before large audiences. The increasing use of special effects and CGI has pushed film toward spectacle (always a possibility for it) rather than the photographic exploration of reality. The availability of videos on TikTok and YouTube, where photographic art films share virtual space with commercials, TV clips, homemade uploads, and everything else, has undermined the distinctiveness of the experience of photographically produced narrative film. Add to all this the tendency under neoliberal market institutions to reduce all values to preferences, expressed in widespread activities of buying and selling things based only on likes and dislikes, with little reference to any objectively freer and more meaningful way of life, and the very idea of there being anything to learn about value can fall under suspicion. Identity politics and subjective preference (group or individual) undermine the project of moving toward a shared culture of freedom, meaning, and justice. Even the words "fair" and "unfair" come to be seen on all sides as subjectively deployed terms of praise and criticism within an unresolvable cultural warfare. Religion, even putatively ecumenicist religion, divides us more than it binds us to common possibilities and projects. Nihilism disguised by egoism threatens to be the order of the day. In this situation, does film have anything left to teach us? Is there even anything to be taught?

There is some hyperbole here, and our cultural situation is less than fully catastrophic. There have, after all, been gains, too, in the pluralization of legitimate identities and the undoing of misbegotten norms. But the directions of worry about both contemporary culture and the powers of art and film are real. Plausible address to them cannot come from either a fearful reversion to fundamentalism (an inverted utopianism) or simply letting a thousand flowers bloom (quietism). It will have to come instead from finding images of freedom from within our cultural situation and imaginatively envisioning and tentatively narrating potentially fruitful courses of development.

One way to scrutinize critically whether and to what extent this possibility remains alive for us is to consider a film, François Truffaut's 1973 *Day for Night* (*La Nuit américaine*) that itself addresses the topic of how a measure of meaning and satisfaction might be found within a common project, at least for a time, among people who are very different from each other and whose actions are pervasively hostage to ill fortune.

It is, of course, a movie about making a movie, in this case *Meet Pamela* (*Je vous présente Pamela*), in production at *Studios de la Victorine*, Nice. Within the film (*Day for Night*), the issue of the point or worth of making a movie is raised directly, when two German actresses, the sisters Greta and Diana, visit the film set (of *Meet Pamela*), accompanied by their agent. The agent reports that Greta has made a political film, while Diana has made an erotic one. He then asks the director Ferrand, "Why don't you make a political film? Why don't you make an erotic film?"[7] The implication or joke here is that the Germans, perhaps as a metaphor for heavy-handed philosophy, have mistaken images of what is important and fail to understand or appreciate art. Parallel to this, the question of the worth of any general course of action in life is raised directly when Joelle (Nathalie Baye), the assistant director, reacting to the news that the script girl Liliane (Dani) (and the girlfriend of Alphonse [Jean-Pierre Léaud], one of the leads) has run off with an English stuntman, thus threatening the production by provoking Alphonse's temporary disappearance, remarks, "I might leave a guy for a film, but I'd never leave a film for a guy."[8] What is worth doing and for what reasons are clearly at issue.

The idea for *Day for Night* emerges in part from one of Truffaut's interviews with Alfred Hitchcock.

F.T. It's often occurred to me that one might make a first-rate comedy on the making of a movie.

A.H. It's a pretty good idea, and the way I'd do it is to have everything take place inside a film studio. But the drama would not be in front of the camera, but off the set, between takes. The stars in the picture would be minor characters and the real heroes would be the extras. In this way you'd get a wonderful counterpoint between the banal story being filmed and the real drama that takes place off stage.[9]

In another interview about *Day for Night*, echoing Hitchcock's suggestion, Truffaut says that "In this film I wanted to show eight characters, because I think the script girl and the prop man are just as important as the
director."[10] In fact in *Day for Night*, the major stars of *Meet Pamela* are of
roughly equal importance with the members of the crew. The most significant characters who encounter one or another kind of crisis are the
lead actors of *Meet Pamela*—Julie (Jacqueline Bisset), Alphonse (Jean-
Pierre Léaud), Alexandre (Jean-Pierre Aumont), and Severine (Valentina
Cortese)—along with Liliane the script girl (Dani), the assistant director
Joelle (Nathalie Baye), the prop man Bernard (Bernard Ménez), and of
course the director Ferrand (François Truffaut). It is perhaps easy to conde-
scend to a film that is described on Wikipedia as a romantic comedy-drama
and to overlook the significance of the problems that trouble the making of
the film within a film: death, alcoholism, adultery, abandonment, and lack of
money (along with a refractory cat). It is, in contrast, say, to a Godard film, a
film with a strongly structured continuous narrative and governing question
("Will *Meet Pamela* get successfully made?"). It wears its issues lightly.[11] Yet
Truffaut had clearly been thinking about this material for some time. "I have
files," he reports,

> some of which go back 15 years. . . . In these 7 or 8 dossiers I have
> accumulated pieces of paper with bits of dialogue, a lot of newspaper arti-
> cles. A cutting from a 10 year old newspaper is among my files. A man pays
> a visit to his parents with a young wife. She runs off with her father-in-law.
> I put this situation in *Day for Night*. Besides this, I go to my office every day.
> I have a production company. I work like a bureaucrat.[12]

Thematically, the underlying issue is the existential one of whether, and,
if so, how, life can be worth living rather than something simply suffered in
silent despair. In a letter to Jean-Louis Bory written shortly after the completion of *Day for Night*, Truffaut confesses that "I pulled myself together
and came to terms with myself thanks to *La Nuit américaine* [*Day for Night*],
whose subject was, quite simply, my own reason for living. (You adore your
mother, I hate mine, even now that she's dead—how could we ever have any
two ideas in common?)"[13] As the critic Anne Gillian aptly notes, "At first sight,
this remark may seem peculiar in the way it links together cinema and motherhood, but in fact the connection is logical. Whether rightly or wrongly,
Truffaut attributed his state of malaise and the failure of his personal life to

the secret surrounding his birth."[14] (Truffaut did not learn the identity of his biological father until 1968, at age thirty-six, and he was passed about among various nannies and his grandmother up until age eight.) "In the absence of a harmonious emotional life, cinema became his 'reason for living.'"[15] As Gerald C. Wood puts it, *Day for Night* enacts

> Truffaut's commitment to art as a source of order and wholeness in the fragmented and chaotic ways of modern life. Truffaut finds in the artist's creation of form out of chaos an image of the integrity otherwise rarely experienced in the twentieth century. . . . [His] understanding of art in *Day for Night* is both more existential and more humanistic than Fellini's or Bergman's. He assumes, like the other filmmakers, the brokenness and absurdity of much of contemporary life—private and public—but is still able to see the imaginative act as a source of order in a chaotic world.[16]

Yet art is also neither a full solution to the problems of life nor a replacement for it. In the Foreword to the published script of *Day for Night*, Truffaut himself points to the fact that "*Day for Night* revolves around one central question: 'Are films superior to life?' It gives no definite answer. For there can be none. No more than there can be to that other equally persistent question: 'Are books superior to films? One might just as well ask a child which parent he prefers!"[17] One has to learn to love and to live with both films and life (as with two parents), so far as possible, and to see how they might mutually enrich each other (like books and movies), instead of escaping from one into the other.

The cross-fertilization of art and life is extended through allusions to other films that appear in both *Meet Pamela* and the filmic surface of *Day for Night*.

> Immediately before the troupe leaves [to shoot the crash scene on exterior location], Truffaut has Jean-Pierre Léaud call down to his girlfriend as Julie looks out the next window, an almost exact replica of a shot at the country home in *Jules and Jim* ([Truffaut], 1961). François Truffaut is studying the living form of cinema he is in the process of re-creating; any film is shaped both by the movie heritage which made it possible and the internal requirements of its genre and structure.[18]

The freeze frame of Julie at her airport press conference echoes the freezes on Jeanne Moreau in *Jules and Jim*. When Ferrand is shown opening books about Carl Dreyer, Ernst Lubitsch, Ingmar Bergman, Howard Hawks, Roberto Rossellini, Alfred Hitchcock, and other film directors that have been delivered to him by mail, followed by a cut to a close-up on the books, the music that plays is the love theme from *Two English Girls* (Truffaut, 1971).[19] The question that Alphonse asks various members of the cast and crew, "Are women magical creatures?," is taken from both *Shoot the Piano Player* (Truffaut, 1960) and *Stolen Kisses* (Truffaut, 1968).[20] Jean-Pierre Léaud is the star of the semi-autobiographical *The 400 Blows* (Truffaut, 1959) and the four subsequent Antoine Doinel films *Antoine Colette* (Truffaut, 1962), *Stolen Kisses* (Truffaut, 1969), *Bed and Board* (1970), and *Love on the Run* (Truffaut, 1979), as well as *Two English Girls* (Truffaut, 1971). Julie's nervous collapse picks up "Jeanne Moreau's attack of nerves on the set of *Jules and Jim*," and the cat that refuses to drink milk from the saucer left on a tray out-side a motel room door is taken from *The Soft Skin* (Truffaut, 1964). The members of this network of allusions interrupt and comment on the plot (the making of *Meet Pamela*), thus reminding viewers of the artifactual filmic surface. "The fact is," Truffaut later wrote to Jean-Pierre Aumont, "that many things in *Day for Night* only really make sense a second time around, and in a way that's the danger in all my films since most people see them only once."[21] In interaction with the plot, these allusions become problem materials for the audience to notice and work with, just as Ferrand must notice and work with continual interruptions to the shooting of *Meet Pamela*.

Women function in *Day for Night* as objects of mystery and attraction, as in Alfonse's "Are women magical creatures?" and in the camera's attentions to the beauty of Julie (Jacqueline Bisset, with whom Truffaut had an af-fair, and whose younger surrogate, Alfonse, sleeps with her in the film). In both *Day for Night* and other films, Truffaut seems, as Sam Solecki puts it, to ask "What is it that makes [women] perennially interesting to his male characters, that is, to himself?"[22] Women are also sometimes the sources of disruption, as when Liliane (Dani), Alfonse's script-girl girlfriend "who cannot be integrated into the group," runs off with the stunt double. As in the films of Howard Hawks, "this character is a woman who disrupts the equi-librium of the group because of her erotic attraction."[23] At the same time the assistant director, Joelle—whose name combines "the masculine 'Jo' and the feminine 'elle'"—is a thoroughly independent woman. "[Joelle's] strength, like that of the director, derives from her love of work; and she is actually the first of Truffaut's women to define herself, happily, through her profession.

He seems to be moving to a deeper understanding of the modern (rather than nineteenth-century) woman, ... where females have identities that are not necessarily directed by or toward desired males."[24] As with the allusions, and more broadly as with works of art, women are interruptive presences in life to be noticed and deciphered, at best partially, as they retain their visual presences, while also sometimes themselves exercising independent agency and will. ("Men are magical also. Everyone is magical—or no one is magical,"[25] Julie later replies to Alfonse.)

The structure of *Day for Night* is that of a continuous narrative of getting from beginning to make the film to completing it, despite the obstacles that arise. Jean-Luc Godard calls it, scornfully, a "film-train" that goes from point A to point B, without stopping to ask "who takes the train, in what class, and who is driving it with an 'informer' from the management standing at his side."[26] (Godard would clearly prefer more narrative discontinuity, class analysis, and intellectual interruptions of the narrative.) Truffaut suggests that the structure is modeled on Howard Hawks' *Red River*. "The movie itself being shot would be the equivalent of the cattle trek from Texas to Missouri in Howard Hawks's beautiful film, *Red River*. My movie would also consist of a long crossing, a difficult journey; and at the end of this trek a real *goal* would also be attained."[27] Citing V. F. Perkins' work on Howard Hawks, Wayne J. Douglass argues that

"The Hawks hero ... does what he can with the materials at his disposal." In other words, he improvises and Ferrand is "famous for improvising." ... Hawks's heroes "are constantly testing their abilities, and, particularly, their limitations. They have to see how far they can impose their own terms on nature and on life."[28]

Or as Truffaut describes Ferrand in the Description of the Characters that precedes the script "Ferrand never acts high-handedly, and seems not to care in the slightest about giving the impression of being the 'Big Chief.' Shooting a film always makes him happy. ... To Ferrand improvisation can only deepen the resonances of a movie script."[29] The movie within the movie, *Meet Pamela*, will be made successfully, and, more broadly (as in Hegel) life will be worth living, if and only if one can coherently impose *enough* of one's terms and forms on the material at hand, even while others have conflicting aims and perfect orderings remain impossible, in both art and life. Like Socrates, Ferrand is, as he puts it, "continuously being asked questions—questions about everything. Sometimes he has the answers, but not always."[30] The less-than-perfect answers that he does have will have to make the film good enough to work and life good enough to be worth living.

The film opens with an image of the soundtrack, itself being recorded in a studio in Paris, showing at the left edge of an otherwise black screen on which the credits are rolling. "Beaucoup silence; beaucoup justesse," the conductor admonishes, as the orchestra tunes up. Here the French "justesse" means accuracy, aptness, precision, and sureness—a virtue for conduct in life and in the making of a film as well as in musical performance. What is to be avoided are unnaturalness, bias, inaccuracy, and ineptness.[31] *Day for Night* dwells on Ferrand choosing a hotel vase for a shot because it looks right, choosing the right gun, the right car (passing by at the right speed) in the opening scene, and the timing of the entry and exit of a lady with a dog. Things must be made, deftly, to look right.

Getting the right look will involve care and artifice as well as the recording use of the camera. The fact that artifice is required, but that the result must look natural, is stressed continuously through *Day for Night*. The opening scene concludes with the shout "Cut" and a zoom out to show that a camera has been shooting what we had been seeing and initially taking to be real: "what appeared to be real life was art making a precise illusion."[32] We are shown the trick candle that illuminates Julie's face in the fancy-dress ball sequence and the gas fire that goes proxy for a real wooden one. In both cases an artificial light source replaces something more natural, suggesting, perhaps, the replacement of the sun by human-constructed fire in the Platonic allegory of the cave, itself legibly an allegory of movie-viewing, but with the twist that this artifice, unlike in Plato's conceit, serves the production of naturalness and artistic truth.[33] The title *Day for Night/La Nuit américaine* refers to the practice of shooting a scene during daylight with filters so that it will appear to have taken place at night. This form of shooting, like the movies in general, which we watch (or used to watch) mostly at night and in dark places, brings together or into communication the daylight world of planning, artifice, and convention with the nighttime world of dreams, fantasy, and desire. The latter world animates the former, redeeming it from flatness and conformity; the former world shapes and controls the latter, redeeming it from waywardness. The artificial-phenomenal can express the erotic-noumenal.[34] Recurrently, we see Ferrand at night asleep and dreaming of himself as a child, furtively approaching and at last reaching a movie theater, where he uses a cane to reach through a grating to a rolling display board, from which he steals publicity stills advertising *Citizen Kane*. Evidently he has been dreaming in some anxiety about whether he will succeed in reproducing a magic of the movies that has haunted and compelled him since childhood.

As *Meet Pamela* is in production, there are continuous threats and obstacles. "Shooting a film," Ferrand tells us in voiceover, "is exactly like crossing the Old West in a stagecoach. At first you hope you have a good trip. But, very soon, you start wondering if you'll even reach your destination."[35] Success requires people with very different, often opposed, skills and temperaments to work together—actors, the director and assistant director, cameramen, makeup girls, prop men, and producers. Many are troubled by self-centered preoccupations. In response to a television crew asking members of the cast what the film is about, Alexandre (Jean-Pierre Aumont) says, "Well, it's a story of a man in his early 50s who has a son. . . .," while Alphonse (Jean-Pierre Leaud) in contrast answers, "Well, it's the story of a young man who marries an English girl. . . ."[36] Later on, at a press conference, Julie Baker (Jacqueline Bisset) says that "*Meet Pamela* is the story of a young Englishwoman who falls in love with the father of her husband and who runs away with him."[37] Each evidently sees things from his or her distinctive point of view. Whether they can work together successfully from these different stances is an open question.

The entire production is repeatedly threatened by contingencies ranging from minor to catastrophic. Sheep momentarily block the street that the cast and crew are using to get to an exterior location shot. A cat repeatedly refuses to drink milk from a saucer as called for in the script, despite the prop man Bernard's (Bernard Ménez) self-exculpation that the cat "hasn't been fed for three days!"[38] The American financiers of the film threaten to withdraw funding. A set of rushes is ruined in a studio fire. Stacey (Alexandra Stewart), who must later on in production appear in a pool scene in a bathing suit, turns out to be pregnant; the shooting schedule cannot be altered, and her visible pregnancy introduces ambiguity into her shots. The son of Séverine (Valentina Cortese) is dying from leukemia, leading her to drink excessively, collapse from nerves, and be unable to complete a scene. Alexandre is killed in a car crash in returning from the airport, where he had gone to pick up his young lover Christian (Xavier Saint-Macary). Alphonse abandons the set and threatens to quit after learning that Liliane (Dani) has left him. He is lured back only by Julie comforting him and spending the night with him. When Alphonse calls her husband (David Markham)—an older psychiatrist who has recently helped her through a nervous breakdown and left his family for her—to reveal the incident, Julie collapses in anxiety at how he will react. She is then coaxed back to work by Ferrand bringing her the (artfully faked) country "tub butter" she had asked for and then reassuring her that "when your husband finds out exactly what happened, he will understand. He'll forget. Everything will be the same as before."[39] This reassurance is then echoed by Dr. Nelson (David Markham), another directorial surrogate, who upon his arrival after being summoned to the set, smiles at her and gives her a pill for her nerves. As Julie had just told Ferrand, after her earlier breakdown on the set of another film, "he tried to make me into a responsible woman,"[40] and she now shows herself to be one in returning to work. Here she echoes the emphasis on the importance of maturity that has been the text of Ferrand's advice to Alfonse to grow up. This advice, as Douglass puts it, "can thus be seen as a kind of auto-critique of Truffaut's early career when he concentrated on youthful, spontaneous, rebellious characters. As he has grown older, Truffaut has begun to emphasize more adult values similar to the ethos of Howard Hawks."[41] Truffaut himself comments directly on the kind of maturity required to make *Day for Night*.

> Nor do I think it would be possible to make *La Nuit américaine* as a first film. Experience and film-craft are required and one obviously has less film-craft at the beginning of one's career. Sincerity is fine for one's first film, but I don't think one can base one's whole career on sincerity. In addition one needs a little technique and a little skill and of course a little luck. Nothing happens without luck.[42]

Throughout the making of *Meet Pamela*, continuous improvisation and adaptation are required. A new cat must be found, Stacey's pregnancy must be written in, and a new ending, with a double standing in for Alexandre and shot from a distance, must be worked out. No script or set of plans is effectively dispositive, in art or in life. The producer Lajoie's wife (Zenaïde Rossi) is unable to see the point of it all, as she yells, "her face contorted with rage,"

> What kind of a world is this, our precious cinema? What kind of a world is this where everybody is on such intimate terms with everybody else, where everybody lies—where everybody sleeps with everybody else! Do you find

all that normal? ... Your precious cinema! To me it's rotten, it stinks to high heaven! I *despise* your cinema.... Yes, I despise it![43]

And yet when things go well—when a suitable cat is found, when newly scripted lines fit into place, when the actors and directors play off each other and a shot works—it is sublime, a point that is made repeatedly by the recurrence of "the Vivaldi-like theme connected with shooting the film"[44] and by the camera panning out and up in satisfaction with the whole. As Ferrand puts it to Alphonse,

> Private life is messy for everyone. Films are more harmonious than life, Alphonse. There are no traffic jams in films, no dead waits. Films move forward like trains, you understand, like trains in the night. People like us are happy only in our work, you must realize that, in our work of making movies.[45]

At least for a time, among this varied cast of people, sense and meaning of the kind anyone needs have been found.[46] The erotic-noumenal has been brought into the phenomenal light of day.

This kind of satisfaction in full cathexis to activity is neither universal nor permanent in life. Severine's son still has leukemia, Alexandre is dead, and Alphonse remains a talented but petulant child. But it is there, achieved in the making of *Meet Pamela* and on screen for us to resonate to in *Day*

Figure 13.1. Alphonse, Julie, and Ferrand work together effectively

Figure 13.2. The camera pulls back in satisfaction as the score swells

for Night. The last lines of the film are spoken by the prop man, Bernard, as a kind of Shakespearean wise fool, speaking a Prospero-like valedictory in response to a television crew's query about Alexandre's death and about whether there were difficulties on the set:

> Not at all, not at all! Everything went perfectly. And what's more, we hope the public will have as much fun watching this movie as we all had making it. [*Bernard's face moves closer to the camera. We realize that he is indeed talking to all of us in the audience . . . not only about* Meet Pamela, *but about* Day for Night *as well.*][47]

As Cavell's reading of the powers of film and his broad account of finding meaning in life critically have suggested, *Day for Night* is there for us as provocation to and pattern for our own fragile, improvisatory, and temporally bounded achievements of felt meaningfulness. Both within the experience of it and after watching it, and within and after any course of experience, there will be odd enchantments and disturbances to be noticed and accounted for. There will be further films to be watched, books to be read, others to be engaged with, and critical vocabularies to be developed, as in Cavell's work and life. Even if it provides no broad institutional-political solution to the problem of identifying with one's courses of activity and finding them worthwhile, photographic-realist film can be a bounded model for life. It can give to the transitory phenomena of life a higher actuality born of the spirit. We can come to enjoy much of the train ride, while also always encountering disruptions and never having perfect control. Nothing happens without luck. As in *Day for Night* and in Cavellian critical practice, making it up responsively and artfully with others as we go along is the path and substance of freedom.

Epilogue

Paradoxes and Possibilities of Freedom, Social and Individual

"beginning no doubt with the strangeness of oneself"
—Cavell, *A Pitch of Philosophy*

There is evidently enough a need for significant change in the political and economic institutions of both the advanced industrialized nations and, for different reasons, less developed ones. Paradigmatically in the United States, high life expectancy and unprecedented opportunities for leisure and enjoyment are available to the relatively well-off, while life expectancy has dropped since 2000 for those in the 50th income percentile and lower, with especially striking drops for racial minorities and in rural populations who frequently lack regular access to proper health care.[1] In both the United States and Europe, economic inequality has increased dramatically since 1970: in the United States in 2020 the richest 10% received 45% of the national income, while the poorest 50% received 14%, compared to 38% for the rich and 20% for the poor in 1970; in Europe the numbers are 35% to the richest 10% in 2020, and 20% to the poorest 50% versus 30% to the richer and 21% to the poorer in 1970.[2] While the spread of capitalism has brought both increased life expectancy and some access to middle-class enjoyments to some portions of the developing world, poverty, inequality, and various forms of political and social authoritarianism remain significant problems. Nation-states, singly or through treaties, seem unable to address effectively the collective decision problem of what to do about anthropogenic climate change and its catastrophic environmental effects.

Dissensus reigns socially, with various kinds of traditionalist-fundamentalists facing off against secular, cosmopolitan individualists (what Jonathan Haidt has dubbed the WEIRD: Western, Educated, Industrialized, Rich, Democratic[3]), among other fractures. What ought to be an argumentative conversation about important matters of public policy devolves into

Anticipations of Freedom. Richard Eldridge, Oxford University Press. © Richard Eldridge 2026.
DOI: 10.1093/9780197841785.003.0018

name-calling, virtue-signaling to the like-minded, and the shouting of conclusions,[4] within what Robert B. Talisse describes as the polarized "political saturation of social space,"[5] fed by increasing segregation of housing, employment, and religious affiliation (or the lack of it) along political lines— what the journalist Bill Bishop dubbed "The Big Sort."[6] In the United States, Republicans shop at Walmart and Dunkin Donuts, while Democrats patronize Target and Starbucks, and each side sneers at the other for doing so.[7] Polarization has Americans locked within "a self-fulfilling cycle of dysfunction" in which "civil war carried on by other [cultural] means threatens to degenerate into civil war carried on by the typical means."[8]

Psychologically and morally, what Robert D. Putnam and Shaylyn Romney Garret call "expressive individualism" rules, with individuals standing on their preferences and declining to interact with others who do not share or support them.[9] Drawing on a comprehensive macrohistory of economic, political, social, and cultural developments in the United States, Putnam and Romney Garrett find an inverted U-shaped curve describing a development toward social cohesion, community, equality, and mutual responsibility rising from 1895 until roughly 1965, followed by a downward slope toward individualism, inequality, and looking out for oneself afterward.[10] They point to "feedback loops" among all four domains and "concatenated causes" (to which corporate power might be added) that make it hard to see how the "moral awakening," "reevaluation of our shared values," "reinvigorat[ion] of democratic citizenship," and "massive grassroots organizing" that they hope for are possible.[11] Mutuality in institutions and practices is undercut by both polarization and individualism. Even family relations are inflected toward transactionality, as moral mentalities become colonized by the economic markets under which people live, encouraging them to ask about any course of action, "What preference satisfactions are in it for me?" Lacking readily available activities within institutions and practices that include mutuality— Putnam's famous work on bowling alone[12]—many individuals are left seeking escapist entertainments and self-narcosis from alcohol and drugs to block the pains of non-recognition. According to the Gallup Poll, in 2023 29% of US adults reported having been diagnosed with depression at some point in their lives, 10% more than in 2015, and 17.8% were receiving or had received medical treatment, 7% more than in 2015.[13] According to a 2021 survey, globally "44% . . . of 18–24 year-olds had mental wellbeing scores within [the] Distressed or Struggling range."[14] Establishing and sustaining a meaningful practical identity—an ensemble of commitments expressed in activities in ways that are broadly found worthwhile by enough others and by oneself—is evidently a significant problem for many. The kids are not exactly alright, and the reasons have to do in some large part with the kind of social world to which they are perforce undertaking to accommodate. Fortunate circumstances—economic, educational, social, and geographic, among others—and good parenting can make big differences, and significant enjoyment in life activities, from work to family life to sports to cooking to service—remains possible enough for many. Yet even those mostly at ease in their social identities frequently remain haunted by senses of undeserved good luck on their part and undeserved suffering elsewhere, while meanwhile the suffering suffer.

In *Envisioning Real Utopias*, Erik Olin Wright makes a number of significant and plausible proposals for structural-institutional reform. He accepts that free markets, by encouraging technological innovation, have "generated . . . enormous advances in human productivity" that have "contributed to enlarging the potential for human flourishing" for many, and he accepts that they have "certain equality-promoting effects" in creating "conditions for a certain real degree of class mobility compared to earlier societies."[15] At the same time, he notes the massive economic inequalities, the routinization of labor, the exploitation, the suffering, and the consequent alienation that they also generate.[16] There is, Wright holds further, no perfect institutional design. It is impossible to "imagine that institutions can be designed in such a way as to produce precisely the kinds of people needed for those institutions to run smoothly and to marginalize any social processes which might undermine or disrupt the institutions . . . [or] to imagine a social system without contradictions, without destructive unintended consequences of individual and collective action, a system in a self-sustaining emancipatory equilibrium."[17] Despite the impossibility of perfect and perfectly self-sustaining institutions, however, productive moves can be made in response to current conditions, according to Wright. There are available "multiple pathways of social empowerment" that can be broadly classified as ruptural (confrontational, revolutionary) strategies, interstitial strategies involving the creative formation of new forms of community within the state (anarchist collectives, agricultural communes), and symbiotic metamorphoses that involve reforming the state democratically from within (proportional representation, participatory budgeting processes for cities).[18] Among these strategies, it is best to do what one can where one can creatively and to hope for the best. "No one of these pathways ... by itself is likely to constitute a viable framework for a socialist economy, but taken in combination they have the potential to shift the underlying configuration of power that controls economic activity."[19]

This is as it may be, and local, creative experiments in forms of social, political, and economic organization are worth taking seriously. But one can also wonder about the extent of their transformational power. There is no clear agent for ruptural, revolutionary change; the working class is if anything more in solidarity with comparatively freer markets than it is inclined to revolution. Local alternative communities face the problem of reproducing themselves over time within and in interaction with the larger economy, and the track record of more or less Fabian communities in reproducing themselves is generally not good; major widenings of them seem unlikely. Interstitial strategies for structural political reform presuppose significant, creative coalition-building, and that, too, is unlikely, given current conditions of bimodal polarization and pervasive economic competition among both firms and individuals. How and where, then, might the relevant motivation to take up these strategies be found or formed on any large scale? Or is there, as Margaret Thatcher famously proposed, no alternative? And if one is then unable to give up the dreams of at least more fully reconciled life and more satisfying practical identity, with one's human powers of meaning-making significantly actualized in mutual-recognition-enabling interactions, is there nothing left but accommodation, melancholy, and alienation? Meanwhile, what Axel Honneth aptly dubs "pathologies of individual freedom"—heteronomy, "bottomless self-questioning, indeterminacy," and an inability to participate wholeheartedly in social life, coupled with "dogmatic, rigid insistence on subjective rights"—persist within a framework of relative legal and economic freedom, along with suffering and radical economic inequality.[20]

In his *Letters on the Aesthetic Education of Man*, Friedrich Schiller (echoing both Rousseau on *amour propre* and Kant on *Streit*) registers and faces up to this situation poignantly and presciently. His description is worth quoting in full for its account of the intensities and kinds of effects of modern socio-economic-political organization on psychological life.

In the very bosom of the most exquisitely developed social life egotism has founded its system, and without ever acquiring therefrom a truly sociable heart, we suffer all the contagions and afflictions of society. We subject our free judgment to its despotic opinion, our feeling to its fantastic customs, our will to its seductions; only our caprice we do uphold against its sacred rights. Proud self-sufficiency contracts the heart of the man of the world, a heart that in natural man still often beats in sympathy; and as from a city in flames each man seeks only to save from the general destruction his own wretched belongings. Only by completely abjuring sensibility can we, so it is thought, be safe from its aberrations; and the ridicule that often acts as a salutary chastener of the enthusiast is equally unsparing in its dese-cration of the noblest feeling. Civilization, far from setting us free, in fact creates some new need with every new power it develops in us. The fetters of the physical tighten ever more alarmingly, so that fear of losing what we have stifles even the most burning impulse toward improvement, and the maxim of passive obedience passes for the supreme wisdom of life. Thus do we see the spirit of the age wavering between perversity and brutality, between unnaturalness and mere nature, between superstition and moral unbelief; and it is only through an equilibrium of evils that it is still some-times kept within bounds.[21]

Schiller sees clearly, moreover, that there is no ready way out of this con-dition through either education or political action in their current shapes of possibility. "In order to love wisdom" and thence to overcome socially inflected egotism, one "would first have to be wise," and within our present form of social life, most of us most of the time are not. Changes in theoretical understandings of values are required to bring about changes in passions, yet changes in passions are required in order to motivate the pursuit of the relevant theoretical understandings. Socially, individual character and polit-ical institutions shape and reinforce each other, under current conditions of alienation and barbarism.

> Intellectual education is to bring about moral education, and yet moral ed-ucation is to be the condition of intellectual education? All improvement in the political sphere is to proceed from the ennobling of character—but how under the influence of a barbarous constitution is character ever to become ennobled? . . . When the craftsman has a timepiece to repair, he can let its wheels run down; but the living clockwork of the state must be repaired while it is still striking, and it is a question of changing the revolving wheel while it still revolves.[22]

It is a question of changing the characters, understandings, and passions of individuals who are already formed within and necessarily subject to the barbarizing effects of economic and political life as they stand. One wonders how Schiller can write at all and further how philosophy at all might address these conditions and productively find an audience.

Nonetheless, Schiller poses a solution, apt or fantastic as it may be: "If man is ever to solve that problem of politics in practice he will have to approach it through the aesthetic, because it is only through beauty that man makes his way to freedom."[23] Already we should note here that the claim specifies only a necessary condition for what Schiller thinks of as genuinely human, non-mechanical society and fully meaningful life, a necessary condition the fulfillment of which is posited as occurring in the future. These points should raise doubt about whether that aesthetically informed future will come and about whether the other conditions that must be in place as well in order to compose a set of conditions that are jointly sufficient for freedom will ever obtain. This same undercurrent of hesitation or self-doubt also marks Schiller's fuller and final formulation of the solution he proposes.

> The aesthetic state alone can make [humanly satisfying and affirmatively willed society] real, because it consummates the will of the whole through the nature of the individual. Though it may be his needs that drive man into society, and reason that implants within him the principles of social behavior, beauty alone can confer upon him a *social character*. Taste alone brings harmony into society, because it fosters harmony in the individual. All other forms of perception divide man, because they are founded exclusively either upon the sensuous or upon the spiritual part of his being; only the aesthetic mode of perception makes of him a whole, because both his natures must be in harmony if he is to achieve it. All other forms of communication divide society, because they relate exclusively either to the private receptivity or to the private proficiency of its individual members, hence to that which distinguishes man from man; only the aesthetic mode of communication unites society, because it relates to that which is common to all. The pleasures of the senses we enjoy merely as individuals, without the genus that is immanent within us having any share in them at all; hence we cannot make the pleasures of sense universal, because we are unable to universalize our own individuality. The pleasures of knowledge we enjoy merely as genus, and by carefully removing from our judgment all trace of individuality; hence we cannot make the pleasures of reason universal,

because we cannot eliminate traces of individuality from the judgments of others as we can from our own. Beauty alone do we enjoy at once as individual and as genus, i.e., as *representatives* of the human genus.[24]

Only within actively self-maintaining aesthetic experience, productive or receptive, do we act and exist in a fully human way, actualizing our powers of satisfying meaning-making without reduction to hedonic tingles, without abstraction, and without competing with others. Here too, however, there is a carefully qualified "can," indicating deferment of realization of the effects of aesthetic activity into the future, and it is easy to wonder whether the attractions and effects of that activity either can or should outweigh the presence and effects of the continuing, contrary forces of the sensuous-hedonic and rational-moral-theoretical lives.

Recently, Samantha Matherne and Nick Riggle have reconstructed and defended Schiller's argument for the importance—personal and political—of active involvements with both works of art and beautiful phenomena more generally (persons and their characters; fine wines and meals; compelling sports performances, and so on). Engagement with such things, they find, puts "us in a state of volitional openness and so pave[s] the way toward the realization of our individual and political freedom."[25] (Note the slightly hesitant "paves the way," echoing Schiller's "can.") To be in a continuing state of volitional openness is to enjoy what one is doing in exercising one's perceptual-sensual and cognitive powers freely and for the sake of active enjoyment and delight in the object, rather than for the sake of hedonic satisfactions, instrumental control, or theoretical understanding, all of which are informed by competitive self-interest. Volitional openness is a matter of "distancing ourselves from our ordinary patterns, values, and commitments—from our 'normal sense of self.'"[26] To be in a state of volitional openness is to be caught up in enjoyments that are liberating because unstained by either self-interest or stern self-regulation. "When we playfully engage with the aesthetic value of the other, we are set free from the compulsion of the sense and form drives that give rise to the egotistical ways of relating to the other."[27] In practice, engaging with aesthetic value in play amounts to enjoying works of art and other aesthetic phenomena with others. Schiller's view, as Matherne and Riggle put it,

encourages us to regard cooking for friends, spinning records, displaying aesthetic objects, throwing intriguing parties, and the like as paradigmatic ways of aesthetic engaging. By being attentive to the social pulse of play in these ways, Schiller thinks that we can attempt to give freedom by eliciting the play drive in others and become the occasion for the kind of loving interaction that plays a crucial role in socio-aesthetic life. . . . For when we playfully engage with the aesthetic value of the other, we are set free from the compulsion of the sense and form drives that give rise to egotistical ways of relating to the other.[28]

Loving interaction, in Schiller's formulation, can help to liberate "potentially and prescriptively, an ideal man, the archetype of a human being . . . that every individual human being . . . carries within him,"[29] as human powers are actualized cooperatively and meaningfully in joint activity.

Matherne and Riggle are clear that episodes of volitional openness and aesthetic engagement are not panaceas for psychological or social ills. They can "pave the way" for genuine freedom, without the individualist pathologies of competitive egoism and alienation, but they are not sufficient conditions for it. "While engaging with aesthetic value continues to be an important component of the political good, it is not sufficient. There also need to be morally grounded political laws and institutions in place that uphold the rights of citizens and citizens who uphold those morally-grounded laws and institutions."[30]

The idea that aesthetic experience, especially when socially shared, leads to richer, fuller lives and that it might at least sometimes have productive effects on social and political sensibilities is worth taking seriously. Social safety nets, substantive fair and equal opportunities to build a meaningful life, and widened democratic control of at least some major aspects of economic life would all help, too; the failures of authoritarianism and unconstrained libertarianism to yield significant, meaningful life for many are obvious enough, even if there is room for continuing debate about the means and ways of fairness. Together more widely enjoyed aesthetic experiences and political reforms might at least mitigate the worst inequalities and sufferings and help to make practical identities and their social circumstances more fully affirmable.

There are, however, also significant reasons to doubt how widespread and substantial for political and economic life such changes might be. First, the idea that aesthetic experience is open to each and all does not imply that either many will in fact pursue it or that its effects when enjoyed will bleed productively into the rest of life. The demands of work and family, the competitive pressures of resource accumulation, and the charms of escapist hedonisms will continue to have their force, and aesthetic experiences will frequently enough be experienced as gratuitous private enjoyments. Second, traces of egoism frequently remain present within both aesthetic experience and sincere, right-minded efforts at political reform. Boastful pride in one's taste in art or wine and enjoyments of political power for its own sake and for the control over others that it affords are scarcely unknown. Third, whatever aspirations for reciprocity and mutual recognition in the satisfying exercise of powers of meaning-making are built into the structures of discursive consciousness and practical identity as such, those structures also include a drive toward distinctive individuation that manifests superiority. (This is the point of Glaucon's rejection of the first, pastoral city in the *Republic* as a city of pigs; it offers no scope for the satisfaction of this drive toward distinctiveness.) Forming and displaying oneself as in some way and in some domain distinctive, accomplished, and commanding admiration and esteem is close enough to being a standing value for human beings that it is unlikely that even the legitimate claims of social reciprocity will or should override it. Yet pursuit of this kind of accomplishment paves the way toward inequalities, class distinctions, and mutual shunning. To cite Erik Olin Wright again, it is impossible to "imagine a social system without contradictions, without destructive unintended consequences of individual and collective action, a system in a self-sustaining emancipatory equilibrium."[31]

How, then, if at all, it is possible to avoid sheer accommodation, quiet desperation, and consequent despair? How, if at all, is it possible to get free of politics-as-usual that "maintains a deep pessimism about human nature and ends up with a version of passive nihilism?"[32] How is it possible to avoid complacency, despair, and withdrawal from political life, on the one hand, and overblown, potentially tyrannical hopes for perfect reciprocity on the other? Stanley Cavell's contribution to political life, and to philosophy insofar as it is caught up in political life and the problems of practical identity, is to enact in his writing a way of addressing and living with these questions, including achieving some onwardness in doing so.

Doing this amounts to what Cavell calls "a criticism of democracy from within" (CHU, 3),[33] from where one already is in being bound up in imperfect relations with others, and not from a place apart. Living alertly and critically with oneself and others must begin from and remain faithful to the thought that one does not, not yet and not ever, fully know oneself in smoothly inhabiting a practical identity unfreighted with oppositions and doubts, with one's skills, habits, preferences, values, and relations with others fully settled. Here, no doubt influenced by his readings of Freud and his experience of psychoanalysis, Cavell explicitly rejects the idea of a fully formed, whole self that is somehow just given for subsequent actions and valuings. "[My] picture of a human life, of my life, as patterns of struggles or detours away from painful and ineffective reparations and from pleasures that are fractured, investments or necessities that are as foreign as they are familiar to me, toward a discovery and acceptance of the reality of my own death, strikes me as intuitively incompatible with such a thing" as any kind of given self.[34] Nor are things much different with the political realm as reciprocally both mirror and cause of the individual psychic-practical realm. The political realm is never wholly formed, and we are never fully housed and at home within it. "The impression I get is of our interactions as constituting an incessant formation and deformation of the public realm, or say a continuous affirmation or denial of its existence."[35] In light of his sense of continuing unsettlements, fractures, and opacities, personal and political, mixed with moments of whole-hearted cathexis and partial reciprocity, Cavell's effort, as Paola Marrati puts it, is to "attempt to find a different answer to our discouragement and a different way to reaffirm a democratic hope at distance equally from any undue idealization of the present and from the escape in false forms of transcendence."[36] As Andrew Norris describes Cavell's stance, "Cavell consistently emphasizes both the ways our common form of life is held together by individual commitments and the manner in which that community can break down into skepticism and confusion, and in which we can find ourselves out of tune with one another, unable to make sense of one another—in which, as he puts it, we can fall into 'intellectual tragedy.'"[37] As a result, the effort toward reciprocity and the formation of more meaningful life, in the form of Cavell's "pairing of the claim to reason and the claim to community, . . . is inherently tentative and exploratory."[38] As in both ordinary language philosophy and Wordsworthian self-forming, self-enacting poetry that seeks to form its audience,

> the claim to community is always a search for the basis upon which it can be or has been established. I have nothing more to go on than my conviction, my sense that I make sense. It may prove to be the case that I am wrong, that my conviction isolates me from all others, from myself. That will not be the same as the discovery that I am dogmatic or egomaniacal. The wish and search for community are the wish and search for reason. (CR, 20)

This may sound like a method for solving political and personal problems of coherence, unity, and satisfaction: just say what *we* do. But it is not, or not exactly that. An appeal to what we say or do is entered tentatively and exploratively, in a situation in which at the moment what we do or have been doing is unclear or contested. It is not a method for the exact characterization of a given external object; we are ourselves at stake in entering such an appeal. There is, moreover, no possibility of settling fully and with unchallengeable assurance in what we say or do; both the self as a locus of commitments and the community as an ensemble of shared repertoires are always changing and open to contestation. Always, "either we transform both or we are lost"[39]—Cavell's version of original sin. "What I have to do is to continually assess my consent in the present, that society is in fact itself always in formation."[40] One can never say—in the words Cavell imagines in the mouth of Torvald in Ibsen's *A Doll's House*—"I have done nothing wrong; I am above reproach."[41] Or, rather, one can say this, but in doing so one will be defensively standing on one's commitments and actions, shunning open engagement with the other, precisely in a situation where an issue about how or whether we are to go on together has arisen.

What is left, then, beyond or beside the formulation of general policies and the design and inauguration of institutional frameworks that make opportunities for meaningful life more available—these retain their importance—is a kind of work on oneself: the achievement and display of imperfect, but more fully responsive and transformative coming to more aptly affirmable commitments in situ, motivated by an initiating disappointment. This is the open-ended work of Cavellian perfectionism, understood, as Marrati puts it, as

> an attitude of thinking, one that Cavell often describes as the Socratic or romantic quest for the "truth of the self." . . . The self is taken [as existing] in a never ending process of becoming, one that is uncompromisingly non-teleological not only because it is not guided by any pre-established norm or ideal but also because every step, or state, of the self has its own consistency and immanent value. . . . The desire for change never comes from abstract pictures of moral values, but from the dissatisfaction with ourselves as we stand, from the sense that something is deeply amiss with the current form of our lives in all its aspects and not only in a few particulars, say in an ugly action we may have committed or in some undignified habit we may have taken on. It is this dissatisfaction with ourselves and things as they are

that gives to the search for a better self the urgency and necessity it has (or lacks).[42]

What is left, then, if not theses that support full and lasting arrivals at free and meaningful life, as instead we remain entangled and complicit in structural oppositions and injustices, are transfigurative movements toward greater meaningful freedom and itineraries of them. This possibility is what Cavell points to in his contemporary refiguration of escape from a Platonic cave of illusion, trance, and dullness.

> I am, one or another day, like any other, brought to my feet suddenly, torn from my ordinary, with some instinct of consciousness that the way we are living partakes of irreality, unnecessary necessaries, an insight that we are, in our distraction by shows and echoes of what seem shadows, lost, out of place, filled with the sense that reality is, as it were, behind us or above us. That I am drawn, in my quest to transform my existence, to walk and look for reality despite the quest's causing me pain, is the sign that I was already in greater pain, without realizing it; I had learned, grown accustomed, to consider the constrictions of pain as the normal condition of the ordinary human dispensation. *As* this realization becomes articulated as my being drawn, or dragged, dragging myself, to a state of illumination, or perspicuity, concerning my fate, I recognize that I now have news that I am compelled to convey. It is a story, however, the members of the audience for which I will have to create—paradoxically, since the story is precisely theirs. So I return to my old home from my new home, leaving the new, as I left the old, in pain. One could say I am at home nowhere or everywhere.[43]

The pain does not go away. Full at-homeness is not achieved. Others are different, caught in their own trances, preoccupations, escapes, and enchantments, and they may not listen or resonate. But a movement has been made, depicted as walking and looking, in continuing pain, in response to being torn from the ordinary. The character of this movement has been articulated as mixing passivity and activity, responsiveness and assertion, being dragged and dragging oneself, toward illumination, or at least a new angle on the course of one's life with others. And then something might happen: resonances might be achieved, and an audience with a measure of mutuality might form itself, passively and actively. Or it might not. Communion may or may not follow, and in any case, it will be indefinitely limited in circumference and caught up in its own partialities and complicities. But then it is not nothing, either.

In a formulation that Paul Standish offers Cavell in conversation, "there must be an assent to the political realm within which one finds oneself, such that the offering of the words is a continual attempt to express or test the possibilities of that assent," to which Cavell responds, "That's absolutely right."[44] No one has the authority of an office to form and express such assent or its content, let alone to compel it in others—the core stance of democracy. "We are," as Cavell puts it in describing "the culture depicted in the *Investigations*, . . . all teachers, and all students—talkers, hearers, overhearers, hearsayers, believers, explainers; we learn and teach incessantly, indiscriminately; we are all elders and all children, wanting a hearing, for our injustices, for our justices" (TNYUA, 75).

That much of the time our conversations as well as our judgments and actions *are* indiscriminate, a matter of chatter or Heideggerian *Gerede*, sometimes innocently so, sometimes embodying failures of alertness, underlying melancholy, and complicity in violence, is the standing situation within which one can nonetheless be struck and a movement can be begun. In his response to Emerson's question "Where do we find ourselves?" in the opening sentence of "Experience," Cavell describes in 2003 an America whose citizens are locked in polarization, polemic, and mutual grievance, unable, it seems, genuinely to think.

> It is a world without truth or falsity, of human significance only in its production of need and relief ("as when, being thirsty, I drink water"), of life and death. . . . We find ourselves aggrieved at being spoken for while being unspoken for; second, manipulated by assurances of our moral purity, and that of our standing America's; third, asked to think of everything but of how to assess our partiality (for example, the partiality of our society's realization of the principles of justice) and to change ourselves; fourth, unconvinced by our own voices unless they are raised polemically, etymologically meaning taking sides in a war, which is to say, unphilosophically.[45]

Whatever the inevitability, in different shapes and with different degrees of violence, of something like this situation, Cavell is not willing to abandon either democracy or the quest for a life of human significance as involving something more than (necessary) animal satisfactions. Where Nietzsche's imaginings of transformations out of present despairs are, as he sees them, vengeful, escapist, and limited to a few, Cavell continues to cast his lot with Emerson, democracy, others, and the ordinary.

> Nietzsche does find us at a dead end—a dead end with Christianity and a dead end with democracy so far as human beings so far have established themselves. That *either* we get to a radical transformation of the human and let God die and regard ourselves as equal to the deed of the killing of God, *or* there is no future . . . is something that I don't believe. In short, I'm much more of an Emersonian than that. Emerson was as appalled by democracy in some ways as Nietzsche might have been if he had experienced it. But appalled is appalled, and I think he preferred to live with it. And the absolute idea that there is something that only he knows and one or two followers is where I can't go with Nietzsche. I see it. I see how close it is. I see the temptation for that. . . . Yes, well, I have said that with the absolute rejection of Christianity comes the absolute rejection of the low. I do mean that implication to be there. Emerson had not come to an absolute rejection of Christianity—the church is another thing.[46]

Abstract theories of justice might be useful in setting boundary conditions on holdings and courses of life up to a point. The worst excesses of suffering and exploitation must be blocked. But abstract theories cannot offer fully dispositive guidance for overcoming oppositions and actualizing distinctively human powers fully, reciprocally, and meaningfully. Granting the fact and value of some (constrained) measures of inequality and of substantial divergences in taste and talent across distinct individuals, difference and opposition are facts of human life. Philosophical arguments about ideal arrangements will be either too weak to yield full resolution of these differences and oppositions, or, if their conclusions are implemented in such a way as to compel agreements, they will support tyranny. It does not follow, however, that philosophical arguments are without point, and Cavell nicely describes the point they can plausibly serve.

> Cynics about philosophy, and perhaps about humanity, will find that questions without answers are empty; dogmatists will claim to have arrived at answers; philosophers after my heart will rather wish to convey the thought that while there may be no satisfying answers to such questions in

certain forms, there are, so to speak, directions to answers, ways to think, that are worth the time of your life to discover. (TS, 9)

To find a direction of thought available to one—opened up to one by another, figured by Cavell as a philosophical friend[47]—and thence to work within it and with it, finding one's course via its refiguration, is to come to words for one's life, for how one exercises one's human powers, happily or tragically, but always partially, in a world with others. Measures of self-scrutiny, change, articulateness, satisfaction, and reciprocity become available in relation to each other. As Larry Jackson puts it,

> In ... a society [of good enough justice], argument and confrontation make possible the conversation of justice by redirecting it away from the impersonal rules and political operations that have no need for my voice to scenes of mutual acknowledgment where the possibilities of language to recount the world are explored and contested. In such circumstances, dissent is not the mark of a society's failures, but a measure of consent to its mode of justice.[48]

It plays an ineliminable and vital role in the exploration of concrete possibilities of satisfaction and acknowledgment. It offers the possibility "'to fall in love with the world,' while at the same time living with doubt."[49] Out of the circumstances of present dissatisfactions, I, or anyone, in pursuit of animation and freedom, might inherit, produce, and use the words that compose a direction of thought, to go on with oneself and with others, amid whatever acknowledgments and avoidances, or mutual recognitions and departures, then ensue.

> In philosophizing, I have to bring my own language and life into imagination, *rather than leaving them inert or dull or unconsidered, merely suffered rather than affirmed.* What I require is a convening of my culture's words— *its accounts of what we count as what and of what we do*—in order to confront them with my words and life as I pursue them and as I may imagine them; and at the same time confront my words and life as I pursue them with the life my culture's words may imagine for me, *eschewing both escapism and despair:* to confront the culture with itself, along the lines in which it meets in me. (CR, 125, with my interpolations in italics)

Such convenings and confrontings are not everything, but they are not nothing. They may occur at moments in anyone's life, and they have their fruits as well as their limits. Without the continuing pursuits of the human and anticipations of freedom that they compose, we are lost; with them we can go on in at least some engagement with immanent possibilities of meaningful human life.

Notes

Introduction

1. J. S. Mill, *Utilitarianism*, ed. Roger Crisp (Oxford: Oxford University Press, 1998), p. 56.
2. G. W. F. Hegel, *Introduction to the Lectures on the History of Philosophy*, trans. T. M. Knox and A. V. Miller (Oxford: Oxford University Press, 1985), p. 9.
3. G. W. F. Hegel, *Phänomenologie des Geistes*, ed. Johannes Hoffmeister (Hamburg: Meiner, 1952), p. 29; my translation.
4. G. W. F. Hegel, *Elements of the Philosophy of Right*, ed. Allen W. Wood, trans. H. B. Nisbet (Cambridge: Cambridge University Press, 1991), §353, p. 377; §360, p. 380.
5. Elizabeth Anderson, *Hijacked: How Neoliberalism Turned the Work Ethic Against Workers and How Workers Can Take It Back* (Cambridge: Cambridge University Press, 2023), p. 245.
6. See G. W. F. Hegel, *Lectures on the Philosophy of World History: Introduction*, trans. H. B. Nisbet (Cambridge: Cambridge University Press, 1975), p. 48: "Spirit is self-sufficient being [*Beisichselbstsein*], which is the same thing as freedom"; and Hegel, *Elements of the Philosophy of Right*, §7, p. 42: "Freedom is to will something determinate, yet to be with oneself [*bei sich*] in this determinacy and to return once more to the universal."
7. Stanley Cavell, "Aesthetic Problems of Modern Philosophy," in Cavell, MWM, p. 73; citing Heinrich Wölfflin foreword to the seventh German edition of *Principles of Art History*, as quoted by E. H. Gombrich, *Art and Illusion* (New York: Pantheon, 1960), p. 4.
8. For further development of this line of thought, see Richard Eldridge, "The Culturally Educated Spirit and Its Fate: Hegel, Diderot, and the Futures of Crises," *Angelaki* 30, 2 (April 2025), pp. 68–78.
9. The point here is not that there are not good morally and legally defensible institutional solutions to these conflicts, and liberal ones at that; the point is rather that these conflicts tend to present themselves as rationally unresolvable for a general public under pervasive conditions of polarization and instrumental material self-seeking, where institutions are subject to interest capture and where the very idea of objectively fair cooperation begins to founder in public consciousness.
10. In *Tolerance: Between Forbearance and Acceptance* (Lanham, MD: Rowman and Littlefield, 2001), Hans Oberdiek presents a powerful argument for the importance of tolerance as an affirmative virtue and habit of mind, but he provides no concrete account of how this virtue might be better cultivated and practiced under generalized conditions of polarization and self-seeking.
11. Jean-Paul Sartre, *No Exit and Three Other Plays*, trans. Stuart Gilbert (New York: Vintage, 1989), p. 45.
12. Martin Heidegger, *Being and Time*, trans. John Macquarrie and Edward Robinson (Oxford: Basil Blackwell, 1962), p. 41.
13. Michel Foucault, "Truth and Power," in Foucault, *Power/Knowledge: Selected Interviews and Other Writings 1972–1977*, ed. Colin Gordon, trans. Colin Gordon, Leo Marshall, John Mepham, and Kate Soper (New York: Pantheon, 1980), p. 132.
14. Robert B. Pippin, *Philosophy by Other Means: The Arts in Philosophy and Philosophy in the Arts* (Chicago: University of Chicago Press, 2021), p. 33.
15. Robert B. Pippin, *Hegel's Practical Philosophy: Rational Agency and Ethical Life* (Cambridge: Cambridge University Press, 2008), p. 5. In *Hegel on Self-Consciousness*, Pippin elaborates and endorses Hegel's argument (in the master-slave section of the *Phenomenology*) that forming and sustaining such a practical identity is an end that is non-optionally built into the structure of reflective, conceptually structured consciousness.
16. Pippin, *Philosophy by Other Means*, pp. 28, 31.
17. Ibid., p. 35.

18. Ibid., p. 152.
19. Ibid., p. 157. In *After the Beautiful: Hegel and the Philosophy of Pictorial Modernism* (Chicago: University of Chicago Press, 2014), Pippin takes up modernist art's aesthetic intelligibility in addressing fractures in modern life and their consequences for practical identity, arriving at Manet's renderings of the "'weakened presence' of animated subjectivity" (p. 57) and Cezanne's bathers as brute presences for whom social meaning is unavailable as exemplary cases (p. 126). Compare also Raymond Geuss's characterization of the situation of the modern artist:"The situation of the modern artist is an impossible one. *Ex professo*, artists try to describe what is there, to depict it, present it, and also to express themselves. Reality, however, does not admit of being depicted, and no one can express themselves adequately. The more artists work, the clearer this will become to them, so their fate is necessarily failure" (*Seeing Double* [Cambridge: Polity Press, 2024], p. 170).
20. Lydia Goehr, *Red Sea-Red Square-Red Thread: A Philosophical Detective Story* (Oxford: Oxford University Press, 2022), p. 611.
21. Ibid., pp. 421, 485.
22. Ibid., p. xli.
23. Charles Taylor, *Cosmic Connections: Poetry in an Age of Disenchantment* (Cambridge, MA: Harvard University Press, 2024), pp. 494, xi.
24. Ibid., p. 98.
25. Ibid., p. 24.
26. Ibid., p. 117.
27. Ibid., p. 267.
28. Ibid., p. 181.
29. Ibid., p. 235.
30. Ibid., p. 331.
31. "Pleasure completes the activity not as the corresponding permanent state does, by its immanence, but as an end which supervenes as the bloom of youth does on those in the flower of their age." Aristotle, *Nichomachean Ethics*, trans. W. D. Ross, in *The Basic Works of Aristotle*, ed. Richard McKeon (New York: Random House, 1941), 1174b, p. 1099.
32. It is worth nothing that this exploration bears more than a passing affinity with what major lyric poets do. See Charles Altieri on the experience of participatory valuation via imagined affections that lyric experience offers, in his *Reckoning with the Imagination: Wittgenstein and the Aesthetics of Literary Experience* (Ithaca: Cornell University Press, 2015), and see also Richard Eldridge "Poetics, Perspective, Truth: The Aesthetic Authority of Lyric," in *The Cambridge Companion to Philosophy and Literature*, ed. Lanier Anderson and Karen Zumhagen-Yekple, forthcoming.
33. This is the primary argument of "Aesthetic Problems of Modern Philosophy" (MWM, 68–90), including the thought that philosophy and its human practitioners frequently refuse this thought, naturally enough seeking a more absolute authority under a fixed doctrine, at their peril.
34. William Wordsworth, "Preface to *Lyrical Ballads*," in Wordsworth, *Selected Poems and Prefaces*, ed. Jack Stillinger (Boston: Houghton-Mifflin, 1965), pp. 446–7, 448. Wordsworth writes "*must be . . . enlightened and purified*" (emphasis added), but the entire Preface is composed in the grip of the thought that these poems might be rejected, given the prevailing habits of life and art on the parts of their intended audiences. In *Hearing Things: Voice and Method in the Writing of Stanley Cavell* (Chicago: University of Chicago Press, 1998), Timothy Gould nicely distinguishes and describes what he calls the method of ordinary language and the method of reading in Cavell, though he fails, I think, to see how intimately related with each other they are as each variations on this Wordsworthian conception of poetic work.
35. Timothy Gould, *Hearing Things: Voice and Method in the Writing of Stanley Cavell* (Chicago: University of Chicago Press, 1998), p. 48. This is, it should be noted, a shift in emphasis, not an abrupt change. Cavell was already an alert, committed, passionate reader of Shakespeare, Beckett, Thoreau, and movies, among other things, prior to *The Claim of Reason*, and in his readings he opened himself to transformation by their words and images as he found them.
36. Ibid., p. 137.
37. Ibid., p. 59.
38. Ibid., p. 55.
39. J. L. Austin, "A Plea for Excuses," in Austin, *Philosophical Papers*, ed. J. O. Urmson and G. J. Warnock (Oxford: Oxford University Press, 1961), p. 127.

40. Gould, *Hearing Things*, pp. 104–5.
41. Wordsworth, *The Prelude*, in Wordsworth, *Selected Poems and Prefaces*, Book XIV, ll. 446–6, p. 366. Note, however, that Wordsworth qualifies this pronouncement with "Should Providence such grace to us vouchsafe" (Book XIV, l. 441, p. 366). For more on continuing undercurrents of anxiety and self-doubt in Wordsworth's writing, see Eldridge, "Internal Transcendentalism: Wordsworth and 'A New Condition of Philosophy,'" reprinted in Eldridge, *The Persistence of Romanticism* (Cambridge: Cambridge University Press, 2001), pp. 102–23.
42. Espen Hammer, commenting on Cavell's 1964 essay "Existentialism and Analytic Philosophy," in his "Logic and Voice: Stanley Cavell and Analytic Philosophy," *Journal for the History of Analytic Philosophy*, 9, 9 (2021); Special Issue: *Recovering the History of Analytic Philosophy with Stanley Cavell*, ed. Edward Guetti and G. Anthony Bruno, p. 111. Gould usefully notes that the existentialist motif in Cavell of self-responsibility conceived as achievable only 'against the grain' yet still relying on and courting resonances helps to explain "the weaving of intimacy and antagonism that constitutes an essential element of his relation to [systematic, academic] philosophy" (p. 14).
43. Espen Dahl, *Stanley Cavell, Religion, and Continental Philosophy* (Bloomington: Indiana University Press, 2012), p. 16.
44. Plato, *Symposium*, trans. Alexander Nehamas and Paul Woodruff (Indianapolis: Hackett, 1989), 192B–C, p. 28.
45. Alexander Nehamas, *Only a Promise of Happiness: The Place of Beauty in a World of Art* (Princeton: Princeton University Press, 2007), p. 53.
46. Andrew Bowie, *Aesthetic Dimensions of Modern Philosophy* (Oxford: Oxford University Press, 2022), p. v. Bowie insightfully describes how such moments of arrest challenge the homogenizations of experience that are encouraged by materialist metaphysics, instrumentalism, and the reduction of all goods to commodities.
47. For an important essay on the making of original sense out of cultural inheritances via free imitation or following after (*Nachahmung*), not mere copying or aping (*Nachmachung, Nachaffung*), focusing on Kant and Wordsworth, see Timothy Gould, "The Audience of Originality: Kant and Wordsworth on the Reception of Genius," in *Essays in Kant's Aesthetics*, ed. Ted Cohen and Paul Guyer (Chicago: University of Chicago Press, 1982). See also the discussion of succession in Eldridge, *An Introduction to the Philosophy of Art*, 2nd ed. (Cambridge: Cambridge University Press, 2014), pp. 59–61, 115–20.
48. These books include the valuable, topically organized studies by Stephen Mulhall, *Stanley Cavell: Philosophy's Recounting of the Ordinary* (Oxford: Clarendon Press, 1999) and Espen Hammer, *Stanley Cavell: Skepticism, Subjectivity, and the Ordinary* (Cambridge: Polity Press, 2002), as well as valuable books focusing on other single topics: Cavell and film (William Rothman and Marian Keane, *Reading Cavell's The World Viewed* [Detroit: Wayne State University Press, 2000]); Cavell and philosophical method (Timothy Gould, *Hearing Things: Voice and Method in the Writing of Stanley Cavell* [Chicago: University of Chicago Press, 1998]); Cavell and literary studies (Michael Fischer, *Stanley Cavell and Literary Skepticism* [Chicago: University of Chicago Press, 1989]), Cavell and American Philosophy (Russell B. Goodman, *American Philosophy and the Romantic Tradition* [Cambridge: Cambridge University Press, 1991]), Áine Mahon, *The Ironist and the Romantic: Reading Richard Rorty and Stanley Cavell* [London: Bloomsbury, 2014]); Cavell and Wittgenstein (Jônadas Techio, *The Threat of Solipsism: Wittgenstein and Cavell on Meaning, Skepticism, and Finitude* [Berlin: de Gruyter, 2020]); and Cavell and politics (Andrew Norris, *Becoming Who We Are: Politics and Practical Philosophy in the Work of Stanley Cavell* [Oxford: Oxford University Press, 2017]). Norris's book contains the fullest reading of Cavell's simultaneous engagements and inheritances of ordinary language philosophy (Austin) and skepticism (Thompson Clarke). (There is a continuing regular stream of conference volumes and collections devoted to Cavell as well as an important online journal of Cavell Studies (*Conversations: The Journal of Cavellian Studies*). Recent PhD dissertations on Cavell have been written in (at least) Norway, Belgium, Brazil, Ireland, Italy, and France, as well as the United States and the United Kingdom.
49. "The unity of the ensemble"—here, of Cavell's pieces—is "constituted in a certain way outside the work, in the subject that is seen in it, or in the judgment that proffers its maxims in it."—Philippe Lacoue-Labarthe and Jean-Luc Nancy, *The Literary Absolute: The Theory of Literature in German Romanticism*, trans. Philip Barnard and Cheryl Lester (Albany: State University of New York Press, 1988), p. 40, commenting on Friedrich Schlegel's fragments.

Chapter 1

1. Cavell's sense of the perennial availability and necessity of movements of both departure and return might usefully be compared to Geoffrey Hartman's reading of Romanticism as involving alternating moments of apocalypse (the unbinding of creative imagination) and *akedah* (rebinding to earth and the common). See Geoffrey Hartman, *Wordsworth's Poetry, 1787–1814*, 2nd ed. (New Haven, CT: Yale University Press, 1964, 1971), esp. pp. ix–xx, 225–42. See also Richard Eldridge, "Internal Transcendentalism: Wordsworth and 'A New Condition of Philosophy,'" in Eldridge, *The Persistence of Romanticism* (Cambridge: Cambridge University Press, 2001), esp. pp. 107–13.
2. Dieter Henrich, "Hölderlin in Jena," trans. Taylor Carman, in his *The Course of Remembrance and Other Essays on Hölderlin*, ed. Eckart Forster (Stanford, CA: Stanford University Press, 1997), p. 112, emphasis added.
3. Stephen Mulhall, *Stanley Cavell: Philosophy's Recounting of the Ordinary* (Oxford: Clarendon Press, 1994), p. 68.
4. Cavell, "An Interview with Stanley Cavell," conducted by James Conant, in *The Senses of Stanley Cavell*, ed. Richard Fleming and Michael Payne, *Bucknell Review* 32, 1 (Cranbury, NJ: Associated University Presses, 1989), p. 50.
5. Martin Heidegger, "The Origin of the Work of Art," trans. Albert Hofstadter, in Heidegger, *Poetry, Language, Thought* (New York: Harper and Row, 1971), p. 54.
6. Ludwig Wittgenstein, *On Certainty*, ed. G. E. M. Anscombe and G. H. Von Wright, trans. Denis Paul and G. E. M. Anscombe (Oxford: Basil Blackwell, 1969), §378, p. 49e.
7. Immanuel Kant, *The Critique of Judgment*, trans. J. C. Meredith (Oxford: Oxford University Press, 1928), p. 56. Cf. Cavell, "Aesthetic Problems of Modern Philosophy," in MWM, p. 94; and Richard Eldridge, "Philosophy and the Achievement of Community: Rorty, Cavell, and Criticism," *Metaphilosophy* 14 (April 1983), pp. 107–25, at p. 121, n.13.
8. Wittgenstein, *Philosophical Investigations*, 3rd ed. (New York: Macmillan, 1953, 1958), §288, p. 99, my translation.
9. See Richard Eldridge, "The Normal and the Normative: Wittgenstein's Legacy, Kripke, and Cavell," *Philosophy and Phenomenological Research* 46 (June 1986), pp. 555–75, at pp. 570–5; and Richard Eldridge, *Leading a Human Life: Wittgenstein, Intentionality, and Romanticism* (Chicago: University of Chicago Press, 1997), pp. 107–8.
10. See Cavell, "Music Discomposed," in MWM, pp. 188–9: "the dangers of fraudulence, and of trust, are essential to the experience of [modern] art," and "modernism only makes explicit and bare what has always been true of art."
11. G. W. F. Hegel, *The Phenomenology of Spirit*, trans. A. V. Miller (Oxford: Clarendon Press, 1977), para. 177, pp. 110–11.
12. Compare Cavell, SW, pp. 107–8: "Our first resolve should be towards the nextness of the self to the self; it is the capacity not to deny either of its positions or attitudes—that it is the watchman or guardian of itself; and hence demands of itself transparence, settling, clearing, constancy; and that it is the workman, whose eye cannot see to the end of its labours, but whose answerability is endless for the constructions in which it houses itself.... The answerability of the self to itself is its possibility of awakening."
13. See Cavell, "The Philosopher in American Life," in IQO, pp. 14–15; and Timothy Gould, *Hearing Things: Voice and Method in the Writing of Stanley Cavell* (Chicago: University of Chicago Press, 1998), esp. chapter 4, "The Model of Reading."

Chapter 2

1. There are a number of interrelated reasons for focusing on a Hegelian understanding of self-hood. (A) It is difficult to make sense of putative entities that do not occupy space and cannot readily be counted, such as a Cartesian soul. No entity without identity. In contrast, human bodies as loci of subjectivity can readily be counted. (B) Insuperable interaction problems (noted by Hegel in the Introduction to the *Phenomenology*) arise if we posit primitive, internal, nonspatial, purely mental representers. These problems include the problem of the external

world, the problem of other minds, and the problem of non-material causality. (C) The positing of such internal representers mistakenly intellectualizes experience into the receipt of discrete data to be assessed, thus denying the multimodal, temporally unfolding character of our bodily involvements with objects. There is no implicit sub-basement to conceptualization. (D) Primitive internal representers make it impossible to account for normativity and relations of material implication. (E) "seems"-language and "appears"-language are temporally and logically posterior to "is"-language. (F) Positing primitive internal representers unhappily encodes and reinforces alienation from materiality, experience, and other subjects. In contrast with Aristotle, who holds a similar view in some respects, Hegel is aware of the possibilities of alienation and of significant historical change in conceptual repertoires. Readers will recognize themes from Wittgenstein, Quine, Davidson, Sellars, and Brandom, among others, here. I do not dwell on these points here given that, first, each is worth an extended argument on its own, and, second, for resistant readers none of them is likely to carry conviction: we might do better to appreciate these points by understanding the practico-conceptual lives of human subjects downstream, as it were, rather than ontogenetically in the terms of ontogenesis that are favored within the natural sciences.

2. Hegel's use of "Sammlung" here bears interesting affinities to Augustine's account in the *Confessions* of the dawning nature of awareness of external objects, recognized under concepts.

To know objects as persisting things apart from me, "and as they actually are, is in reality only to take things that the memory already contained, but scattered and unarranged, and by thinking bring them together, and by close attention have them placed within reach in that same memory: so that things, which had formerly lain there scattered and not considered, now come easily and familiarly to us. And my memory carries an immense number of things of this sort, which have already been discovered and, as I have said, placed within reach—the things we are said to have learned and to know. Yet if I ceased to give thought to them for quite a short space of time, they would sink again and fall away into the more remote recesses of the memory, and I should have to think them out afresh and put them together again from the same place—for there is nowhere else for them to have gone—if I am to know them: in other "words they must be collected out of dispersion, and indeed the verb to cogitate is named from this drawing together. For *cogito* (I think) has the same relation to *cogo* (I put together) as *agito* (I excite) to *ago* (I drive) and *factito* (I keep doing) to *facio* (I do). But the mind of man has claimed the word *cogitate* completely for its own: not what is put together anywhere else but only what is put together in the mind is called cogitation." (As the editor notes, the point here is that *cogito* is an intensification [and persistence] of *cogo* [that yields a stable product].) Augustine, *Confessions*, 2nd ed., ed. Michael P. Foley, trans. F. J. Sheed (Indianapolis: Hackett, 2006), p. 199.

3. G. W. F. Hegel, *Vorlesungen über die Ästhetik*, Vol, III, ed. Karl Markus Michel and Eva Moldenhauer (Frankfurt a. M.: Suhrkamp, 1986), pp. 164–5; my translation.

4. For a full explication of Hegel's individual developmental psychology or account of Subjective Spirit, as he lays it out in the Anthropology and Phenomenology sections of Part III of his *Encyclopedia of the Philosophical Sciences*, see Richard Eldridge, "Hegel's Account of the Unconscious and Why It Matters," *Review of Metaphysics*, 67, 3 (March 2014), pp. 491–516.

5. Lambros Malafouris, "Between Brains, Bodies, and Things: Tectonoetic Awareness and the Extended Self," *Philosophical Transactions of the Royal Society of London B: Biological Sciences*, 363, 1499 (June 12, 2008), pp. 1993–2002, p. 1999. Malabouris presents what he describes as "a view of selfhood as an extended and distributed phenomenon that is enacted across the skin barrier and which thus comprises both neural and extra-neural resources" (p. 1993).

6. Though it might go without saying, it is also worth noting that the Freud in whom I am interested here is not Freud as a neurophysiologist or scientist, but rather Freud as a reader of pressures on subject formation and of the expression of those pressures in various domains of the lives of subjects.

7. Hegel, *Philosophy of Mind*, trans. William Wallace and A. V. Miller (Oxford: Clarendon Press, 1971), §406Z, p. 116. For an excellent account of how, after 1926, Freud came to regard anxiety (arising in the continuing course of subject formation and development) as the cause of repression, rather than vice versa, see Marcia Cavell, *Becoming a Subject: Reflections in Philosophy and Psychoanalysis* (New York: Oxford University Press, 2008). Somewhat more strongly than Freud, Hegel stresses that the fragile achievement of psychic health is also a fragile sociopolitical achievement, bound up with occupying social roles under which one wins recognition.

8. Stanley Cavell, "Companionable Thinking," in *Philosophy and Animal Life*, ed. Cary Wolfe, Cora Diamond, Stanley Cavell, and Ian Hacking (New York: Columbia University Press, 2008), p. 121.

9. For a substantial elaboration and defense of Cavell's reading of both Wittgenstein and the motivation of skepticism, see Richard Eldridge, *Leading a Human Life: Wittgenstein, Intentionality, and Romanticism* (Chicago: University of Chicago Press, 1997), chapters 8 and 9.

10. Plato, *Symposium*, trans. Alexander Nehamas and Paul Woodruff (Indianapolis: Hackett, 1989), 175D, p. 5.

11. Ludwig Wittgenstein, *Philosophical Investigations*, rev. 4th ed., trans. G. E. M. Anscombe, P. M. S. Hacker, and Joachim Schulte (Oxford: Basil Blackwell, 2009), §68, p. 37e.

12. Cavell, "Companionable Thinking," p. 110.

13. Ibid., p. 96.

14. Pierre Hadot, *Philosophy as a Way of Life*, ed. Arnold Davidson, trans. Michael Chase (Oxford: Blackwell, 1993), p. 83.

15. Ibid., p. 102.

16. Hadot, *Philosophy as a Way of Life*, pp. 107–8, 270–1.

17. Ibid., pp. 212, 273–4.

18. Compare Georg Lukács, *The Theory of the Novel*, trans. Anna Bostock (Cambridge, MA: MIT Press, 1974) on the transcendental homelessness of the modern subject in contrast with the more fully role-identifying subject of Ancient Greek epic.

19. Hegel, *Phenomenology of Spirit*, trans. A. V. Miller, rev. ed. (Oxford: Oxford University Press, 1977), p. 43. The German reads: "Denn die Natur dieser [der Humanität] ist, auf die Übereinkunft mit anderen zu dringen, und ihre Existenz nur in der zustande gebrachten Gemeinsamkeit der Bewußtsein[e]" (Hegel, *Phänomenologie des Geistes*, ed. Eva Moldenhauer and Karl Markus Michels [Frankfurt a. M.: Suhrkamp, 1986], p. 65). Miller's translation best captures this.

20. Ibid., p. 43.

Chapter 3

1. Bertrand Russell, "My Mental Development," in *The Philosophy of Bertrand Russell*, vol. 5 of The Library of Living Philosophers, ed. Paul Arthur Schilpp (Evanston: The Library of Living Philosophers, 1946), p. 12.

2. Norman Kemp Smith, "The Present Situation in Philosophy," *The Philosophical Review* 29, 1 (1920), pp. 1–26; henceforth PSP, followed by page number.

3. J. L. Austin, "Are There *A Priori* Concepts?," in *Philosophical Papers*, ed. J. O. Urmson and G. J. Warnock, 2nd ed. (Oxford: Oxford University Press, 1970), p. 41.

4. This is, in fact, a controversial point, and defending it will require—what philosophy does not?—appealing to a mixture of descriptive and stipulative, ideal, coherence-seeking considerations. For example, what about language of thought hypotheses involving Chomskyan tacit-knowledge? And what about concept-possession on the parts of non-linguistic animals? (See Noam Chomsky, "Recent Contributions to the Theory of Innate Ideas," *Synthese* 17, 1 (1967), pp. 2–11). Austin must be assuming something like the distinction Brandom draws, following Sellars, between sapience and sentience (see Robert Brandom, *Making It Explicit: Reasoning, Representing, and Discursive Commitment* [Cambridge: Harvard University Press, 1994], pp. 4–6). Full-blooded concept possession on the part of a sapient being requires both sensitivity to issues about correctness and some degree of awareness of relations of material implication among concepts, such as *red* implies *not-green*. A merely sentient, non-sapient animal fails to fulfill these conditions. Those who—unlike Austin, Wittgenstein, and Brandom—are concerned to fit human conceptually structured performances (judging and acting) fully into a material world, wherein all changes of material state ultimately take place in accordance with an exceptionless law of nature, will resist claims about the distinctiveness of human performances and appeals to normativity and holistic awareness. For a good survey of the Austinian-Wittgensteinian sense, together with an account of the depth of the difficulty in defending it within the context of a culture that includes strong strands of scientific materialism, see Charles Taylor, *The Language Animal: The Full Shape of the Human Linguistic Capacity* (Cambridge: Harvard University Press, 2016).

5. Austin, "Are There *A Priori* Concepts?," pp. 41–2.

6. See Ludwig Wittgenstein, *Philosophical Investigations*, trans. G. E. M. Anscombe, P. M. S. Hacker, and Joachim Schulte, ed. P. M. S. Hacker and Joachim Schulte, rev. 4th ed. (Malden, MA: Wiley-Blackwell, 2009), §§86, 199; henceforth PI, followed by section number.

7. W. V. O. Quine, "Natural Kinds," in *Ontological Relativity: And Other Essays* (New York: Columbia University Press, 1969), pp. 114–38, esp. 123–4; and *The Roots of Reference* (La Salle, IL: Open Court, 1974), p. 19.

8. Again, building on Wilfrid Sellars on material inference (see "Inference and Meaning," *Mind* 62, 1 [1953], pp. 313–38), Robert Brandom has emphasized these features of genuine concept possession in distinguishing between *sentience* and *sapience* (*Making It Explicit*, pp. 4–6). More broadly, Donald Davidson's argument for anomalous monism stresses that some degree of coherent patterning among propositional attitudes (psychological states) is necessary in order for any subject to "possess" such attitudes and states at all (see Donald Davison "Mental Events," in *Essays on Action and Events* [Oxford: Clarendon Press, 1990], pp. 207–24). Davidson writes, "It is a feature of physical reality that physical change can be explained by laws that connect it with other changes and conditions physically described. It is a feature of the mental that the attribution of mental phenomena must be responsible to the background of reasons, beliefs, and intentions of the individual. There cannot be tight connections between the realms *if each is to retain allegiance to its proper source of evidence*" (p. 222; emphasis added). The point about the irreducibility of psychological to physical idioms holds, even if we hold that the in-principle availability of an exceptionless physical law to explain any physical event is itself a working assumption within physics that has proved to pay, rather than something we know to be true or to be sufficiently explanatory of everything we want to understand.

9. G. E. Moore, *Principia Ethica* (Cambridge: Cambridge University Press, 1903), pp. 6–7.

10. See Tom Regan, *Bloomsbury's Prophet: G.E. Moore and the Development of His Moral Philosophy* (Philadelphia: Temple University Press, 1986), pp. 59–61.

11. G. E. Moore, *Some Main Problems of Philosophy* (London: George Allen and Unwin, 1953), pp. 30–1.

12. See Paul Levy, *Moore: G.E. Moore and the Cambridge Apostles* (New York: Holt, Reinhart, and Winston, 1980), and Regan, *Bloomsbury's Prophet*.

13. Moore, *Principia Ethica*, pp. 7–8.

14. See, in particular, J. L. Austin, *Sense and Sensibilia*, ed. G. J. Warnock (Oxford: Clarendon Press, 1962).

15. Ibid., pp. 115–16.

16. Ibid., p. 8.

17. Gilbert Ryle, *The Concept of Mind* (London: Hutchinson, 1949), p. 15.

18. Ibid.

19. Compare Austin's account of complexities of usage that undermine the doctrine *unum nomen, unum nominatum* in his "The Meaning of a Word," in *Philosophical Papers*, pp. 71–5.

20. Donald Davidson, "Afterthoughts," in *Subjective, Intersubjective, Objective* (Oxford: Clarendon Press, 2001), p. 156.

21. Bertrand Russell, *The Problems of Philosophy* (London: Williams and Norgate, 1912), p. 91.

22. See Bertrand Russell, *Why I Am Not a Christian: And Other Essays on Religion and Related Subjects* (London: Simon and Shuster, 1957).

23. Russell, *The Problems of Philosophy*, pp. 39–41.

24. For Russell's use of human mortality as a general law, see ibid., p. 131; Russell discusses Faraday in Bertrand Russell, "The Place of Science in a Liberal Education," in *Mysticism and Logic: and Other Essays* (London: Longmans, Green, 1918), p. 34.

25. Bertrand Russell, "Logic as the Essence of Philosophy," in *Our Knowledge of the External World* (Chicago: Open Court, 1914), p. 56.

26. See Bertrand Russell, *My Philosophical Development* (New York: Simon and Shuster, 1959), pp. 134–5.

27. Russell, "Logic as the Essence of Philosophy," p. 51.

28. Ibid., pp. 45–6.

29. Rudolf Carnap, *The Logical Structure of the World*, trans. Rolf A. George (Berkeley: University of California Press, 1967), p. 5.

30. Ibid., p. 6.

31. Ibid., pp. 122–36.

32. Rudolf Carnap, "Empiricism, Semantics, and Ontology," in *Meaning and Necessity: A Study in Semantics and Modal Logic* (Chicago: University of Chicago Press, 1956), p. 207.

33. W. V. O. Quine, *Word and Object* (Cambridge: MIT Press, 1960), p. 275.
34. W. V. O. Quine, "Two Dogmas of Empiricism," in *From a Logical Point of View* (Cambridge: Harvard University Press, 1953), p. 44.
35. See ibid. For a rich, complex, plausible picture of the multi-aspectual, always unfinished development of scientific theories, emphasizing the creative tinkering of engineers under the pressures of nature, see Mark Wilson, *Wandering Significance: An Essay on Conceptual Behavior* (Oxford: Clarendon Press, 2006).
36. See Quine, *Word and Object*, p. 221.
37. Morality, for example, according to Quine, lacks normative authority and is instead a matter of "each of us . . . pursuing exclusively his own private satisfactions," subject to modification of those pursuits "by word of mouth, by birch rod and sugar plum, by acclaim and ostracism, fine, imprisonment" (W. V. O. Quine, "On the Nature of Moral Values," in *Theories and Things* [Cambridge: Harvard University Press, 1981], pp. 60–1). Outcomes of various systems of reward and punishment might be studied empirically, and individuals or groups might pursue their private satisfactions by urging moral systems on others, but for Quine there are no further facts of the matter of morality other than facts of preference and outcome. Beliefs are to be cashed out first as dispositions, then ultimately as underlying neuro-physiological states with law-governed causal antecedents and effects (see W. V. O. Quine, "Mind and Verbal Disposition," in *Mind and Language*, ed. Samuel Guttenplan [Oxford: Clarendon Press, 1975], pp. 83–95).
38. Quine concedes this point (see *Word and Object*, p. 221).
39. P. F. Strawson, *Analysis and Metaphysics: An Introduction to Philosophy* (Oxford: Oxford University Press, 1992), p. 19; henceforth AM, followed by page number.
40. Historically, this idea of informal, nonreductive explanations of a family of terms appears in the reply of Grice and Strawson to Quine's "Two Dogmas of Empiricism" (see H. P. Grice and P. F. Strawson, "In Defense of a Dogma," *Philosophical Review* 65, 2 [1956], pp. 141–58). Grice and Strawson elaborate the idea of informal explanation and offer examples of three independent and non-reducible networks of related terms: the alethic modal network, the assertion-related network, and the moral network (pp. 147–9).
41. Strawson notes that Kant is the obvious inspiration for this idea (AM, 26). He further notes, echoing his *Individuals: An Essay in Descriptive Metaphysics* (London: Methuen, 1959), that the existence of a world without sounds or colors is conceivable (AM, 25–6).
42. While I share Strawson's sense of practical absurdity here, I also feel a certain disappointment and vertigo in the thought that this practical sense might be used to justify a claim about what human beings fundamentally are as free and rational agents, as though I had been given a description of the standing practical problem of using the intentionality-responsibility-morality network of explanation—a problem I already had—when what I wanted and was promised was a justification of its applicability in virtue of the existence of a stable, well-bounded network of concepts with a fixed place in human life. Human reason has this peculiar fate.
43. In developing a kind of philosophical anthropology, emphasizing continuing practical conflicts about what we say and do in applying concept words, Cavell might be taken to be doing something *like* Strawsonian connective analysis, but to be correcting Strawson's offhand dismissal of "that kind of more or less systematic reflection on the human situation which one finds in the work of, say, Heidegger, Sartre, and Nietzsche" as not analytical (AM, 2). When it comes to a metaphysics of human life in and with language, reflection on practical situations is not easily hived off into a separate enterprise as Strawson casually supposes. Or one might say that Cavell is doing something *like* Austinian ordinary language philosophy, but with a fuller sense than Austin of the open-ended, rhetorical-persuasive, and unending character of appealing to what we say, where such appeals are motivated by and attempt to address agonized and contested matters of shared practice and of relations with others. Or as Cavell puts it, an appeal to what we say is entered, on behalf of oneself and others, when we are *seeking* agreement, when "what they [and I with them] had not realized was what they were saying, or, what they [and I with them] were *really* saying, and so had not known *what they* [or I] *meant*. To this extent, they [and I] had not known themselves, and not known the world. . . . [The task is to] coax the mind down from self-assertion—subjective assertion and private definition—and lead it back, through the community, home" (MWM, 40–3).
44. The actual remark from *The Blue Book* is "I know what a word means in certain contexts" (Ludwig Wittgenstein, *The Blue and Brown Books: Preliminary Studies for the Philosophical Investigations* [Oxford: Basil Blackwell, 1958], p. 9).

45. Compare this with Wittgenstein's claim that "to understand a language means to have mastered a technique" (PI, 199).
46. Cavell describes a pretend game of *pasting labels on things* (see CR, 174).
47. Compare this with Wittgenstein's remark that our use of the word "game" "is not everywhere bounded by rules; but no more are there any rules for how high one may throw the ball in tennis, or how hard, yet tennis is a game for all that, and has rules, too" (PI, 68).
48. Note that "indefinite" does not mean "infinite," but rather "not organized in such a way that we can enumerate all instances and directions of projection in a closed list or according to a definite algorithm" (which itself would not require projection). Martin Gustafsson's essay, focusing on chapter 7 of *The Claim of Reason*, is invaluable in developing Cavell's account of projective imagination (see Martin Gustafsson, "Familiar Words in Unfamiliar Surroundings: Davidson's Malapropisms, Cavell's Projections," *International Journal of Philosophical Studies* 19, 5 [2001], pp. 643–68).
49. Similar points can be made about a variety of Germanic- or Middle-English-derived verbs of active bodily motion: for example, "guide," "put," "pass," "lift," "drop." In each case, we must project the application of the verb on the basis of a similarity that we readily grasp but that is not readily specifiable according to a rule.
50. This, of course, explains the failure of Moore and Russell to construct a language consisting only of names for sense-data.
51. Note that while the construction of a dictionary, like the construction of a map, is a cognitive enterprise that can be carried out more or less well, it is also controlled by users' interests and purposes. There is no universal dictionary, just as there is no universal map.
52. We might add to this list "right," "excusable," "permissible," "just," "fair," "justifiable," and all the others words about which philosophers dispute.
53. In his early essay "Aesthetic Problems of Modern Philosophy" (in MWM, pp. 73–96), Cavell criticizes Cleanth Brooks and Yvor Winters for just this kind of moralism, in their fits of theorizing in proposing fixed formulae for what counts as a poem, thereby avoiding the complexities of engaging with the details of particular difficult cases.
54. It is no accident that Cavell initially trained, both practically and in the university, as a musician, improviser, and composer—that is, in regions of practice where an ear for musical cadences is essential (see LDIK, 418).
55. Alva Noë, *Strange Tools: Art and Human Nature* (New York: Hill and Wang, 2015), p. 16.
56. Ibid., p. 17. Noë was a student of Cavell's, and his view of philosophy as an activity of clarification of commitments that is akin to (modernist) art (and art criticism) is a development of Cavell's views in his "Aesthetic Problems of Modern Philosophy." As Cavell puts it there, "The problem of the critic, as of the artist [and of the philosopher working in and from ordinary language], is not to discount his subjectivity, but to include it; not to overcome it in agreement, but to master it in exemplary ways. . . . The implication is that philosophy, like art, is, and should be, powerless to *prove* its relevance; and that says something about the kind of relevance it wishes to have. All the philosopher, this kind of philosopher, can do is to express, as fully as he can, his world, and attract our undivided attention to our own," therein helping to move us from perplexity, divided attention, and incoherent practical commitments into greater clarity (MWM, 94, 96). For further developments of Cavell's conception of elucidatory, detail-oriented criticism as philosophy, see Richard Eldridge, *Leading a Human Life: Wittgenstein, Intentionality, and Romanticism* (Chicago: University of Chicago Press, 1997), pp. 4–5, and Ted Cohen, *Thinking of Others: On the Talent for Metaphor* (Princeton: Princeton University Press, 2008), pp. 22–4.
57. For instance, Cavell writes, "The philosophical appeal to what we say, and the search for criteria on the basis of which we say what we say, are claims to community. And the claim to community is always a search for the basis on which it can be or has been established. I have nothing more to go on than my conviction, my sense that I make sense. It may prove to be the case that I am wrong, that my conviction isolates me, from all others, from myself. The wish and search for community are the wish and search for reason" (CR, 20).
58. See Arnold Isenberg, "Critical Communication," *The Philosophical Review* 58, 4 (1949), pp. 330–44, esp. 336.
59. Were we actually to accomplish the full clarification of all conceptual-practical commitments that are necessary and sufficient for fully reasonable and meaningful life, then we would be living in the possession of Hegelian absolute knowledge, within the fully realized concrete universal—an unlikely and in fact undesirable outcome (see G. W. F. Hegel, *The Phenomenology of Spirit*, trans. A. V. Miller [Oxford: Oxford University Press, 1977], §§788–808).

60. R. G. Collingwood captures this point well in remarking that philosophy is the expression of intellectual emotions or emotions attendant upon reflecting on the coherence of one's conceptual commitments, while literature is the expression of emotions of consciousness or emotions attendant upon the experience of particular objects (including persons) and incidents, but "in the limiting case where each was as good as it ought to be, the distinction would disappear" (R. G. Collingwood, *The Principles of Art* [Oxford: Clarendon Press, 1939], p. 298; see pp. 266–8 and 297–8 for the distinction between intellectual emotions and emotions of consciousness).

61. Interestingly, Strawson offers as an aside that what matters in the work of Descartes is not any proofs full stop, but instead his "conscious or unconscious propaganda in favor of a certain direction of development in the natural sciences" that took the form of "dramatic expression [of] his doctrines about the essential nature of knowledge and existence" (AM, 15). Alert readers will not have missed that I have offered no proofs about the natures of concepts and conceptual analysis, but instead a kind of narrative of practices of conceptual analysis, coupled with an effort to sketch out a direction in which that narrative and those practices might most reasonably develop.

62. For examples of what (I think) a *fully textured* analysis of a concept, developed in relation to histories of practices, looks like, beyond the more-closed analyses of concepts and conceptual analysis on offer in early analytic philosophy, see Richard Eldridge, *An Introduction to the Philosophy of Art* (Cambridge: Cambridge University Press, 2014) on art, esp. pp. 284–6, which summarize and extend the book as a whole; and Richard Eldridge, "'A Danger at Present Unperceived': Self-Understanding, Imagination, Emotion, and Social Relations in *Emma*," in *Jane Austen's Emma: Philosophical Perspectives*, ed. E. M. Dadlez (Oxford: Oxford University Press, 2018), pp. 109–33, on self-understanding.

Chapter 4

1. This way of opening the subject is adapted from Russell B. Goodman, "Cavell and American Philosophy," in *Contending with Stanley Cavell*, ed. Russell B. Goodman (New York: Oxford University Press), 100–17.

2. See Cornel West, *The American Evasion of Philosophy: A Genealogy of Pragmatism* (Madison: University of Wisconsin Press, 1989), for a reading of a central evasion of epistemology in American philosophy, coupled oddly with the thought that religiously inspired social prophecy is pursued nonetheless. Though West is right that both of these tendencies are in place in American thought, there is more tension between them than he supposes, as the evasion of foundationalist epistemology pushes toward the rejection of social visions and in favor of utilitarianism, while the pursuit of social prophecy seems to require an epistemology of larger visions in order to be credible.

3. Though this is the standard picture in American departments of philosophy, it bears noting that it is in many ways unfair to the richness and visionariness of the actual writings of Peirce, James, and Dewey, among others. On James see, for example, Charles Taylor, *Varieties of Religion Today: William James Revisited* (Cambridge, MA: Harvard University Press, 2002); on Dewey, see Goodman, "Cavell and American Philosophy."

4. Compare Jay Bernstein's similar picture of American professional philosophy in his "Aesthetics, Modernism, Literature: Cavell's Transformations of Philosophy," in *Stanley Cavell*, ed. Richard Eldridge (Cambridge: Cambridge University Press, 2010), pp. 107–42.

5. See Stanley Cavell, "Being Odd, Getting Even: Descartes, Emerson, Poe" in his *In Quest of the Ordinary: Lines of Skepticism and Romanticism* (Chicago: University of Chicago Press, 1988).

6. See Richard Eldridge, *Leading a Human Life: Wittgenstein, Intentionality, and Romanticism* (Chicago: University of Chicago Press, 1997), passim, for an elaboration of the relevant concept of *expressive freedom*, and especially also pp. 108–12 on Cavell in relation to this concept. The pursuit of expressiveness comes to the fore in Cavell's discussion of Thoreau in (SW, 55, 57).

7. For a reading of Cavell's understanding of artistic modernism, as the pressure toward it and the possibility of it are described by Wordsworth and by Kant, see Timothy Gould, "The Audience of Originality: Kant and Wordsworth on the Reception of Genius," in *Essays in Kant's Aesthetics*, ed. Ted Cohen and Paul Guyer (Chicago: University of Chicago Press, 1982), pp. 179–93.

8. Stephen Mulhall, *Stanley Cavell: Philosophy's Recounting of the Ordinary* (Oxford: Clarendon Press, 1994), p. 58. Interjection added.
9. Immanuel Kant, *Critique of Pure Reason*, trans. and ed. Paul Guyer and Allen W. Wood (Cambridge: Cambridge University Press, 1997), B 131–2, p. 246.
10. Ibid., A 546–7 = B 574–5, p. 540.
11. Henry David Thoreau, *Walden*, chapter 5, para. 11, "Solitude," cited in (SW, 102).
12. Ted Cohen pressed me, rightly, to strengthen this point.
13. Again, a worry aptly urged on me by Ted Cohen.
14. I specifically note, however, that Plato's texts, with their dramatic structures of conversation, their allegories, and their frequent inconclusiveness are richer and more literary than a Plato*nist* doctrine of the good sometimes takes them to be.
15. Mulhall, *Stanley Cavell*, p. 252.
16. Simon Critchley, *Very Little . . . Almost Nothing: Death, Philosophy, Literature* (London: Routledge, 1997), p. 130.
17. For an eloquent expression of this thought, balanced against the contrary thought that we also need to and can care about some things together, see Ted Cohen, "High and Low Thinking about High and Low Art," *The Journal of Aesthetics and Art Criticism* 51 (Spring 1993), pp. 151–6.
18. Here, along with Russell Goodman, I have the sense that Cavell and Cavell's Emerson and Thoreau are perhaps less far from Dewey and James, and from Rorty's Dewey in *Achieving Our Country*, and from Cornel West's "prophetic pragmatism," than is sometimes thought to be the case. Dewey and James and Rorty and West, rightly read, *do* urge the perfectionist pursuit of freedom, in and through continuing uncertainties, not just "coping." Situating these figures within the tradition of Emerson and Thoreau will mean, however, moderating their voluntarism and utilitarianism and noticing how they remain haunted by both skepticism and its perfectionist partial overcoming, even when and where they seek to deny this haunting.

Chapter 5

1. Richard Poirier, *Poetry and Pragmatism* (Boston: Harvard University Press, 1992), p. 155.
2. John Dewey, *Art as Experience* (New York: Penguin Putnam, 1980), p. 338.
3. Robert Brandom, *Making It Explicit* (Cambridge, MA: Harvard University Press, 1998), p. 129.
4. Dewey, *Art as Experience*, p. 352.
5. Friedrich Waismann, "How I See Philosophy," in *Logical Positivism*, ed. A. J. Ayer (New York: The Free Press, 1959), p. 375.
6. W. V. O. Quine, "Two Dogmas of Empiricism," in Quine, *From a Logical Point of View* (New York: Harper, 1963), p. 22.
7. W. V. O. Quine, *Word and Object* (Cambridge, MA: MIT Press, 1960), p. 275.
8. Monroe Beardsley, "The Concept of Literature," reprinted in *The Philosophy of Literature*, ed. Eileen John and Dominic McIver Lopes (Malden, MA: Blackwell), p. 57B.
9. Ibid.
10. Ibid., p. 51A.
11. Sacvan Bercovitch, *The American Jeremiad* (Madison: University of Wisconsin Press, 1978), p. 177.
12. *The Bible: Authorized King James Version with Apocrypha*, ed. Robert Carroll and Stephen Prickett (Oxford: Oxford University Press, 2008), p. 257.
13. Bercovitch, *The American Jeremiad*, pp. 4, 1, xiv.
14. Perry Miller, *Errand into the Wilderness* (Cambridge, MA: Harvard University Press, 1956), p. 15.
15. Bercovitch, *The American Jeremiad*, p. 38.
16. Ibid., p. 11.
17. Ibid., pp. 6–7.
18. Ibid., p. 55.
19. Ibid., p. 141.
20. Ralph Waldo Emerson, "The American Scholar," in Emerson, *Selections from Ralph Waldo Emerson*, ed. Stephen E. Whicher (Boston: Houghton-Mifflin, 1957), pp. 73, 65, 64.

21. Emerson, "Nature," in *Selections from Ralph Waldo Emerson*, pp. 21–2.
22. Ibid., p. 24.
23. Ibid., pp. 24–5.
24. Emerson, "Experience," in *Selections from Ralph Waldo Emerson*, p. 261.
25. Emerson, "History," in Emerson, *Essays and Lectures*, ed. Joel Porte (New York: Library of America, 1981), p. 239.
26. Emerson, "Skepticism," in *Selections from Ralph Waldo Emerson*, p. 267.
27. Henry David Thoreau, *Walden* in Thoreau, *Walden and Other Writings*, ed. Brooks Atkinson (New York: The Modern Library, 1992), p. 8.
28. Ibid., p. 5.
29. Ibid., p. 91.
30. Ibid., p. 86.
31. Ibid., p. 61.
32. Thoreau, "Life Without Principle," in *Walden and Other Writings*, p. 768.
33. Thoreau, *Walden*, pp. 154–5.

Chapter 6

1. The critical, as opposed to dogmatic, epistemological significance of juxtaposed readings of our condition, amounting to a perspicuous representation of it, is the main theme of Eldridge, "Hypotheses, Criterial Claims, and Perspicuous Representations: Wittgenstein's 'Remarks on Frazer's *The Golden Boughs*,'" *Philosophical Investigations* 10 (1987), pp. 226–45.
2. Ludwig Wittgenstein, *Philosophical Investigations*, 3rd ed., trans. G. E. M. Anscombe (New York: Macmillan, 1958), pt. 2, p. 214e. Throughout this short summary of Wittgenstein on the physiognomy of words, I rely on Stephen Mulhall's discussion in sections entitled "The Experience of Meaning" and "The Physiognomy of Meaning" in his *On Being in the World: Wittgenstein and Heidegger on Seeing Aspects* (London: Routledge, 1990), pp. 35–45.
3. T. S. Eliot, "The Love Song of J. Alfred Prufrock," reprinted in *The Norton Anthology of English Literature*, 3rd ed., vol. 2, ed. M. H. Abrams et al. (New York: Norton, 1974), p. 2167.
4. Cavell, in James Conant, "Interview with Cavell," in *The Senses of Stanley Cavell*, ed. Richard Fleming and Michael Payne (Lewisburg: Bucknell University Press, 1989), p. 50. Compare CR, 207: "[Wittgenstein] never underestimated the power of the motive to reject the human: nothing could be more human. He undertook, as I read him, to trace the mechanisms of this rejection in the ways in which, in investigating ourselves, we are led to speak 'outside language games,' consider expressions apart from, and in opposition to, the natural forms of life which give those expressions the force they have."
5. Martin Heidegger, *Being and Time*, trans. John Macquarrie and Edward Robinson (New York: Harper and Row, 1962), p. 32.
6. Stanley Cavell, "A Conversation with Stanley Cavell on Philosophy and Literature," in *The Senses of Stanley Cavell*, ed. Richard Fleming and Michael Payne (Lewisburg: Bucknell University Press, 1989), pp. 3, 14.
7. See Richard Eldridge, *Leading a Human Life: Wittgenstein, Intentionality, and Romanticism* (Chicago: University of Chicago Press, 1997), pp. 8–9 and pp. 17–20, on the essential connection between conceptual consciousness and moral consciousness.
8. On how a commitment to freedom is worked into the structure of conceptual consciousness according to Kant, see Onora O'Neill, "Reason and Autonomy in *Grundlegung* III," in O'Neill, *Constructions of Reason* (Cambridge: Cambridge University Press, 1989), pp. 51–65, especially p. 63, and more generally, Richard Velkley, *Freedom and the End of Reason* (Chicago: University of Chicago Press, 1989), especially pp. 1–11.
9. Hegel announces the great "turning point" [*Wendung*] in *Phenomenology of Spirit*, trans. A. V. Miller (Oxford: Oxford University Press, 1977), para. 177, p. 110. See the discussion of this turning point in Eldridge, *Leading a Human Life*, pp. 27–33.
10. Apropos of passages in Cavell's partly autobiographical *A Pitch of Philosophy* that voice versions of these questions, I have in mind pp. 6, 22–3, 56–7, and especially 169. On how these questions animate Wordsworth's *Prelude*, in specific responsiveness to a felt sense of having possibly done or been nothing, see Richard Eldridge, *On Moral Personhood: Philosophy Literature, Criticism,*

and *Self-Understanding* (Chicago: University of Chicago Press, 1989), pp. 106–11. On how responses to these questions remain conjectural and require tendentious narrative revisions of one's course so as to bring out its reasonableness, but in being revisions remain haunted by their erasures, see Eldridge, "Wordsworth and 'A New Condition of Philosophy,'" *Philosophy and Literature* 18 (1994), pp. 50–71.

11. Friedrich Hölderlin, Letter No. 117 to Immanuel Niethammer, February 14, 1796, and Letter No. 172 to his Brother, January 1, 1799, both in Friedrich Hölderlin, *Essays and Letters on Theory*, ed. and trans. Thomas Pfau (New York: SUNY Press, 1988), pp. 131, 137.
12. Hölderlin, "Judgment and Being," in *Essays and Letters on Theory*, p. 37.
13. Hölderlin, "On Religion," in *Essays and Letters on Theory*, pp. 94–5.
14. Hölderlin, "Remarks on *Antigone*," in *Essays and Letters on Theory*, p. 116.
15. Dieter Henrich, "Hegel and Hölderlin," in *The Course of Remembrance and Other Essays* on Hölderlin, ed. Eckart Forster, trans. Taylor Carman (Stanford, CA: Stanford University Press, 1997), p. 114. Henrich has drawn the phrase "an eccentric path" out of the preface to the "Fragment of *Hyperion*."
16. Henrich, "Hölderlin in Jena" and "Hegel and Hölderlin," in *The Course of Remembrance and Other Essays on Hölderlin*, pp. 112, 127–8. Note the specifically Emersonian sound of Henrich's phrase "to withstand what is greatest, and yet to be humbled by what is smallest."
17. See the editor's note to this fragment in Friedrich Hölderlin, *Hölderlin, Hyperion and Selected Poems*, ed. Eric L. Santner (New York: Continuum, 1990), p. 300.
18. Hölderlin, "The fruits are ripe . . . [*Reif sind . . .*]," in *Hölderlin, Hyperion and Selected Poems*, pp. 174–7.
19. The translator unhelpfully adds "in mind" to "borne," where Hölderlin's sense is that preserving prophetic thoughts in mind is as much a matter of stance or bodily bearing in motion through life as it is anything mental or internal.

Chapter 7

1. Brett Millier, *Elizabeth Bishop: Life and the Memory of It* (Berkeley: University of California Press, 1992), pp. 1–27, esp. pp. 9, 22.
2. See Walter Benjamin, "On Language as Such and on the Language of Man," trans. Edmund Jephcott, in Benjamin, *Selected Writings: Vol. 1, 1913–1926*, ed. Marcus Bullock and Michael W. Jennings (Cambridge, MA: Belknap Press, 1996), pp. 62–74.
3. Cavell, "Excerpts from Memory," *Critical Inquiry* 32, 4 (Summer 2006), p. 804.
4. Cavell, "Excerpts from Memory," p. 791.
5. Friedrich Nietzsche, *The Twilight of the Idols*, trans. Duncan Large (Oxford: Oxford University Press, 1998), p. 16.
6. Walter Benjamin, "Critique of Violence," trans. Edmund Jephcott, in Benjamin, *Selected Writings*, p. 250.
7. Betsy Erkkila, "Bishop, Modernism, and the Left," *American Literary History* 8, 2 (Summer 1996), p. 302.
8. Ibid., p. 285.
9. David Kalstone, "Questions of Memory, Questions of Travel," in *Elizabeth Bishop*, ed. Harold Bloom (New York: Chelsea House, 1985), p. 53.
10. April Bernard, "A Genius Ill-Served," *The New York Review of Books*, 58, 5 (March 24, 2011), p. 16A.
11. Ibid., pp. 16A, 16C.
12. Dana Gioia, "Wherever Home May Be," *The Wall Street Journal*, February 5, 2011.
13. Bonnie Costello, *Elizabeth Bishop: Questions of Mastery* (Cambridge, MA: Harvard University Press, 1991), p. 2.
14. Ibid., p. 6.
15. Neil Besner, "Brazil in Bishop's Eyes," in *"In Worcester, Massachusetts": Essays on Elizabeth Bishop*, ed. Laura Jehn Menides and Angela G. Dorenkamp (New York: Peter Lang, 1999), p. 75.
16. Elizabeth Bishop, "Arrival at Santos," in *Elizabeth Bishop: Poems, Prose, and Letters*, ed. Robert Giroux and Lloyd Schwarz (New York: Penguin, 1991), pp. 65, 72.

17. Kim Fortuny, *Elizabeth Bishop: The Art of Travel* (Boulder: University Press of Colorado, 2003), p. 33.
18. Costello, *Elizabeth Bishop*, p. 142.
19. Millier, *Elizabeth Bishop: Life and the Memory of It*, p. 239.
20. Elizabeth Bishop, "Letter to Marianne Moore," March 3, 1952, in Bishop, *Poems, Prose, and Letters*, p. 779.
21. Costello, *Elizabeth Bishop*, p. 152.
22. Millier, *Elizabeth Bishop: Life and the Memory of It*, p. 24.
23. Costello, *Elizabeth Bishop*, p. 152.

Chapter 8

1. Stanley Bates usefully challenges the assumption that characters are not people and argues that our very idea of what a character *is* is formed as strongly by our experience of figures in literary texts, where plot abstracts and highlights related but temporally separated displays of temperament, interest, and so on, as by experience of actually existing people. "Character," in *The Oxford Handbook of Philosophy and Literature*, ed. Richard Eldridge (Oxford: Oxford University Press, 2013), pp. 393–419.
2. Kenneth Burke, "Othello: An Essay to Illustrate a Method," in *Kenneth Burke on Shakespeare*, ed. Scott L. Newstok (West Lafayette, IN: Parlor Press, 2007), p. 85.
3. Stephen Greenblatt powerfully describes the development of what he calls Shakespeare's "new technique of radical excision" enabling "an intense representation of inwardness" in his essay "The Death of Hamnet and the Making of Hamlet," *The New York Review of Books* (October 21, 2004), p. 47.
4. For an excellent survey of subject development that brings together Cavell's work on language with Freud's developmental psychology, see Marcia Cavell, *Becoming a Subject: Reflections in Philosophy and Psychoanalysis* (Oxford: Oxford University Press, 2008). A second dramatic picture of subject development as it occurs through learning language within a field of contestation and accommodation occurs in R. G. Collingwood's Hegel- and Spinoza-inspired account of language learning in *The Principles of Art* (Oxford: Clarendon Press, 1938), pp. 227–8, 239–40. Finally, compare Charles Petersen's very apt summary of Cavell's Freudian-inflected understanding of the stages of subject development:

   First, an ambition [Cavell] finds fundamental to the human condition: the desire to make the world more present, to experience the world even more directly, to know that another loves you, say, to the same degree that you love him. Second, since making the world more present becomes impossible, and we cannot know the love of another in the same way we know our love for that other, we arrive at the feeling of fraudulence (where others, since we can't confirm their love, can't confirm our love, so we doubt that even we do love), and skepticism (where others, since we can't confirm their existence, can't confirm our existence, so we doubt that we exist). Ever since Descartes first asked how he could be certain the world was not the work of a demon—the famous line of inquiry that led to modern skepticism—this problem has seemed little more than an intellectual exercise. Cavell makes skepticism fundamental, a relation to the world that comes not from the intellect but from (frustrated) desire. The third stage, then, is the attempt by philosophers (and writers of all kinds) to solve skepticism, to rid themselves of doubt and achieve certainty by abstracting the world, which Cavell interprets as a redoubling of skepticism—an attempt to again make the world more present not by acknowledging that frustrated first attempt but by ignoring it, or avenging it, 'a kind of violence the human mind performs in response to its discovery of its limitation.' This is Cavell's diagnosis of logical positivism, the philosophy of his peers. Next follows the fourth stage, represented by the work of the ordinary language philosophers: an attempt to return to all that had been left behind through the abstraction of everyday life. But this return is radically altered by the initial run-in with skepticism, such that what had become ordinary becomes uncanny, and the philosophers of ordinary language, as it were, discover for the first time the ordinary, the everyday, all that had previously been taken for granted. They thus point the way, though without going far enough. After skepticism, Cavell writes, 'the everyday is what we cannot but aspire to, since it appears . . . lost to us'; but the answer to skepticism is not a 'philosophical construction,' not a treatise or a single technique, but the wholesale 'reconstruction or resettlement of the everyday.'

"Must We Mean What We Say?: On Stanley Cavell," *n + 1* (February 11, 2013), https://nplusone mag.com/online-only/online-only/must-we-mean-what-we-say/.

5. Anthony J. Cascardi aptly notes that "The disclosure of our commitments in what we say, together with an account of what it means to honor or to skirt them, is as important as anything in Cavell's work. . . . Cavell portrays his engagements with Shakespeare as unavoidable because it is Shakespeare who, above all writers, explores the full range of the commitments that language entails. The power of Shakespeare's work rests on his ability to envision characters who live out the fate of their words relentlessly, without compromise or escape, or who suffer disastrously from their failure to do so." ("'Disowning Knowledge': Cavell on Shakespeare," in *Stanley Cavell*, ed. Richard Eldridge [Cambridge: Cambridge University Press, 2003], pp. 190–205, at p. 190.)

6. Cavell's evident thought here is that there *is* some alternative open to us between Humpty Dumpty's world- and other-denying claim to be absolute master of what words mean and W. C. Fields's sullen, depressive, alcoholic resentfulness at the antics of children and café waitresses.

7. Cascardi registers this point in noting that "Cavell's analyses of Shakespeare are rooted in a conviction that Shakespeare's characters *must* mean what they say, and mean it thoroughly, unless of course they are in a posture of avoidance, in which case their words may reveal whatever it is they might wish to disown. It bears upon us as readers and critics of these plays to suppose this and nothing less." ("'Disowning Knowledge': Cavell on Shakespeare, p. 193.)

8. J. M. Bernstein dwells on Cavell's perception that modernity is an age of subjectivity prominently foregrounded and individualized, but therein also prominently detached from love and community. Cavell's "idea of saving 'love for the world [until it is responsive again]' is intended as a way of expressing, at least, that love of the world is no longer possible because the world is no longer lovable, . . . and hence that our attachment to life, however fierce and insistent, is smaller, meaner, narrower. . . . [Cavell's claim is] that love, or what we think of as love, and subjectivity as we have inherited it from the exemplary instances of Hamlet and Descartes, are all but incommensurable. . . . *Hamlet* begins, and so modernity begins, with the loss of the king-father and the queen-mother, that is, not only with the loss of the ideal god-like father and goddess-like mother, but thereby with the loss of father and mother as the (representative) sources of ideality, sources of meaningful order." ("How Tragedy Ends," in *Stanley Cavell: Philosophy, Literature, and Criticism*, eds. James Loxley and Andrew Taylor (Edinburgh: Edinburgh University Press, 2012), pp. 106–22, at pp. 106, 108, citing Cavell, "A Matter of Meaning It," in MWM, pp. 213–37, at p. 229.)

9. In Richard Eldridge, *Leading a Human Life: Wittgenstein, Intentionality, and Romanticism* (Chicago: University of Chicago Press, 1997), I trace, following Cavell, the continual surging forth of this effort and its foundering in *Philosophical Investigations*.

10. Cascardi notes correctly that "Cavell's work is to dismantle the opposition between skepticism and epistemology, rather than to oppose skepticism by proposing an alternative to epistemology. . . . In Cavell's readings, Shakespearean tragedy and romance are interpreted as presenting openings into the problems of skepticism and knowledge that lie beyond, or beneath, what philosophy conventionally imagines to be at stake in them. . . . Shakespeare's texts ask us to take account of the full measure of what skepticism means and thereby challenge us to confront those things for which epistemology has come to be a cover. . . . What epistemology *avoids* must be something that 'knowing' cannot provide. Indeed, knowing serves as the excuse, the cover, or the alibi for what ought to be acknowledged." ("'Disowning Knowledge': Cavell on Shakespeare," pp. 191, 192, 194.)

11. This should not rule out the further thoughts that men and women, say, or the masculine and the feminine, may experience this fatedness differently. As Cascardi puts it, "The idea, not inconsistent with some feminisms, is that men are rather less certain than women of their bodily existence and continuity with others, and in the face of those uncertainties are drawn to what the world has come to call 'heroism,' 'achievement,' or 'originality.'" ("'Disowning Knowledge': Cavell on Shakespeare," p. 199. It is surely no accident that Shakespeare's tragic protagonists are (all but) all men.

12. Derek Gottlieb, in *Skepticism and Belonging in Shakespeare's Comedies* (London: Routledge, 2016) follows out this thought in taking Cavell's work in *Pursuits of Happiness* to provide a lens for re-reading Shakespeare's major comedies, themselves a major inspiration (by way of Northrop Frye) for Cavell's comedy of remarriage book.

Chapter 9

1. Stephen Mulhall, *On Film*, 2nd ed. (Milton Park, UK: Routledge, 2008).
2. Paisley Livingston, *Cinema, Philosophy, Bergman: On Film as Philosophy* (Oxford: Oxford University Press, 2012).
3. Thomas Wartenberg, *Thinking on Screen: Film as Philosophy* (London: Routledge, 2007).
4. See my review essay on Wartenberg's book "Philosophy In/Of/As/And Film: Thomas Wartenberg's *Thinking on Screen: Film as Philosophy*," *Projections: The Journal for Movies and Mind* 3, 1 (2009), pp. 109–16, followed by Wartenberg's reply ("Response to My Critics," 117–25) to my remarks along with those of Cynthia Freeland ("Comments on Thomas Wartenberg's *Thinking on Screen: Film as Philosophy*," 100–109) for an airing of the issue about the importance of the artistic use of images to original (rather than merely illustrative) thinking in films.
5. See, for example, Laura Marcus, "Cinematic Realism," in *A Concise Companion to Realism*, ed. Matthew Beaumont (Malden, MA: Wiley-Blackwell, 2010), pp. 195–210. William Rothman, along with Marian Keane, has done much to produce a more comprehensively integrated reading of Cavell on film. See William Rothman and Marian Keane, *Reading Cavell's "The World Viewed": A Philosophical Perspective on Film* (Detroit: Wayne State University Press, 2000), and William Rothman, "Cavell on Film, Television, and Opera," in *Stanley Cavell*, ed. Richard Eldridge (Cambridge: Cambridge University Press, 2003), pp. 206–38.
6. Or more recently, the digital recording of light rays. While film stock's ways of registering light are distinctive and open to significant artistic-expressive uses, most of the points about photographic capturing of reality transfer also to at least digital image *recording*, though not to CGI production, which is quite another matter. It is noteworthy that, like cartoons, CGI feature films have so far been most successful when in the registers of fairy tale or fantasy. For a useful investigation of the similarities and differences (especially with regard to continuous shooting) of digital recording versus film-stock recording, see the PBS documentary *Side by Side: The Science, Art, and Impact of Digital Cinema* (dir. Chris Kenneally, Los Angeles: A Company Films, 2012), first aired on US television on August 30, 2013, after a première at the International Filmfestspiele Berlin, February 15, 2012.
7. André Bazin, "The Ontology of the Photographic Image" (1945), in *What Is Cinema?*, trans. Hugh Gray (Berkeley: University of California Press, 1967), pp. 9–16; reprinted in *Critical Visions in Film Theory*, ed. Timothy Corrigan, Meta Mazaj, and Patricia White (New York: Bedford/St. Martin's, 2010), pp. 310–4. All subsequent citations refer to this edition.
8. Ibid., p. 312.
9. Ibid., p. 311.
10. Ibid., p. 312.
11. Ibid., pp. 312, 311.
12. Ibid., p. 311. The influence on Bazin of Hegel's account of artistic practices as rooted in the worshipful representation of life, as in ancient Egyptian burial practices, is evident here.
13. Ibid., p. 312.
14. Ibid., p. 313.
15. Ibid.
16. André Bazin, "The Evolution of the Language of Cinema" (1950–55), in *What Is Cinema?*, 23–40; reprinted in Corrigan, Mazaj, and White, *Critical Visions*, pp. 314–24. All subsequent citations refer to this edition.
17. Ibid., pp. 315, 316.
18. Ibid., p. 317.
19. Ibid., p. 319.
20. Ibid., pp. 320–2.
21. Stanley Cavell, "Nothing Goes without Saying," *London Review of Books*, January 6, 1994, 3–5.
22. Stanley Cavell, "Fred Astaire Asserts the Right to Praise," in *Philosophy the Day after Tomorrow* (Cambridge, MA: Harvard University Press, 2005), pp. 61–82.
23. Rothman and Keane, *Reading Cavell*, p. 62.
24. Stephen Mulhall, *Stanley Cavell: Philosophy's Recounting of the Ordinary*, 2nd ed. (Oxford: Clarendon Press, 1994), p. 225.
25. Here, I take it, Cavell is gesturing toward the possibilities of non-dialogue sound film and non-photographically produced film, possibilities that have been realized, respectively, for example, in *Koyaanisqatsi* (dir. Godfrey Reggio, 1992) and in cartoons and now CGI films.

26. Rothman and Keane, *Reading Cavell*, p. 19.
27. Ibid., p. 71.
28. Ibid.
29. Rothman, "Cavell on Film," p. 212.
30. Stanley Cavell, "What Photography Calls Thinking," *Raritan* 4 (1985), p. 14.
31. David Bordwell, "The Art Cinema as a Mode of Film Practice" (1979), in *Poetics of Cinema* (London: Routledge, 2007), pp. 151–70; reprinted in Corrigan, Mazaj, and White, *Critical Visions*, pp. 559–73. All the subsequent citations refer to this edition.
32. Ibid., pp. 561, 560.
33. Ibid., pp. 561, 563.
34. Noël Carroll, "Film in the Age of Postmodernism" (1985), in *Interpreting the Moving Image* (Cambridge: Cambridge University Press, 1997), p. 331.
35. Ibid., p. 310.
36. Carroll, "Introduction to *Journeys from Berlin/1971*" (1981–82), in *Interpreting the Moving Image*, p. 234.
37. Carroll, "Film in the Age," p. 305.
38. Ibid., p. 332.
39. Ibid., pp. 331–2.
40. Bordwell, "Art Cinema," p. 561.
41. Even blockbuster-oriented Hollywood continues to have its moments. Are *Ocean's Eleven* (2001) and *Mr. and Mrs. Smith* (2005) readable as comedies of remarriage set inside the genres of, respectively, the heist flick and the action thriller?

Chapter 10

1. Edwin Curley, "Cavell and the Comedy of Remarriage," *Philosophy Research Archives* 14 (1988–89), pp. 581, 592.
2. Noel Carroll, "Review of *Pursuits of Happiness*," *The Journal of Aesthetics and Art Criticism* 41, 1 (Autumn 1982), pp. 104B, 105A.
3. Curley, "Cavell and the Comedy of Remarriage," p. 600.
4. Lucas Thompson mounts an extended argument on behalf of *Love Crazy* as well as noting *That Uncertain Feeling* and *The Palm Beach Story*, "Marriage as Madness: 'Love Crazy' and the Hollywood Comedy of Remarriage," *Conversations: The Journal of Cavell Studies* 8 (2020), pp. 92–135.
5. I take these terms from Nelson Goodman's valuable account of visual depiction versus verbal description in *The Languages of Art*, 2nd ed. (Indianapolis: Hackett, 1976).
6. Alice S. Rossi, *The Feminist Papers* (New York: Bantam Books, 1974), p. 616, cited in PH, p. 17.
7. Cavell takes the terms *Hebraism* and *Hellenism*, and the descriptions associated with them, from Matthew Arnold's *Culture and Anarchy*, ed. Jane Garnett (Oxford: Oxford University Press, 2009).
8. Cavell, "Falling in Love Again," *Film Comment* 41, 5 (September–October 2005), p. 54A.
9. Ibid.
10. Ibid.
11. United States Census Bureau, "Figure MS-2: Median Age at First Marriage, 1890 to Present," accessed at: https://www.census.gov/content/dam/Census/library/visualizations/time-series/demo/families-and-households/ms-2.pdf.
12. Robert D. Putnam and Shaylyn Romney Garrett, *The Upswing: How America Came Together a Century Ago and How We Can Do It Again* (New York: Simon and Schuster, 2020), pp. 164, 138, 304. It should not go without saying, and Putnam and Romney Garrett take care to say it, that these developments involved significant improvements in the lives of women and racial minorities who had been significantly blocked from full entry into economic and political life.
13. Andrea C. Westlund, "The Reunion of Marriage," *The Monist* 93, 3–4 (July–October 2008), p. 560.
14. Interestingly, two forms of practice in contemporary life where this kind of trust and faith still seem viable are participation in team sports and participation in musical performance. These

can be important educative experiences. But they are also often experienced as offering forms of relationship and satisfaction that are disjoined from economic, political, and familial life.

15. Cavell, "Falling in Love Again," p. 54A.
16. Ibid., p. 54B.
17. Ibid., emphasis added.
18. Friedrich Nietzsche, *On the Genealogy of Morals*, ed. Keith Ansell-Pearson, trans. Carol Diethe (Cambridge: Cambridge University Press, 2006), p. 3.
19. Television comedies and dramas continue to explore characters and relationships, and they have the flexibility of open-endedness in doing so. The price of this flexibility, however, is frequently less achievement of dramatic closure. I am not aware of any television views that are clearly and directly concerned with remarriage, even if restorations of broken or threatened relationships are common.

Chapter 11

1. David Bordwell, "Intensified Continuity: Visual Style in Contemporary American Film," *Film Quarterly* 55, 3 (Spring 2002), p. 16.
2. Ibid. Bordwell cites the work Elizabeth Cowe, Thomas Elsaesser, and Peter Kramer as advancing this argument (n. 2, p. 26).
3. Ibid., pp. 16, 20, 21.
4. Ibid., pp. 22, 23, 24.
5. Ibid., pp. 24, 25.
6. William Rothman and Marian Keane, *Reading Cavell's The World Viewed* (Detroit: Wayne State University Press, 2000), p. 132.
7. These may not be the only forms of heroism achieved in the pursuits of just and meaningful life: one hopes not. But what successor forms of heroism have wide credibility among both mass and art audiences?
8. Carlo Ginzburg, *The Cheese and the Worms: The Cosmos of a Sixteenth-Century Miller*, trans. Anne C. Tedeschi (Baltimore: Johns Hopkins University Press, 1980).
9. Pierre Hadot, *Philosophy as a Way of Life*, ed. Arnold I. Davidson, trans. Michael Chase (Malden, MA.: Blackwell, 1995), pp. 107, 128–40.
10. René Descartes, "Preface to *The Search After Truth*," in *The Philosophical Works of Descartes*, Vol. 1, trans. Elizabeth Haldane and G. R. T. Ross (Cambridge: Cambridge University Press, 1911), p. 305.
11. Robert B. Pippin, "The Idea that Films Could Have a Bearing on Philosophy," in *Inheriting Stanley Cavell: Memories, Dreams, Reflections* (New York: Bloomsbury, 2020), p. 185.
12. The practices of modern, mathematical-experimental-physical science are undoubtedly both widely useful, with important qualifications, in making human life longer and easier, and they offer distinct, non-hedonic satisfactions that are bound up with understanding, but they do not bind human beings to any particular, meaningful interpersonal, social, and political activities and relationships.
13. Richard Rorty, "From Epistemology to Romance: Cavell on Skepticism," *The Review of Metaphysics* 34, 4 (June 1981), pp. 759–74 at p. 770.
14. Rothman and Keane, *Reading Cavell's The World Viewed*, p. 10.
15. Ibid., p. 35.
16. For excellent accounts of this possibility—for how art can matter for and within the rest of life, see Anthony Aumann, *Art and Selfhood: A Kierkegaardian Account* (London: Lexington Books, 2019), and Charles Altieri, *Reckoning with the Imagination: Wittgenstein and the Aesthetics of Literary Experience* (Ithaca: Cornell University Press, 2015). Altieri (p. 199): in reading, as the "self-aware quickening of appreciative attention . . ., we become aware of how we are modified by our valuing the text because we recognize ourselves as possessing certain powers and as capable of certain gratitudes."
17. As technologies of production, distribution, and communication have advanced, globalization and neoliberalism have yielded increasing economic inequality and political polarization, exacerbated by AI-driven marketing and media filters, among other things. For a brief survey of

these developments, see Richard Eldridge, "Is Democracy Still Possible?" *Los Angeles Review of Books*, March 21, 2021, https://lareviewofbooks.org/article/is-democracy-still-possible/.

18. Two earlier interesting cases are *Remember the Titans* (2000) and *The Fugitive* (1993). Here it is impossible to doubt that Herman Boone/Denzel Washington, Samuel Gerard/Tommy Lee Jones, and Richard Kimble/Harrison Ford are working along with others for the world's good. But neither of these movies tracks how they each came to be able to do this; instead, they work more as character studies that build on the already established photographic magnetisms of their stars. It is also noteworthy that there is a significant amount of compelling long-form television produced especially for cable channels in the last twenty-five or so years: *The Sopranos* (1999–2007), *The Wire* (2002–2008), *The Americans* (2013–2018), *Breaking Bad* (2008–2013), and *Better Call Saul* (2015–2022), among others. But it is equally noteworthy that the principal figures in these series are at odds with American life, often violently. As Martin Shuster puts it, these series respond "to an omnipresent loss of normative authority, of a robust failure of humans to feel at home in their world: to trust their governments, their leaders, their role models, their traditions and, ultimately, even their senses," where "the family emerges as the sole site where normative authority still exists" (Martin Shuster, "Our Golden Age of TV: Amid Collapse, a New Family Emerges," *aeon*, May 16, 2018, https://aeon.co/ideas/our-golden-age-of-tv-amid-collapse-a-new-family-emerges. For further development of this argument, see Shuster, *New Television: The Aesthetics and Politics of a Genre* [Chicago: University of Chicago Press, 2017].) Finally, two more hopeful cases are *Treme* (2010–2013) and *Derry Girls* (2018–2022), with its astonishing final episodes mapping the developments of its characters onto the ratification of the Good Friday Agreement and vice versa.

19. Greta Gerwig, *The Directors Guld of America Podcast: The Director's Cut*, "Podcast #64: Interview with Adam Buxton," February 2018, archived at https://soundcloud.com/adam-buxton/ep64-greta-gerwig, and transcribed at https://collider.com/little-women-ending-explained-book-changes/.

Chapter 12

1. "The Halted Traveler" is the title of Part I: Thesis, of Geoffrey Hartman's epochal *Wordsworth's Poetry 1787–1814* (New Haven: Yale University Press, 1971 [1964]). Cavell and Hartman both participated in a ten-month symposium in Jerusalem on the play of negativity in literature and literary theory that culminated in a conference in June 1986. That conference in turn yielded the volume *Languages of the Unsayable: The Play of Negativity in Literature and Literary Theory*, ed. Sanford Budick and Wolfgang Iser (New York: Columbia University Press, 1987). The symposium participants included, in addition to Cavell, Hartman, and the editors, Jacques Derrida, Frank Kermode, Gerald Bruns, Jonathan Culler, Shira Wolosky, and Neil Hertz, among others. Hearsay as it reaches me has it that Cavell was the central figure to whom others deferred.

2. William Wordsworth, "Preface to *Lyrical Ballads*," in Wordsworth, *Selected Poems and Prefaces*, ed. Jack Stillinger (Boston: Houghton Mifflin, 1965), p. 460.

3. Hartman, *Wordsworth's Poetry 1787–1814*, p. 3.

4. Ibid., p. xxii.

5. Ibid., p. xvi.

6. *Apocalypse* and *akedah* are Hartman's two master terms for describing Wordsworth's primary, competing registers of precipitated but active response (*Wordsworth's Poetry 1787–1814*, pp. 225–33). *Apocalypse* names the unleashing of potentially world-transfiguring imaginative energies; *akedah* names the rebinding of agency to the earth and communal life.

7. Hartman, *Wordsworth's Poetry 1787–1814*, p. 218.

8. Ibid., p. 5.

9. Cavell writes further in "Philosophy and the Unheard" of his "vision of the human as caught between a sense of inexpressiveness suggesting suffocation and a sense of uncontrollable expressiveness threatening exposure" (HT, 262) and of "the modern ego entangled in its expressions of desire" (HT, 267). Evidently, actively maintained, continuously meaningful, and emotionally apt human life is more or less continuously absent or under threat for Cavell.

10. In their Introduction to *Here and Now*, the editors Nancy Bauer, Alice Crary, and Sandra Laugier, commenting on the crucial passage, nicely observe that, for Cavell, "it makes sense to hold that philosophy, and more exactly ordinary language philosophy, can be asked to supply the kind of reclamation of, or reconciliation with, sensibility that we may also seek in music" (HT, 11).

11. See Kristeva, *Desire in Language: A Semiotic Approach to Literature and Art*, ed. Leon S. Roudiez, trans. Thomas Gora, Alice Jardine, and Leon S. Roudiez (New York: Columbia University Press, 1980).

12. Compare Wordsworth's paradoxical attempts to reconnect his now individuated sense of self to an originary, libidinally suffused naturalness, projected onto Dorothy and onto numinous nature more generally, while yet retaining a mature identity. For an account of this, see my *Literature, Life, and Modernity* (New York: Columbia University Press, 2008), pp. 95–7, drawing on and revising the work of John Barrell, *Poetry, Language, and Politics* (Manchester: Manchester University Press, 1988).

13. There is an echo here of Wittgenstein's phrase "das erlösende Wort [the redemptive or liberating word]" in the *Big Typescript*: "The philosopher strives to find the liberating [*erlösende*] word, that is, the word that finally permits us to grasp what until now has intangibly weighed down our consciousness" (Wittgenstein, "Philosophy: Sections 86–93 of the so-called *Big Typescript*," in Wittgenstein, *Philosophical Occasions, 1912–1951*, ed. James Klagge and Alfred Nordmann [Indianapolis: Hackett, 1993], pp. 165, 164]). Martin Luther uses "Erlöser" for what the King James Bible renders as "redeemer," as in Job's "I know that my redeemer liveth" (Job 19:25, KJV). See James C. Klagge, *Wittgenstein in Exile* (Cambridge: MIT Press, 2014), pp. 125–6.

14. Wittgenstein to Maurice Drury, as reported in M. O'C. Drury, "Conversations with Wittgenstein," in *Recollections of Wittgenstein*, ed. Rush Rhees (Oxford: Oxford University Press, 1984), p. 160.

15. John Cage's "Organ2/ASLSP (As Slow as Possible)," in "performance" (mechanical sound generation with rare human interventions) in Halberstadt, Germany, since 2001 and scheduled to conclude in 2640, interestingly lacks hearable development.

16. Ted Cohen nicely captures this point in writing that "being human requires knowing what it is to be human, and that requires the intimate recognition of other human beings" in both their shifting likenesses to and differences from oneself over time. This requires "investing your self" imaginatively and emotionally in what is going on with them, a kind of investment that is also required by metaphors and works of art. "The metaphors, the art, the people would all be dispensable if their measure could be taken by a formula. There are no formulas for this, thank God." Ted Cohen, *Thinking of Others: On the Talent for Metaphor* (Princeton: Princeton University Press, 2008), pp. 85–6.

17. William Wordsworth, *The Prelude Or, Growth of a Poet's Mind*, in *Selected Poems and Prefaces*, Book II, lines 279, 277–8; p. 213.

18. Ibid., Book I, lines 267–9; p. 199.

19. Ibid., Book XIV, lines 126–7, 114–16, 119–23; p. 359.

20. Richard Eldridge, "Internal Transcendentalism: Wordsworth and 'A New Condition of Philosophy,'" in Eldridge, *The Persistence of Romanticism* (Cambridge: Cambridge University Press, 2001), p. 123.

Chapter 13

1. It is an interesting and important question whether, and if so to what extent, this remains true. Long form television offers greater possibilities of extended character development than movies meant to be entirely viewed in a single sitting, but such movies have, perhaps, possibilities of sharper dramatic closure. For a useful investigation of how long form television has investigated free life, see Martin Shuster, *New Television: The Aesthetics and Politics of a Genre* (Chicago: University of Chicago Press, 2017).

2. Hamlet is a natural figure for this condition.

3. Compare WV, 118: Photographically produced movies "do not . . . have to establish presentness to and of the world: the world is there. They do not have to deny or confront their audiences: they are screened." Following Bazin, Cavell argues that the omnipresent possibility of asking, about

an object, "what lies adjacent to that area?" or about an object in it, "what does it occlude?" [WV, 23–4] indicates that a really existing object has been captured, as a result, as Bazin had put it, of "a kind of decal or transfer" (André Bazin, "The Ontology of the Photographic Image" (1945), in *What is Cinema?*, trans. Hugh Gray [Berkeley: University of California Press, 1967], p. 13).

4. There is an echo here of Kant's claim in *The Critique of the Power of Judgment* that the experience of beauty in nature discloses that humanity and nature as such share an obscure metaphysical substrate, in such a way that humanity and nature feel, as it were, made for each other, and nature feels good enough to live in. See Immanuel Kant, *The Critique of the Power of Judgment*, ed. Paul Guyer, trans. Paul Guyer and Eric Matthews (Cambridge: Cambridge University Press, 2000), 5:253, p. 227.

5. Compare CR, 207: "Nothing is more human than the wish to deny one's humanity, or to assert it at the expense of others."

6. Cavell is here appropriating the phrase "purposefulness without purpose" from Kant's *Critique of the Power of Judgment*'s "purposiveness without a purpose [*Zweckmäßigkeit ... ohne Zweck*]," Kant, *Kritik der Urteilskraft* (Frankfurt am Main: Suhrkamp, 1974), §10, A34 = B34, p. 135.

7. François Truffaut, *Day for Night*, trans. Sam Flores (New York: Grove Press, 1975), p. 52.

8. Ibid., p. 125.

9. François Truffaut, *Hitchcock*, trans. Helen G. Scott (New York: Simon & Schuster, 1967), p. 172.

10. François Truffaut, *Interviews*, ed. Ronald Bergan (Jackson: University of Mississippi Press, 2008), p. 91.

11. Truffaut writes to the journalist, novelist, and *Cahiers du Cinéma* film critic Jean-Louis Bory: "Since I left school at 14, I could not logically aspire to the kind of intellectual pursuits of a Robbe-Grillet or of my friend Rivette. The stories I tell have a beginning, a middle and an end, even if I am quite aware that, in the final analysis, their interest lies elsewhere than in their plots." François Truffaut, *Correspondence: 1945–1984*, ed. Gilles Jacob and Claude Givray, trans. Gilbert Adair (New York: Cooper Square Press, 2000), p. 424.

12. Ibid., p. 122.

13. Ibid., p. 426.

14. Anne Gillian, *Totally Truffaut*, trans. Alastair Fox (New York: Oxford University Press, 2020), p. 162.

15. Ibid.

16. Gerald C. Wood, "The Life of Art in François Truffaut's *Day for Night*," *Interpretations* 11, 1 (1979), pp. 67, 70.

17. Truffaut, *Day for Night*, p. xii.

18. Wood, "The Life of Art in François Truffaut's *Day for Night*," p. 70.

19. Annette Insdorf, *François Truffaut* (Boston: Twayne Publishers, 1978), p. 191.

20. Sam Solecki, *A Truffaut Notebook* (Montreal: McGill-Queens, 2015), p. 179.

21. Truffaut, "Letter to Jean-Pierre Aumont," May 1973, cited in Gillian, *Totally Truffaut*, p. 161.

22. Ibid.

23. Wayne J. Douglass, "Homage to Howard Hawks . . . . François Truffaut's *Day for Night*," *Literature/Film Quarterly* 8, 2 (1980), pp. 72–3.

24. Insdorf, *François Truffaut*, pp. 142, 141.

25. Truffaut, *Day for Night*, p. 137.

26. Jean-Luc Godard, "Letter to François Truffaut" (May 1973), in Truffaut, *Correspondence*, p. 383.

27. Truffaut, "Foreword," *Day for Night*, p. ix.

28. Douglass, "Hommage to Howard Hawks . . . . François Truffaut's *Day for Night*," p. 74, citing V. F. Perkins, *"Hatari!,"* in *Movie Reader*, ed. Ian Cameron (New York: Praeger, 1972), pp. 68, 63.

29. Truffaut, *Day for Night*, p. 12.

30. Ibid., p. 36. I owe the comparison to Socrates to Paul Deb.

31. Anne Gillian notes that "The soundtrack gives us [the composer of the score Georges] Delerue's instructions to his orchestra. All of them have to do with the tempo of the piece: 'slowly and relaxed,' 'attack,' 'legato, no breaks.' For Truffaut, directing a film means mastering its momentum in time and space from scene to scene—in other words, its rhythm." (*Totally Truffaut*, p. 163.)

32. Wood, "The Life of Art in Truffaut's *Day for Night*," p. 67.

33. Paul Deb aptly suggested these comparisons to Plato.

34. As in Cavell's account of the tumbling of the walls of Jericho in *It Happened One Night* (PH, 80–1).

35. Truffaut, *Day for Night*, p. 35.

36. Ibid., p. 25.

37. Ibid., p. 69.
38. Ibid., p. 90.
39. Ibid., p. 152.
40. Ibid., p. 151.
41. Douglass, "Hommage to Howard Hawks .... Francois Truffaut's *Day for Night,*" p. 75.
42. Truffaut, *Interviews,* pp. 137–8.
43. Ibid., p. 146.
44. Ibid., p. 173.
45. Ibid., p. 135.
46. As Alexandre (Jean-Pierre Aumont) remarks to Dr. Nelson about actors, but in a point that is meant to apply to everyone in their own inhabitations of social roles: "We must show that we *love* each other as well. '*Mon chéri* ... (*in English*) my darling ... my love ... you are magnificent (*in French once more*).' We seem somehow to need that . . . ." (p. 92). Truffaut notes that "I hide behind all the characters. . . . So in *Day for Night* I have a younger representative in Léaud and an older one in Aumont ... to whom I give a lot of my thoughts." Truffaut, *Interviews,* p. 91.
47. Ibid., p. 173.

Epilogue

1. See Rai Chetty, Michael Stepner, Sarah Abraham, Shelby Lin, Benjamin Scuderi, Nicholas Turner, Augustin Bergeron, and David Cutler, "The Association Between Income and Life Expectancy in the United States, 2001–2014," *Journal of the American Medical Association* 315, 16 (April 26, 2016), pp. 1750–66. Erratum in: *Journal of the American Medical Association* 317, 1 (January 3, 2017), p. 90. See also Anne Case and Angus Deaton, *Deaths of Despair and the Future of Capitalism* (Princeton: Princeton University Press, 2021).
2. Thomas Piketty, *A Brief History of Inequality,* trans. Stephen Rendall (Cambridge, MA: Harvard University Press, 2022), p. 154.
3. Jonathan Haidt, *The Righteous Mind: Why Good People Are Divided by Politics and Religion* (New York: Pantheon Books, 2012).
4. See Scott F. Aikin and Robert B. Talisse, *Political Argument in a Polarized Age: Reason and Democratic Life* (Medford, MA: Polity Press, 2020), especially chapter 6, "Simulated Argument."
5. Robert B. Talisse, *Overdoing Democracy: Why We Must Put Politics in Its Place* (Oxford: Oxford University Press, 2019), p. 71.
6. Bill Bishop, cited in Talisse, *Overdoing Democracy,* p. 75.
7. Talisse, *Overdoing Democracy,* p. 84.
8. Ibid., pp. 120, 124.
9. Robert D. Putnam and Shaylyn Romney Garrett, *The Upswing: How America Came Together a Century Ago and How We Can Do It Again* (New York: Simon & Schuster, 2020), p. 154.
10. Ibid. The relevant graphs appear in chapter 2 for economic life, chapter 3 for political life, chapter 4 for social life, and chapter 5 for cultural life. A summary graph showing developments in all four domains on separate but closely converging lines appears on p. 285.
11. Ibid., pp. 290, 306, 329, 331.
12. Robert D. Putnam, *Bowling Alone: The Collapse and Revival of American Community* (New York: Simon & Schuster, 2000).
13. https://news.gallup.com/poll/505745/depression-rates-reach-new-highs.aspx.
14. https://sapienlabs.org/wp-content/uploads/2022/03/Mental-State-of-the-World-Report-2021.pdf.
15. Erik Olin Wright, *Envisioning Real Utopias* (London: Verso, 2010), p. 46.
16. Ibid., pp. 37–45.
17. Ibid., p. 370.
18. Ibid., p. 369. Wright offers a diagram of available pathways on p. 304.
19. Ibid., p. 368.
20. Axel Honneth, *Pathologies of Individual Freedom: Hegel's Social Theory,* trans. Ladislaus Löb (Princeton: Princeton University Press, 2010), pp. 41, 35.

21. Friedrich Schiller, *Letters on the Aesthetic Education of Man*, in Friedrich Schiller, *Essays*, trans. Elizabeth M. Wilkinson and L. A. Willoughby, ed. Walter Hinderer and Daniel O. Dahlstrom (New York: Continuum, 1993), Fifth Letter, p. 97.
22. Ibid., Ninth Letter, pp. 108–9.
23. Ibid., Second Letter, p. 90.
24. Ibid., Twenty-Seventh Letter, pp. 176–7.
25. Samantha Matherne and Nick Riggle, "Schiller on Freedom and Aesthetic Value: Part II," *The British Journal of Aesthetics* 61, 1 (January 2021), p. 39.
26. Ibid., p. 19.
27. Ibid., p. 24.
28. Ibid., pp. 32, 26.
29. Schiller, *Letters*, Fourth Letter, p. 93.
30. Matherne and Riggle, "Schiller on Freedom and Aesthetic Value: Part II," p. 28.
31. Wright, *Envisioning Real Utopias*, p. 370.
32. Richard Bernstein, *Pragmatic Encounters* (New York: Routledge, 2016), p. 188. In her "Changing Politics: Thoreau, Dewey and Cavell, and Democracy as a Way of Life," *Contemporary Pragmatism* 15 (2018), p. 180, Naoko Saito cites this passage in introducing her account of the distinctive approach to politics offered by Thoreau, Dewey, and Cavell in contrast to "politics-as-usual."
33. Compare Andrea Novakovic's Hegel-derived picture of immanent criticism of sociopolitical life in her *Hegel on Second Nature in Ethical Life* (Cambridge: Cambridge University Press, 2015), especially chapter 3, "Critique."
34. Stanley Cavell, "The Incessance and the Absence of the Political," in *The Claim to Community: Essays on Stanley Cavell and Political Philosophy*, ed. Andrew Norris (Stanford: Stanford University Press, 2006), p. 288.
35. Ibid., p. 273.
36. Paola Marrati, "The Ordinary Life of Democracy," *Contemporary Political Theory* 11 (2012), p. 399.
37. Andrew Norris, "Introduction: Stanley Cavell and the Claim to Community," in *The Claim to Community*, p. 6, citing Cavell, CR, p. 19.
38. Ibid., p. 3.
39. Stanley Cavell, "Stanley Cavell in Conversation with Paul Standish," *Journal of Philosophy of Education* 46, 2 (2012), p. 164.
40. Ibid., p. 159.
41. See Cavell, CHU, pp. 101–26 and Cavell, CW, pp. 177–8. Cavell's point here is targeted against John Rawls, whose pictures of democratic and moral life he finds to be too proceduralist and moralistic. As Andrew Norris (*Becoming Who We Are: Politics and Practical Philosophy in the Work of Stanley Cavell* [New York: Oxford University Press, 2017], p. 126) and Alexander Lefebvre ("Stanley Cavell, John Rawls and Moral Perfectionism in Liberal Democracy," *European Journal of Political Theory* [2024], pp. 6, 14), have argued, Cavell misreads Rawls on the claim to be "above reproach." That claim is imagined by Rawls as directed not to another, but instead to oneself, in an effort to assuage otherwise crippling self-guilt. This is surely correct. But one may also wonder with Cavell whether such an effort at self-reassurance might also be tinged with avoidance of the other. Lefebvre then urges the fusion of "Rawls' brand of liberalism, . . . including its psychological depth, moral subtlety and political hopefulness" with the "moral perfectionist energy and insight" defended by Cavell (p. 2).
42. Marrati, "The Ordinary Life of Democracy," pp. 397–8. Drawing on unpublished notes of conversations with Cavell and on both the overall design and the concluding words of *A Theory of Justice*, Lefebvre finds a similar direction of perfectionist thinking in Rawls's conception-based conception of liberalism, driven by an ideal of more affirmable life pursued against a background of disappointment. "Rawls can be seen as laying out a regimen of what could be called spiritual exercises. . . . The connection between personal transformation and a just society is at the root of Rawls's conception-based approach to justice as fairness, his dialectic of desire and disappointment, and the spiritual exercises he devises" (pp. 15, 17).
43. Cavell, "The Incessance and Absence of the Political," pp. 279–80.
44. Standish and Cavell, "Stanley Cavell in Conversation with Paul Standish," p. 158.
45. Cavell, "The Incessance and Absence of the Political," pp.316–17, citing Emerson's "Experience."
46. Cavell, "Stanley Cavell in Conversation with Paul Standish," pp. 164–5.

47. See Cavell, CW, pp. 446–7 on the role of philosophical friend in the reported conversations that compose the *Republic*, and pp. 362–7 on Aristotle on philosophical friendships of virtue.

48. Larry Jackson, "Reading Silence [excerpt from *Skepticism and Redemption: The Political Enactments of Stanley Cavell*—PhD dissertation, Johns Hopkins University, 2013], *Conversations: The Journal of Cavellian Studies* 5 (2017), p. 92, https://doi.org/10.18192/cjcs. v0i5.2409.

49. Saito, "Changing Politics," p. 180, citing Cavell, *The Claim of Reason*, p. 431.

Index

For the benefit of digital users, indexed terms that span two pages (e.g., 52–53) may, on occasion, appear on only one of those pages.

acknowledgment 22–23, 25–26, 29–31, 95, 106–7, 172
alienation 15–16, 85–86
Almodóvar, Pedro 169, 176–78
Altieri, Charles 222n.32, 238n.16
America 7–8, 14–15, 64–66, 67–69, 73, 74–75, 77–78, 84–86, 216
Anderson, Elizabeth 1–2
anthropology, philosophical 14, 228n.43
Aquinas, Thomas 131–32
Aristotle 146–47, 222n.31, 224–25n.1
arrest 12–13, 14–15, 179–80, 182–83
Austin, J. L., 8–9, 17, 27, 42, 44–45, 47–48, 54, 72, 84, 89, 92, 94, 105–6, 118–19, 120–21, 180–81
automatism 141–42, 143–44, 146–47, 175–76
avoidance 22–23, 25–26, 30–31, 106–7

Bates, Stanley 234n.1
Bazin, André 141–44, 151, 167
Beardsley, Monroe 82–83, 84, 96
Beckett, Samuel 153
Benjamin, Walter 119–20, 122, 130
Bercovitch, Sacvan 84–86
Bernard, April 124
Bernstein, J. M. 230n.4, 235n.8
Bernstein, Richard 243n.32
Besner, Neil 124–25
Bishop, Elizabeth 114, 123–30
Bloom, Allan 186
Bordwell, David 149–50, 151, 167–68
Bowie, Andre 12–13
Bradley, A. C. 131–32
Brandom, Robert 79–80, 224–25n.1, 226n.4, 227n.8
Brooks, Cleanth 90–91
Burke, Kenneth 131–32

Carnap, Rudolf 42, 50–52, 54
Carroll, Noël 149–50, 157–58
Cascardi, Anthony J. 235n.5, 235n.10, 235n.11
Cavell, Marcia 225n.7, 234–35n.4

Cohen, Ted 11, 231n.12, 231n.13, 240n.16
Coleridge, Samuel Taylor 72, 94, 132
Collingwood, R. G. 230n.60, 234–35n.4
Costello, Bonnie 124–25, 128–30
Critchley, Simon 77
criteria 23–25, 26–27, 58, 79–80, 93, 103
Cuarón, Alfonso 169, 176–78
Curley, Edwin 157–58

Dahl, Espen 10
Damasio, Antonio 32–33
Davidson, Donald 48–49, 224–25n.1, 227n.8
Deb, Paul 241n.30, 241n.33
deconstruction 105
Deleuze, Gilles 167
Descartes, René 39, 71, 80–81, 131–32, 170–71
Dewey, John 79–80, 84, 96
Douglass, Wayne J. 197, 199–200, 241n.23

ego, the 13, 34–35, 94
Eliot, George 120–21
Emerson, Ralph Waldo 35, 64–67, 70, 71–74, 76, 77–78, 84, 86–88, 92, 118–21, 136, 145, 216–17
Empson, William 131, 132
Erkkila, Betsy 123–24
existentialism 4, 10–11

Fields, W. C. 135–36
Fortuny, Kim 126–27
Foucault, Michel 4
freedom 1–2, 30–31, 34–35, 65, 67, 73–74, 76, 89–90, 105–7, 108–9, 112, 146–47, 150–51, 154–55, 160–62, 188, 192–93, 207, 219
  expressive 13, 14–15, 21, 23
Frege, Gottlob 80–81
Freud Sigmund 17, 34–36, 40–41, 89–90, 118–19, 212–13
futurity 120–21

Garrett, Shaylyn Romney, 160–62, 205–6
Gerwig, Greta 177–78

Geuss, Raymond 222n.19
Gillian, Anne 194–95, 241n.31
Ginzburg, Carlo 170
Gioia, Dana 124
Godard, Jean-Luc 197
Goehr, Lydia 5–6
Goodman, Russell 230n.1, 231n.18
Gottlieb, Derek 235n.12
Gould, Timothy 9, 222n.34, 222n.35, 223n.42, 223n.47
Gustafsson, Martin 229n.48

Hadot, Pierre 38–40, 170
Haidt, Jonathan 204–5
Hammer, Espen 10
Hartman, Geoffrey 179–80, 224n.1
Hawks, Howard 195–97, 200
Hegel, G. W. F., 1–2, 3–4, 13, 21, 28, 29–30, 32–33, 34–35, 40–41, 50, 106–7, 131–32, 188, 197–98, 229n.59
Heidegger, Martin 4, 25, 65, 72, 94, 103–4, 216
Henrich, Dieter 22–23, 109
Hitchcock, Alfred 193–94
Hölderlin, Friedrich 6, 22–23, 108–9, 110–13
Honneth, Axel 207
Hume, David 115, 131–32

Ibsen, Henrik 214
idealism 42–44
immigrancy 7–8, 14–16, 35, 36, 37–39, 104, 107, 113, 119–21
inequality, economic 1–2, 204, 206–7
Innsdorf, Annette 241n.19, 241n.24
Isenberg, Arnold 229n.58

Jackson, Larry 218
Jefferson, Thomas 73–74

Kalstone, David 123–24
Kant, Immanuel 13, 26–27, 67–68, 70, 71–72, 107–8, 207
Keane, Marian 143–44, 146–47, 168–69, 175–76
Kiarostami, Abbas 169, 176–78
Knight, G. Wilson 131, 132
Kristeva, Julia 183–85

Lacoue-Labarthe, Philippe 223n.49
Lefebvre, Alexander 243n.41, 243n.42
Lévi-Strauss, Claude 4, 182–85
liberalism 1–2, 3–5, 7, 64, 78, 165, 221n.9, 243n.41, 243n.42
Lincoln, Abraham 73–74

Livingston, Paisley 140
Lukács, Georg 3–4, 226n.18
Luther, Martin 118–19, 170

Madison, James 73–74
Malafourdis, Lambros 32–33
Marrati, Paola 212–13, 214–15
Marx, Karl 118–19, 131–32
Matherne, Samantha 210–12
medium, artistic 140–41, 143, 144–47, 149–50, 173–74, 188
Mill, John Stuart, 1
Millier, Brett 114, 127–28, 129
modernism 9, 10–11, 16, 27, 39–40, 65, 114, 116–17, 118, 120–21, 130, 146, 148–49, 150, 158, 166–67, 169, 174–77, 190
modernity 39–40, 121, 136, 169–71, 172, 190, 207–8
Moore, G. E. 42–44, 45–47, 49, 50, 54
Moore, Marianne 123–24, 128
morality 7
Mulhall, Stephen 24, 68, 76, 140, 144
music 32–33

Nancy, Jean-Luc 223n.49
naturalism 42–43, 63–64, 131–32
Nehamas, Alexander 12–13
New Criticism 105
New Historicism 105
Nietzsche, Friedrich 39–40, 103, 119–20, 164–65, 183–85, 216–17
Noë, Alva 57–58
Norris, Andrew 212–13, 243n.41

Oberdiek, Hans 221n.10
ordinary, the 9–10, 22–23, 24–26, 30–31, 58, 89–90, 136–37
orientation 3–4, 8–9, 38–39, 71–72, 82–83, 89–90, 91–92, 96, 107, 108–9, 119–20, 134–35, 138–39

Paideia 13
Panofsky, Erwin 145
perfectionism 16, 35, 115
Petersen, Charles 234–35n.4
philosophy 7, 11, 26, 27–29, 30–31, 37–39, 57–59, 65, 81–82, 83–84, 92–93, 119–20, 157–58, 181–82, 212, 217–18
American 63–65, 79–80, 84, 88–89, 106, 115, 117–18
ordinary language 8–9, 21, 36, 37–38, 48–49, 54, 72–73, 99, 132, 189, 212–13, 240n.10
sites of 179–80

Piketty, Thomas 242n.2
Pippin, Robert B., 4–5, 170–71, 222n.19
Plato 3–4, 5, 12, 36–37, 50, 65–66, 70, 76,
    80–81, 107, 118–19, 134–35, 198–99,
    211–12, 215
Poirier, Richard 79
Poizat, Michel 182–85
polarization 1–2, 204–6
post-structuralism 4
practical identity 4–5, 69, 205–6, 212
Putnam, Robert 160–62, 205–6

Quine, W. V. O. 42, 44–45, 51–52, 54, 63–64,
    81–82, 83, 84, 88–89, 96, 224–25n.1

Rawls, John 243n.41, 243n.42
reason, claim of 26–27, 58, 89–90
Riggle, Nick 210–12
Rilke, R. M. 6
romanticism 10, 11–12, 72, 100, 107, 110, 129,
    169, 214–15
Rorty, Richard 172
Rossi, Alice S. 159–60
Rothman, William 143–44, 146–48, 168–69,
    175–76
Rousseau, Jean-Jacques 65–66, 67–68, 101,
    118–19, 207
Russell, Bertrand 42–44, 45–46, 49–50, 52, 54
Ryle, Gilbert 42, 47–48, 54

Saito, Noriko 244n.49
Sartre, Jean-Paul 4
Schiller, Friedrich 207–12
Schlegel, Friedrich 76
selfhood 32–33, 36, 37–38, 40–41, 69, 71, 103–
    4, 138–39, 145–47, 150–51, 154–55, 169,
    172, 176

self-understanding 15–16, 17
Sellars, Wilfrid 224–25n.1, 227n.8
Shuster, Martin 239n.18, 240n.1
skepticism 11, 14–16, 24–26, 36–37,
    39–40, 42–43, 101–2, 103, 104, 108–9,
    112–13, 131–32, 137, 171, 172, 185–86,
    191, 212–13
Smith, Norman Kemp 42–43, 44
Solecki, Sam 196–97, 241n.20
Standish, Paul 216
Stevens, Wallace 90–91
Strawson, P. F. 52–54
structuralism 4

Talisse, Robert B. 204–5
Taylor, Charles 6, 226n.4
Thatcher, Margaret 207
Thompson, Lucas 237n.4
Thoreau, Henry David 65–66, 70–72, 74, 76,
    77–78, 84, 87–88, 92, 94, 119–20

Uncanny, the 25, 58

Waismann, Friedrich 80–81
Wartenberg, Thomas 140
West, Cornel 230n.2
Westlund, Andrea C. 162
Winters, Yvor 90–91
Wittgenstein, Ludwig 10, 11, 17, 22, 25–27, 35,
    36–37, 54–55, 65–66, 72, 79–80, 84, 89,
    94, 96, 100–1, 105–6, 118–20, 136, 153,
    183–86, 216
Wood, Gerald C. 194–95, 241n.18
Wordsworth, William 8–9, 11–12, 14–15, 72,
    94, 115–16, 126–27, 179–80, 181–82, 186–
    87, 212–13, 240n.12
Wright, Erik Olin 206–7, 211–12